Reflections, Man & Boy

by

RON FORSYTH

Camden, Maine

Cover photograph and design by Lee Thomas Kjos

ISBN: 0-89272-626-1

First American Edition
Originally published in Australia in 1997 by the
Sporting Shooter's Association of Australia

Printed at Versa Press, Inc., East Peoria, IL

3 2 1

Countrysport Press
Camden, ME
www.countrysportpress.com
Orders: 800-685-7962
a division of Down East Enterprise,
publishers of *Shooting Sportsman* magazine
www.shootingsportsman.com

Library of Congress Control Number: 2003109707

Dedication...

— firstly to Arthur, who helped me by seeing the man in the boy and teaching him, and secondly to Wal, who carried on the lesson by seeing the boy in the man; both have forgotten more about this way of life than I'm ever likely to know, and this book is a mark of my respect, and acknowledgement of many a good day in the field;

— but also to all those folk everywhere who with skill and perhaps a little awe take game from the wild to eat it, as man always has done, and always will do.

... and Author's Note:

There are those who are going to ask if these tales are true.

All who love stories learn that sometimes to recount a tale just the way memory offers it up is to tell a greater truth than it would have been possible to convey if the exact chronological facts had been described in detail and everything else excluded.

My answer to those who need to know is that the large majority of these stories are indeed true.

All the rest are very true.

Contents

Foreword

by Bill Shelton,
National Vice President,
Sporting Shooters Association of Australia

In six decades or so of knocking about in this Australia of ours from the Eastern beaches to Kimberley country, I've met all sorts of characters from boss drovers to Aboriginal stockmen, from bush people to city folk, worked for managing directors of multinationals, known all sizes and persuasions, seen the good and the bad.

This book is written by one of the good ones, who seem to be becoming rarer as the years go by. It is by a bloke who I judge has a feeling for and understanding of not only the natural world of our bush country but, more importantly, its people. He has lived and worked in three states as a musician, factory hand, teacher and even as the obligatory taxi driver. Ron Forsyth is a man of many parts — amateur ballistician, acknowledged expert on shotguns and shooting, and also philosopher with a longstanding interest in jazz music and psychology. A childhood car accident left him without much opportunity to participate in team sports, but with a feeling for history and an expanding wish to understand the natural scheme of things.

This collection of timeless short stories, undoubtedly of real life events, will revive old memories for some and serve to explain and expound those days gone by to the current generation who unfortunately for them can't know the bush of yesterday.

The word 'whimsy' is in this book's sub-title for a good reason. It is by an Australian, but hunters everywhere have thought about the themes that are presented in it. When you read it you're going to laugh, but you're also going to cry. The themes are of the real world — real people, dogs and guns, and love and understanding of them all.

At the heart of it there is an awareness of what has always sent people into the bush with a gun. Like many others, I too have had to live in the city, but even in the bricks and mortar I've always been able to experience the bush by means of a book.

Ron Forsyth is well known to readers of the *Australian Shooters Journal.* He began writing on shotguns in the seventies when he discovered there was almost nothing Australian being written about them, and now his articles are widely read and quoted. I have had the pleasure of taking a few birds with him and to say Ron Forsyth is a competent field shot is to say Don Bradman could bat a bit.

Sad, but not Broken

We walked up the quail in the fairly dark winter daylight of mid-afternoon. Two good dogs we had, and he's a better shot than I am. It was good walking, though, and when the day drew on the clouds started to move apart from time to time.

The better light didn't help him, though, and I'd thought it might have. Usually he's at least two or three birds ahead of me; but he wasn't that day.

From the time we started off, I was convinced it was going to be a different kind of day. I just knew. I hoped it'd be a good one, and it started out to be, at least for me. I didn't inadvertently leave the safety on, not all day long. I didn't fumble for cartridges when I needed to reload in a hurry. The wind helped me by staying steady; it meant I didn't have to worry about constantly checking it to see what it was up to, what it would make the birds do as they rose. When I had a double rise, I took them both without struggling to get my feet right or having to look for the dogs to see that one of them hadn't run in. There were no puncture marks in my hide from walking into boxthorns, and I didn't stumble down any rabbit holes. No nails came up in my boots, and the dog took notice when I called.

All the while, over in his half of the partnership, that day — well, there was nothing I could put my finger on, even on reflection, with the benefit of perspective. It could only be described as a day when he couldn't connect. We all have them, and sometimes, for more than a few of us, they're days that turn into months. Not with him, though. Normally his safety was off as his gun touched his shoulder, his cartridges all accessible; normally he could see the dogs without looking, and the way his feet were pointing was a model for mine.

Not this day.

I think it boiled down to being a bit behind them, but at the time it wasn't that simple. As we took it in turns to walk in for the first shot over the pointing dog we talked about what was going wrong. We considered timing, thought about how well scent was holding on the grass, analysed the way the dogs were working. None of it helped.

Most of us learn that it's normally best to shoot our way out of a bad run, just keep doing it, and after a while the rhythm comes back with no more effort than keeping on breathing. It usually happens by itself. This day, though, with the damp on the grass and the clouds beginning to roll back, the birds were plump and strong as they are in early winter, and they rose with a vengeance, power in their stroke as they purred away over the rolling hills. Still for some reason I managed to hit them, and still he missed.

We're never competitive, he and I. Glad to say, it's something that never happens. If one of us had a bad run, then he'd find that he'd be getting the easier approach and a few more of the undisturbed birds; he'd find that the other had fallen back to look under a bush for a fox den, or stopped a dog to take a grass seed out of its eye, until perhaps his confidence started to improve and things began to work for him again.

But this time, as we went on and he was still not coming to grips with them, we approached our joint bag limit so it would have to end soon, and the clouds rolled back and put paid to the bad light of the black day that had been threatening rain but never giving it. With the poor light went his last excuse; we could see them, all right, so it wasn't that.

He even went back to the vehicle and changed guns, put the Merkel away and took out the Westley, the dear old gun that he saves for special occasions, so as not to put too much wear over its ninety-year-old steel. It was after that when I saw him grinding his teeth, saw the muscle flex in his jaw two or three times as he went in past the dog to take a shot. It's a good sign with him. It means he's fed up and he's digging his heels in, so that things are about to change. It means he's turning serious.

He fringed a couple more, I had to help out on a third. I tried standing aside, and I tried walking in with him; together we blamed the dogs for not setting well, we blamed the wind — we did it all, and none of it helped. It was just a bad day for him.

All the while, as it was worse for him, I shot better than I usually do. It seemed a twist of the knife. Then there came the incident that I'll never forget. It was on the side of a long slope that fell away to the left, and the two dogs were both holding a bird, rock hard on point.

He walked in to take the flush, and he was just a few feet past me when it rose. I'd followed the dogs closely, so again I could clearly see the muscle flex in his jaw as he concentrated. I thought to myself as it rose that it was a quail due to be dead before its third wingbeat.

When it was in the air, his swing seemed fluid enough; yet the pattern from his cylinder barrel still smacked the wet green grass over a yard behind it, and I distinctly saw his eyes narrow and his mouth disappear in a line as his decades of discipline told, and he half dropped the gun, and went through the mount again to re-establish his timing. He drove off his back foot and his hips worked the gun ahead as the bird rolled with the breeze behind and powered away in a hard curve to the left, not flying straight ahead. He flung in the second barrel with his mouth grim.

At that particular moment from out of the belly of Time and riding the wind there fell from the sky a peregrine falcon, with his eyes only on his prey, a quail in full flight. It is the only time I've ever seen a quail on which a raptor stooped. It happened precisely at the time that someone was shooting at it, and on the only thoroughly bad day I've ever seen that someone have.

How long does it take to snap a shot at a fast quail? A half a second sees most of it over with. We hunted for well over four hours that day, and four hours is just on fourteen and a half thousand seconds, and if we divided that up into half seconds, that's one chance in twenty-nine thousand the falcon had of getting it wrong. But he did, and flew straight into that second barrel, four feet behind the quail — again — and he never knew what hit him. He was going about his business, and then he was no more.

I had an unhappy friend. It's not hard to understand why. We like the birds of prey and we wish them no harm; they only do with their beaks and talons what we do with our shotguns. It was the most capricious of accidents, and yet probably in his mind, his unusually defective swing seemed somehow all the more to blame for the turn taken by events.

****

Perhaps the clouds came back. I can't say I remember. No, on that occasion his shooting didn't get any better, and when at last we made our way back to the car, it was mostly in silence. I suppose we each had things on the mind. I can't speak for him, though I'll bet he kept on thinking specifically of that falcon, and not his bad swing, because that's what I was thinking of, and in many respects we're so much alike.

Yes, I had that falcon on my mind. I was thinking of how much it had to teach me.... thinking that when it's my turn to get out of bed on a day I'm fated not to see the sun set on, I hope it's a day like that, with a cool wind, and all my personal force, whatever it may be, still with me, and all my focus on a goal that I know best. That's how it is in nature — or, at least, how it can be.

I want to ride the wind of my destiny, and after I'm gone, when my friends remember me, I want them to be as I am when I remember the falcon.

Sad, but not broken.

A Blur on Legs

I was five when my mother died unexpectedly, and my father brought me up alone. In the years later, I was known as the son of the man with the big crossbred dog. The burden of looking after us both must have been heavily borne sometimes.

From time to time I went down to Melbourne on the train, when he unloaded me onto relatives so he could have a spell, and one of the early times I went stays with me.

I remember the railway station, with the hiss and the rush of steam; blackness of soot comes back with the picture, as does the trouble I had keeping up, while my father took me up and down the platform, his eyes scanning the crowd. I didn't understand then, just went as I was bidden, and his hand was warm over mine.

It wasn't all that big a town, but a lot of people congregated there, and mostly I remember legs, serge, severe suits on men and women.

His tread firmed, and he put me in front of a big man with blond hair. His name was Sandy McLennan and he was boarding the train.

"Would you take the lad to town with you, Sandy, keep an eye on him?"

Yes, he would, said Sandy, and I went with him into the compartment and took a seat beside him. He was my custodian to safety at the other end, and received his instructions carefully. The trip was uneventful for me, so he must have done just as he said he would. I remember his big hands on my shoulders were red and gnarled.

Thirty years later, I reminded my father of the incident, and reminisced with him about the way he'd taken me to the station confident that he'd see someone he knew, and I'd be watched over on the journey. The times were different, it's true, but people have never taken chances with their children. I idly asked him why he'd let me go on the train to Melbourne with Sandy McLennan.

"Because Sandy was a man who did what he said he'd do", he told me, before he added as an afterthought "....and he could fight like a threshing machine."

I saw no reason to question him any more.

****

I was doing what I often did, walking on the street, maybe a year or two later as I was getting on for about ten, when I next saw Sandy McLennan. He stopped his big old Dodge and just scooped me up. There was a doe-eyed whippet on the leather back seat, and I didn't know it at the time but there was a .22 Winchester Rimfire in a case, as well. In a while, when we pulled up at the paddock we were going to, he took it out and showed me, and explained its longer chamber to me, told me that it would be different from the .22 we'd have at home, standing somewhere in a corner, explaining that the bullets wouldn't interchange. Perhaps my father had already told him about my air gun and the way I was allowed to use it. I don't know.

He was right, though, there was a .22, the old Winchester '06 slide action that was propped in a corner by the sideboard in the living room. The bullets were in the drawer beside, and I knew that I was never to handle the rifle without an adult present. It was no hardship, because any time I wanted to see it I only had to ask, and it would be presented to me, shown safe, and I could aim it, imagining that one day I'd shoot rabbits the way the adults in my life did.

So it came to be that I first went afield after a dog while I was in short pants. A whippet is a dog not often seen now. She was his pride and joy, though he never said so. Even at that age I knew by the way he looked at her. He recognized what she was for, and she understood, too, which made for a wonderful economy of emotion between them. Sandy's whippet was delicate and finely proportioned, and when she stood on the top of a grassy hill outside town, Sandy beside her, she assumed a force I'd never seen before in a dog. She became transformed. From slender and vulnerable in the back seat of the old car, she turned into an annexe of Sandy, an increase of his powers.

We walked up and down gently rolling hills until the moment came when we put up a rabbit, and she watched him for her instructions. At a nod of his head, she was gone, the fastest thing I'd ever seen on four legs, maybe to this day. The rabbit had bolted from a squat near the top of a hill, just in the lee of the wind, and we had a perfect position to see it happen, the short, breathless chase across the flats, the rabbit trying to shift the game into the tussocks so the twisting and turning would defeat the dog, and the dog trying to carry it out onto the open ground, where the end would be swift and sure, with one quick snatch and a toss of her practised muzzle meaning it was all over.

She stopped beside the rabbit after the single snapping bite that killed it, and together we walked down to fetch the carcass. She sat panting by it with her ribs heaving, and waited for the praise she knew would be hers. When he patted her he took her whole face in his two hands.

In a while the whole process was repeated, and Sandy walked with two rabbits in one hand, their legs notched, the rifle balanced easily in the other. He stopped at two kills, perhaps afraid that if the dog ran after any more her delicate mechanism, that I pictured as clockwork, would somehow wear out. I was disappointed that there had been no need to fire the rifle, but he noticed that, and before we went to the car, he picked a white rock nearly a hundred yards away in front of a big, moist bank of earth, and when I'd had three shots at it he said that was enough. He let me pocket the spent copper cases, and we drove home, the dog smiling as she slept.

Two days later, I was walking from the playground at the top of the street and Sandy drove down to our house, arriving before me. He lived with just his wife, no children of his own, and probably she'd sent him down on the errand, knowing our circumstances. He stepped out of the car carrying a casseroled rabbit, done up in an earthenware pot.

"That's fair," Sandy said when I arrived and looked in at it. "One for us and one for you."

It was more than fair. We ate it appreciatively that night, my father and I. He was never much of a cook, and he enjoyed it as much as I did. In a day or two it became my job to return the pot to Mrs McLennan, washed, so that I could thank her for us both.

In the year or two that followed and before they moved away, whenever I would pass the McLennans on the street, I was conscious of something that has stayed with me to this day. Sandy McLennan might have been a rough labouring man, but when he looked at his dog, it worshipped him, and when he fed it at night he was only doing what the dog in its turn did for him.

I know it now, but I think it is far more important that I also knew it then. When I took back the casserole dish, and made the thanks that one neighbour gives to another for a kindness shown, a chapter had been closed. I'd had no grasp of these things till one day a man who lived nearby had seen a boy on the street with time on his hands, and nothing ever after would be the same. A dog, a black blur on legs, had fed us all. Something in me had been satisfied.

En Passant

When I arrived in the big city and stayed with my grandmother for the long holidays, between my tenth and thirteenth years, I was soon bored. That's what happens at this age. Summer was long, but there was relief in sight in the form of a blacksmith whose name was Fred Smith, a man retired from his forge.

One time when he was bored, he put on his wire-framed reading glasses and learned 'Horatius at the Bridge' and all the time I knew him he could recite it by heart. Boredom offended something in him and he saw no need for it in a boy. He was the only man I ever saw do cartwheels, and he was eighty-one years old at the time. He lived alone on the lot next door, his family all gone, and was building his own house, so he lined and finished the first room, living comfortably enough in it while he worked on the rest. His dog was a blue heeler, and every morning he'd taunt him and stir him up before letting him off his chain for a footrace to the bottom of the long gravelled driveway, where he'd pick up his delivered milk. The dog always won, but I noted he didn't stop doing it.

He was working on the roof and it was from its apex that he toppled when he had the stroke. He landed in a gorse bush and I was the one who found him spreadeagled there, speechless, on his back. His grey eyes were wide with fright. I went for an ambulance, and we had bonded.

He lived in the single room from then on, and his lively intelligence stayed with him if his physical sprightliness left. He closed his mind to unreasonable sanguine expectancy and he lived within the new perimeters life had set for him.

Among other things, he told me that it was time I learned to play chess. I did, and he had no mercy on me. He said life was too hard for anyone ever to expect a free ride, even when they were only learning the rules, and defeat was as much a part of life as success, and I was to accept it. I did, again and again, interminably, every time he said 'checkmate'; then, at the end of the holiday time I went home and I found a folding money gift in my suitcase, put there with a note from him, apologizing for seeming hard on me.

For three years he took part in my education. He provoked me, goaded me, laughed at and with me, showed me respect, pined for his past sometimes when the shadows were long, read, threw ideas at me, taught me more chess.

One day he moved one of his pawns past mine and with a cock-eyed motion across the board he took it. *En passant* — it was a move that always seemed anomalous to me. "Arn pazarn", he pronounced it, because his education was all from his own reading, and he'd never heard French spoken. In the manner of many social chess players of the day, he believed that for it to be a legal move, the words had to be uttered, so that's what he did: "In passing". It came as a shock. It didn't seem to fit in with the otherwise orderly rules. It looked back-handed to me, the kind of manoeuvre that would be dreamt up by a southpaw. Having to speak aloud in a foreign language at the same time didn't make a grasp of it any more accessible. I hadn't expected it, and it seemed to me another purpose-built affirmation that in the company of the young, people always assume they can change the rules to their advantage.

Nothing could have been further from his intentions. I spent hours staring at his wooden, ornate chessboard. It taught me patience and till then I'd never known such determination as I felt in in my quest at least one time to defeat him. He'd made the whole set by hand, shortly after the turn of the century, and I had no reason to suppose it was his most valued possession, and none to suppose it wasn't. He owned very little.

Then one day, for the first time he brought out and showed me his rifle. It was a single shot .22 Brevette, made in Belgium. It was delicately built, with exquisitely filed open sights. We were in the end of suburbia, but he let me shoot it, nobody paying much attention in those days, and in retrospect his only interest was in watching how safely I handled it. I'd already told him I'd had an air gun since I was nine, but I suppose he'd decided to make sure.

On a subsequent holiday, perhaps six months later, as I was about to leave to go home and back to school, he called me in to give me two gifts. Neither was wrapped, because I think it was an old and lonely man's pleasure to watch my face when I saw them.

He gave me both his rifle and his chess set, simply, undemonstratively. My first .22 meant more to me than any gift I've ever received in my life. It was to go home with me on the train, broken down in my suitcase, a ticket to a new world, and I had instructions to tell my father that it was mine to use only when he saw fit to allow it.

It dawned on me that if I were to take them, then the old man wouldn't have them, and so I asked him why he was giving them to me. He told me he was admitting himself to a rest home, and to my thirteen-year-old experience that was explanation enough. All he asked, he said, was that I write to him.

****

I like to think of myself as a man who has no regrets. I like to say when pressed that always, whatever it was, whatever of my life and times the discussion is running over, I did the best I could with what I had to work with, and there's no point in recriminations. As I recall these events, though, it's a boast that starts ringing hollow.

He was dead in ten weeks, and he must have known he was going to be, but, to my shame, he was gone without any letter from me. I was too young to understand, I tell myself, too young. Yet if people were somehow allowed to nominate just one mistake in life that they could rescind, I think that one would be mine.

I shot many and many a rabbit with that little rifle till it was retired, worn out, and my daughter will have the chess set.

"In passing".... we all are. But my word, Fred, you were a sound and gracious human being.

Arthur - A Study in Mentors

There were a lot of good bushmen in my early life, and it's something worthy of acknowledgement. I remember Mister Schenk with fondness, as one who did sterling work. My school mate was his grandson, and so I found myself in his care going rabbiting on weekends.

I don't even recall his given name because I can't have heard too many adults call him by it, he never informed me of it, and it wasn't for me to ask. To my young high school eyes, he was identified by his blue boiler suit, so much so that I wondered when he died in his eighties if they'd buried him in it. He took mineral water for his arthritis and if one of his joints became too bad he'd go out into the yard and cause a co-operative bee to sting it. He said it worked.

What was important to us was that he knew the bush and the creatures in it and on weekends he took us into it. I suspect that he perceived by instinct that it would be wrong not to. We needed to go there and that was the end of it. He was a grown man at the turn of last century and he patiently educated his young charges about the changes he'd seen, about what he saw as a loss of principle in the unfolding new world, about the gangs that roved in the cities and the way they behaved, making him believe in the validity of his choice of a farming life. He was always happy to take us back there, out of the town, and if we could bring home blackberries or mushrooms as well as rabbits then he was a doubly happy man.

We plugged along in his six-cylinder Pontiac, which he drove in first gear and third, never using second. Perhaps it was a belief in frugality that led him to save it. He took us to places that I realize now had importance for him; to us they were just places, settings to find furred targets that tasted good.

He walked round and round the tussocky country he took us into, and he never shot and in fact never even took a rifle. That wasn't what he was there for. I couldn't understand it then, but I do now. While we kids bolted across country and covered ground, always racing for the next hill against the failing of the light, he was happy to see us go, and equally happy to hear us come back foot-sore and bone tired to tell him what we had seen. While we were covering miles, he meandered in what looked to us like tedious circles and he never took himself out of sight of the car. We didn't have the patience for stalking.

His first question always used to be about how many rabbits we had. We'd lay down the slain and tell him the total. We might have six between us, but he'd have eight or ten. His tally was not made up of the ones he shot, but the ones he could've shot despite his shaky hands, through the eye, sitting in their squats, from just a few feet away. We used to protest it wasn't fair that he never actually pulled a trigger on the rabbits he saw, and we had to have ours in the hand. He almost always ended up with a better score in his way than we did in ours, stumbling around the fallen trees like lost baby elephants. When we'd been beaten in yet another of our contests, he'd give his dry little chuckle, but the thought that he'd have lied to us or even exaggerated his non-bag was just out of the question; he wasn't capable of it. We gradually learned the sense in his stalking methods and overcame the exuberance of our own.

Two events stand out in my memories of him; one was the day he started talking to another rabbit shooter who pulled up alongside us as we organized our rifles at the back of the car before we walked off, and I glanced his way in time to see him looking uneasy. His wife had come out for the run that day, and she was sitting in the passenger seat with her window down. The other rabbit shooter was near her, and I saw the old man's brow knit up and knew something was making him indignant. I wandered around just in time to hear him tell the brash younger man that if he swore in front of his wife once more he intended to punch him on the nose. He was past eighty at the time.

I observed a couple of things from that. The rabbit shooter began minding his mouth. Also, needless to say, his wife thought the world of him.

The other incident I remember showed his childlike absorption in the natural world he took us out to expose us to. He found two tiny lizards at war one day, and he lay on the ground like a child, chin cupped in his hands, lost to the world, to watch them sort it out. He encouraged our wonder.

I think fondly of old Mister Schenk, but his real work was preparing the way for Arthur, who made the bigger impact. He came a little later and was the one who captured my youthful energy and sent it more substantially towards the bush, and the way he did it was once again by example.

Arthur fought in a war and when he came back he had not a lot of hearing left to speak of, or to, and a profound inner life that I was able at least to glimpse if not tap into. When pressed he talked engagingly of fish and of streams and lakes and ducks and foxes.

He told me once of the only plague of hares I ever heard of, the way it passed through the district he lived in. If I had to give evidence on my own behalf as a boy, I'd at least have to agree that I did listen. I found it remarkable to hear of the way the hares could be seen moving through any part of the landscape, almost any day, just by walking up onto a hill and looking down. They'd come past a few at a time, going mainly in circles, and he learned how to trap them by seeing the line they were taking and running down the hill to position himself on it ahead of them with a rabbit trap. There'd be one making stew inside the hour.

With his oilskin coat he was the one who taught the young would-be hunter that rain wouldn't do him any lasting harm. When it was cold and wet we had no shooting opposition in his favourite paddocks. I was to learn that he could smell rabbits, and that when his nose sent him towards a set of tussocks in the winter drizzle it was because he already knew what was in them. He shot a wickedly choked old Italian hammergun and used heavy loads of number three shot. When he laid a pattern over a rabbit, unless he shot it up front it wasn't worth picking up. If he missed any more than one shot in a day, he could have been thought of as having a bad one; it took me a long time to wake up to the fact that like a lot of successful shotgunners, he was choosey about his shots. This he let me discover for myself.

Perhaps in life's grand scheme it didn't amount to much, a skinny kid and a squarely-built man in waterproofs carrying shotguns and three or four pairs of rabbits, putting down squelching footprints in soft green-covered loam. It meant a lot to me, though. I knew from him that this was right and proper. When we did this together, and he took me and his old double-barrelled hammergun out to one of his favourite rabbiting spots, we owed no apologies, and by common but unspoken agreement, none of his problems from the workday or mine from adolescence were going to break into our time in the paddock. Clouds were not allowed on that horizon.

In those formative years of mine there was a long stretch of months when every weekend he laid another slab of concrete in the yard of his new house. It took me a little while to calculate that it was going to take him some time to work his way around it all, mixing and laying a square a week, but in time I saw this was a regular event and then I made it my business to turn up in the morning and pick up a shovel.

I found that as a result I often ended up in his car in the afternoon of the same day being taken out to shoot a rabbit. This was part of an early and healthy discovery of the laws of cause and effect. Again it's hardly earth-shaking information, but it seems to me now that all too often the young are denied an environment where they can learn that when people help lay concrete, they may be rewarded with some rabbit shooting.

I didn't learn anything about perfecting my swing from Arthur; nor did I learn about shot sizes or chokes. Instead, I learned a principle when I needed to know it: what I did with a shotgun had value. Every head of game I brought home was an achievement and gave a sense of participation in a scheme that had run well enough without me in the past, but was nevertheless prepared to admit me without judgement. This wasn't the way I entered the adult world, but it was the way I put my toe over the threshold.

There were other things to learn from him, some of them later. In his retirement he bought his wife, my aunt, the refrigerator he'd always promised her. The shop attendant gave it to them at wholesale price, even though they'd been retail customers when they'd bought it. When she saw the difference, she concluded there was some mistake, and called into the shop next time she was passing. But the salesman only smiled and said he'd given them the best price he could and still keep his job, because he recognized Arthur; when he was a small boy in a big family his father had been a potato farmer, and Arthur was the local mechanic. When times were tough, the bills they were supposed to receive to keep the decrepit old farm truck running somehow had a way of getting themselves lost. He was just repaying the favour.

One day Arthur and I were in his car and topped a rise before a sweeping bend on the way to our Saturday afternoon shoot. In the still of the country road we came across a car on its roof on the grassy verge with a wisp of smoke coming from where it shouldn't and a large woman sprawled half upright, leaning against one wheel, her equally large friend lying further away on the grass, both of them with glazed eyes. A quick survey of the scene showed that they'd blown a tyre and the car had rolled, and they'd both been flung out the passenger door, to land heavily enough to knock them silly. He looked at the smoke, looked at me, made his estimate of our chances and told me to step lively. I did as I was told and kept up with him. I'd never seen him move so fast. He went straight to the one by the car, and took the heavy end, which was just as well, while I lifted her legs. She didn't protest, didn't cooperate. We had her fifty feet away from it when it exploded in a fireball, and in an instant the paint peeled off unforgettably as the extraordinary heat rolled over us. He'd taken a considered risk with his life and mine, and as a result had won hers. When we drove away anonymously, the sirens by then wailing closer, she still hadn't realized what she'd been saved from. I pondered on it, and decided that considered risks are the province of the experienced. It wasn't for me to know then that one day a couple of decades later I'd come on a car accident, see that familiar wisp of smoke, and have a rough idea of how many seconds I had to do something about it.

Sometimes these days when I hear some televised politician instructing us self-righteously about what's erroneously termed gun control, I wonder if I might be a misplaced pawn on God's chessboard. My government seems to want to take away my guns, on the basis that they threaten the public good; and it's then that I wonder, this old adolescent, privileged to have spent time in the company of wiser men, people of childlike curiosity and mature courage, yes, wonder just how it is I could have been so foolish as to have suffered from misplaced values all this time.

Tommo

In my day, some people turned to shooting to eat; some began more to stave off boredom. Others followed a family connection, a tradition they couldn't break, shooting clay targeets or military rifle or smallbore. There were many like me. In time, I shot rabbits for money — ferreted them, too, and trapped them, and generally breathed their air, sneezed their fur from up my nose, and what's worse, found their fleas all over my ankles like a blanket, sometimes.

Took them with a rifle, took them with a shotgun... in the summer mornings, when I'd try to be in the paddock by six, and have to pedal twelve or fifteen miles on a fixed-wheel bicycle to get there, it's safe to say I set the alarm clock for early; in winter, climbing out of bed on a Saturday morning and contemplating the same trip after discovering a cold, heavy drizzle had started unheralded overnight, there was only one spur, and that was the arrangement of the day before, a promise given, not something to renege on.

The money for the casual rabbiting boy was poor, but the discipline was priceless, because it was all internal. I didn't like the rain and the heat, but I liked the success.

What crystallized it, though, my motion towards the bush?

****

Last night when I was out in the car near my duck hole, an hour or so before sunset, I saw a blue-winged shoveller fly, saw the fast, driving wings, and it came back, the real reason. Perhaps as close as I'll ever come to it, anyway.

****

We came to be good mates. We were barely fifteen at the beginning. I carried my old single shot rifle and stood in awe of his Hollis hammergun. He was the senior partner.

To be where we had to go we'd mount bicycles and we'd travel miles, which are longer than kilometres, and harder to pedal over.

And the rain was wetter in those days, and the frost was colder... Yes, I know; I plead guilty, and I'll try to romanticize nothing. But even when I grit my teeth and cut all this back to bare bones, it still comes out as a good life. We never came to be masters of the rabbit game but we were set to take bachelors' degrees. At the end of most weekends, at least, we had the first prerequisite: we stank to the sky.

We juggled rabbits and traps and ferret boxes and all the gear we needed on bicycle handlebars; we walked ourselves to weariness, before pedalling home in stiff head winds; we nearly drowned in creeks, we slid alarmingly on steep paths running on precipitous, rocky cliffs and we never thought it all a struggle. I don't know why. I'd put the dog on someone who asked me to do it now.

I assumed at the time that there were many of our own age who were like we were, but later on it dawned on me that in fact it wasn't everybody who did what we did and saw value in what we saw. Only some. I salute Tommo's wise parents, who were smart enough to be conspirators in the march toward our rabbiting goals. They were numbered in the front ranks of those adults who gave meaning to what we did, with their honest appreciation of how our activities were directing us in our lives. They must have believed our achievements were teaching us values that would be important to us later. Their acknowledgement of our hunting needs was never grudging, and mild irony was their sternest reproach. They were practical and gentle people, and I'd like to think that in the way we grew up, we might not have given them any special reward, but at least we left behind no reason for reproach. Sometimes he and I would ride to where we were going, spend the day there, and by arrangement they'd drive out to collect us in the dark. This gave us an extra productive hour or two in the paddock, and I used to feel at the time that such would be the kind of concession that the saintly could look forward to receiving in heaven, assuming saints rode bicycles.

They'd come and they'd pick us up with our load of rabbits and eels and sometimes even the odd trout, all garnered by two boys who hadn't started shaving, and it was provender of ours to deploy, for sale, for our families to eat, as gifts. Just however we saw fit. When we came home, I felt like Ulysses, home from the sea — Ulysses with a single shot .22.

I remember the black night after one such rabbiting day in winter. They picked us up in their old green Chev and as we rolled over one of our landmark hills, it turned its hundred thousand miles on the odometer. They'd seen it coming, waited on it patiently, and as the numerals rolled around, all the family cheered in salute of the old car's valour. This rabbiting, I mused, was surely a family affair. It might've been cold outside, but it was warm in the car.

The creeks we were always poking around in gave us a sense of place and belonging, and one in particular was a source of many of our triumphs. It stood to show us things we didn't know, and yet somehow thought important. A plane flew up it one day, while we were in it, on the side of its wide banks, ferreting. We heard the rumble of an approaching motor and couldn't place it. No wonder. It was below ground level, until it came round the gentle bend downstream, and there it was, a fair dinkum aeroplane. It twisted and rolled its way past, close enough for us to make brief eye contact with the pilot. No wonder he looked a bit preoccupied. I don't know who he was trying to impress, or if it was worth it, but I conclude he was taking a risk. He went beyond, staying in the wide, meandering creekbed, and flew out of our ambit, just another of the unexpected things that happened.

And this is the way it went. In our rabbiting lives, we never knew what would come up next. All manner of people, bush folk and farmers, the rich and the poor, the sympathetic and the sour, had one flimsy thing in common that they probably never even knew about: they went past us, and as kids we watched them.

It was good for us to be picked up hitch-hiking by a farmer, or go trying to put together a row of permissions to enter adjoining properties at night to go spotlight shooting with a motorcycle battery; I recall acceptances, sometimes near-joyous, and the odd rejection, too (almost always because there were no rabbits, not because we were young), the occasional hand to dig out a ferret gone walkabout, and never, never patronization. One day a farmer listened to us as we asked permission to camp a few days in his wool shed, and walked away before we'd finished. We threw quizzical looks at each other, thinking we'd offended him. But all he did was go to the implement shed, start his Ferguson tractor, and then bring it over to us, still standing where he left us. In front of our widening eyes he told us it had plenty of fuel and we should put it back where it belonged when we were ready to go home. The next night we sat like old members of the family by the fire in his sitting room, tousle-haired guests, enthralled while he played concertina and his neighbour violin, in between limitless helpings of their wives' home-made cake. We neither of us knew how to drive a tractor when we'd stood outside his shed, but two days and fifty rabbit warrens later that had all been rectified.

The world seemed rich with characters.

Roy Bell was another, a rabbiter with a stiff leg from the war, and a family of ten to feed. He was the only man I ever saw who could set a rabbit trap one-handed. If we could fit into his twenty-year-old car with no top gear or door linings, then he'd take us with him. There were a couple of poles slung transversely through it, poking out all four wound-down windows, and an indeterminate number of his tribe would clamber in around them, bringing in their perpetual squabble. They never took into account the way those same poles would be carrying thirty or forty pairs of rabbits on the trip home, and if the journey out was crowded, the one back was unforgettable, and all the more if it was in summer.

We'd trundle a few kilometres to where he'd have his trapline, and if the hubbub became too much for him, he'd slow the car to a walk, reach back with one hand for a fistful of hair, open the door and sling it out with the body attached underneath it, and we'd proceed to the accompaniment of at least a lesser degree of pandemonium. Innocent or guilty, the bruised ex-passenger would walk home along a road empty of all but powdery dust. Roy's family wasn't prone to tragic frailty.

He carried a bolt action, open-sighted .22 as he walked the line, and he head-shot any sitter he spotted. He'd smoothly ease the pole off his back, dropping ten or fifteen pairs of rabbits to the ground, and he'd shoot. Even on the run, a rabbit up to sixty or seventy yards away was likely to be in for more than a fright. It had to be. I was there at the end of one day and happened to see him performing the ritual bullet hand-over to his wife. Her count showed him three rounds down for the day, and hands on hips she was shrill as she wanted to know the individual fate of them. She was deaf to his protests ("Struth, woman, give a man a fair go!") because bullets cost money ("Why don't yer wake up to yerself, Roy?") and he ought to keep his mind on the job.

They say that behind every good man there stands a woman.

At the end of the day they'd sit on creaky kitchen chairs and eat a rough meal, spreading their thick bread with the ubiquitous staple, Vegemite, or with stiff hunks of jam gouged out of open, sticky tins in the centre of the bare wooden table. Afterwards they'd repair to the next room, where the whole family, or however many could be run to earth, would skin the day's catch, preparing the rabbits for the butcher shop Roy supplied, and then pegging out the skins for sale to a merchant. Even the six-year-old wielded a razor blade.

No, none of these folk ever patronized us; like adolescents everywhere we stood looking for an entrance to the adult world, and as we slipped into it we were lucky enough to be able to stand alongside a few people who understood our interests.

This history was part of what made me an interested observer, but it didn't make me a committed hunter. It's one thing to be initiated by a few adults into a wider world, another to enter that world on equal footing with one's peers. The first is a treat or an experiment, but the second is a decision and a commitment.

****

One day on the side of our big creek Tommo and I had amassed a large pile of rabbits, a good load for two.

He was carrying the old Hollis in his right arm, muzzies down; this I remember, because he had to lug the clumsy wooden ferret box on its long leather strap over his back, and also the mattock, the ferreter's friend, on which was slung a whole row of paired rabbits, and this protruded backwards over his left shoulder.

It was late autumn, clear and cold; the sun had been shining but was setting, and the cold, fast stream of the big creek was enough to take the breath away, and it was made all the worse by the breeze that was intensifying as night came on.

We were on course to exhaustion, a state I recall well from those days when with more energy than sense we'd work ourselves to a standstill through late afternoon, and then eat, wait for nightfall and go spotlighting rabbits on foot till dawn.

As we trudged around the creek this day, bearing our load, a blue-wing shoveller rose off a tiny inlet where it had settled. Tommo obviously didn't think about it; he raised the hammergun and cocked it some way or another, and then swung on the rising duck and shot it, all one-handed. It was a triumph, a rabbit shooter's crowning glory, and it was to taste like it, too, when his grandmother solemnly served us half each at the table next evening.

After it was added to the already considerable bag, we picked our way through the rocky hillside to the point where the creek had to be crossed. It was a part of the journey we didn't relish, but like misplaced shoveller ducks it was just something that happened, and we tried to regard it as neutrally as we could.

I don't know.... boots didn't seem to fit as well in those days. There were blisters on heels, maybe from holes in socks, I can't recall. The water from the crossing always made it worse, anyhow, the walk back in the cold with blistered feet, boots wet through.

This night, as that is what it fast became, we'd stood higher up, watching the current. Perhaps there was something particular about the day that moved him; perhaps there wasn't. We'd made the crossing plenty of times before. But this time, Tommo, who was bigger than I was, just plunged across the stream first while I was still finding a way down the sheep path I'd selected. When I got there, he ploughed back, without his gear.

"No sense both of us getting wet," he said, and he motioned me aboard. I rode him over, and then in a final trip he picked up the gear I'd left on the bank.

It cemented a friendship. At fifteen it was an uncharacteristic thing for one boy to do for another, if my reading of the age group today is anything to go by.

Ultimately, what struggled up the far hill was one wet boy and one grateful dry one, a pile of rabbits and a blue-winged shoveller that lost its way once too often. I can't speak for Tommo; he went overseas not all that long after and maybe that changed a few things. But I can speak for me, and say that the dry half of the combination that trudged heavy-footed in the direction of the sun's last light was by then confirmed, a rabbit shooter always.

Rabbits and the Street

I was still a boy. We were going rabbit shooting, and we knew we'd find a few. I was happy. It's one thing to go rabbiting, but it's another to be completely certain of rolling along into a good afternoon's shooting and to look forward to the reward of stews and happy dogs and farmers' smiles, all for doing a public duty that you've lain awake at night anticipating.

There were just the two of us, and as we passed in the car through the tar and cement we came on a knot of street thugs, a city-generated blue coloured encrustation that seemed to have trickled out of the bad housing and then glued itself to the dirty bricks of the hotels and the empty buildings.

On this day before my mentor had bundled me off in the car he'd just had what might be called a lively discussion with a friend of the family, who'd found out that he was going rabbit shooting. She'd tried to give him a hard time. She was scandalized — obviously hadn't known he shot at all. She reacted powerfully against the idea of hunting anything. Cruelty, rabbits never hurt anybody, pick on somebody your own size.... It was an unusual attitude for those days, and I think he was embarrassed for her more than for himself.

What peeved her more than anything was that he was taking me with him, just a teenager, having all this exposure at a tender age to what she saw as a distasteful practice. It was her vocation to save the world, and she likely went on to land a good position working for the government. She's probably even now protecting us all from ourselves, Superintendent of Standards somewhere behind a spacious desk in the Department of Everything.

As we slowed to negotiate the sad spectacle of the street kids, something happened. Young folk have always congregated on street corners in cities, and I can't say I paid a lot of attention to them. I more or less took them for granted. They didn't belong to my world. I'd passed through that temptation. My father had taken me aside about then, and told me that he wanted me not to associate with a previously good friend of mine from school. Up till then we'd occasionally been taking him fishing, and, surprised, I asked him why. He said that he was spending too much time on the street and his eyes were turning wild, and no good was going to come of it. Offered as yet another unwelcome insight from the adult world, I thought this was mad, but I did as I was told, at least partly because my friend promptly left school.

The next time I saw him he was walking home, seven miles out of town, having just had every tooth top and bottom on the left-hand side of his mouth knocked out in a fight; apparently he'd made the mistake of keeping on getting up. A few months later he was involved in a murder.

That was him, an ex-friend. As for me, I was going rabbit shooting.

So on this day, we rolled on through the city and I came to realize he was driving in silence. There was something on his mind. I waited till he was ready.

"I was in a street gang once," he said, a few blocks later, obviously having followed my eyes to see what I was looking at.

He was a pillar of society and past sixty, so this took me back a bit. But I sensed a story coming and made quick carry-on noises, and I was happy to find that he kept going.

"We spent our time on street corners. I was thirteen when I started and fourteen when I stopped. All the others were older. I was on the outer, but I was learning fast."

I wondered out loud what youths used to do on corners fifty years before, and he told me.

"We drank anything we could afford. We fought with other kids, and we fought with each other when we couldn't find anybody else to fight with.

"We stole from bakers and from greengrocers' carts. We stood over strangers our own age and we beat them up when we thought we'd get away with it.

"Mostly nothing happened to us to hurt us. We just got worse and worse over about a year or so.

"First it was other kids we roughed up. Then it was old women, for their handbags. I didn't like that much, but I didn't stop it, either...."

I'd forgotten rabbit shooting and I looked around, not to see the city I knew; I saw it as it once was, as though by gaslight in the dusk, run down even then, the odd T-model Ford, full of bored teenagers in dungarees and Tasmanian Blueys, short back and sides and roll your own. I asked what happened.

"Local copper," he said. "Turned the corner one Saturday afternoon. We were all there. Walked up to Nobby, six foot three, fastest hands I ever saw. He'd already worked out Nobby was the leader. Had his truncheon out, behind his back, and the first thing Nobby knew was his collarbone breaking. Whack! Whack! Once each side of his neck, and both Nobby's arms just fell down useless. Hadn't seen that before, I can tell you.

"Never said much. Just held Nobby's head up with the front end of his truncheon stuck under his chin, looked him in the eyes, and they were going kind of glassy, and said 'Now, listen, son, I've got somethin' to tell you. Leave old ladies in peace. Your mother'll have to wipe your backside for you every morning for the next six weeks, and every time she does, you think of me.' Then he turned around and walked off."

It was a powerful story, but I sensed it hadn't finished, even though no more words were coming. So I prodded a bit. "Did you stay with the gang?"

"What gang?" he asked. "It'd broken up before poor old Nobby'd got led away.

"But anyway, the next Saturday must've been the policeman's day off, and he turned up on our doorstep just after breakfast. Knew my old man. Said he had something better for me to do than stand around on street corners making trouble."

I watched through the car window as another one, just such a corner, went by, again dressed up in the black and the blue of aimless adolescents. In those days they weren't so liable to be high on something, but they had the same lost look as they've got today, and I doubt there was a lot of difference.

"I never stood on another street corner again," he said. "Y'see, he took me rabbit shooting. That was fifty years ago. I'm still doing it."

We drove on out of the city, and as the houses thinned out I thought about them both, the rabbits in the bush and the other kind of rabbits, the ones that hang out on street corners.

Most of all, I thought about the middle aged woman he'd argued with, whose misguided sentimentality helped to keep them both, the long-eared and the short, where they were — and are.

Bad Economics

We all have our days when the gun barrel is crooked and the game has the last laugh. If we complain about our lot in the matter of game and hunting, that's probably one of the things that we have in common with our ancestors. Anyone thinking it's hard to afford ammunition, or that the properties aren't there to gain access to, or that in some other way life's got him in its sights, perhaps ought to take some advice and realize that it's no new phenomenon. Most of us shoot from budgets that are less than limitless, and in all this we're like every other generation of people ever to shoot for the pot.

I wonder if Donnie is still alive. He was what could be termed accident prone. He finished one leg of his career, as it were, by finishing one of his legs, which he did when he rode his old Indian motorcycle into a horse, a meeting that had sorry consequences in leaving him with a limp and doing I don't know what to the horse.

The time in question was the late thirties, the tail end of the Depression, when people were only able to struggle on and hope for better days. They weren't tough in terms that most of us could summon up, but truly tough, as the history books testify, when people went without food, and ate whatever they could catch.

Donnie took it into his head to go and shoot a few rabbits at a place called Green Hills, which today is covered all over with little boxes made of ticky-tacky, and they all look just the same, as the old song says. In those days it was covered in rabbits instead. I suppose they all looked the same, too.

No houses stood in the way of the innocent rabbit shooter then, and he was welcomed in most places he went because the rabbits were such a pest that every one taken off a property was seen as one less mouth to feed.

All the problems with finding a rabbit to shoot related strictly to money; it took money to buy and to fuel the transport that put the shooter in the right place. Finding the money to buy the cartridges for the gun was an even bigger problem, because they were scarce then and were to go on to be even more so during the course of the war.

People made do, and they managed by helping one another. Donnie found himself in the paddock with a cheap Belgian hammergun, borrowed, and a handful of cartridges, probably scrounged out of someone's rundown garden shed, and with a knife, and his mate. Neither of the two could be called your expert rabbiter, but the object of shooting a feed was far more easily attained in those days so the skills of the modern rabbit purist weren't an ingredient necessary for success.

They went out to the spot uneventfully, and not long into the shoot, which took place in winter time, Donnie came on a rabbit sitting very tight in a tussock, as they do in winter, loath to run out into the cold until pushed to it.

Because of the scarcity of ammunition and the straitened times, Donnie had good reason to put a rabbit in the bag and still save a cartridge when he thought he saw the opportunity.

It was a rabbit the same as a few million others, and I suppose he saw its eye in the tussock, or else a shaft of pale winter sun outlined its ear in the resinous grass. It was motionless in its place, and no doubt it watched him as he laid the gun down and took out the knife he was carrying. He made an energetic dive on the tussock, blade first, with the idea of bagging it by this more unconventional means. Apparently Donnie was always leaping somewhere or other. He never lacked dash. It was only the direction his spasmodic energy took that gave cause for worry.

It doesn't take too much imagination to work out that he had about the same chance of success as he had of flying over the nearest gum tree. The bunny headed for parts unknown, and Donnie rose to his feet with nothing more than some mud to wipe off, and more work ahead of him if he was to make a meal of some underground mutton.

He picked up the gun, and found himself standing there with it, and an open folding knife still in his hand. He placed the gun butt on the ground by his left leg, wedged the muzzles under his shoulder to hold the gun still and prevent it from falling on the wet grass, and reached his right hand round past the gun to his left side so he could put the knife away in his left-hand pants pocket.

His mate was watching, but even later didn't know what it was that came in contact with what, whether the gun was cocked and his hand or knife hit a trigger, or whether it was hand or knife that whacked a hammer. Whatever it was, the report was just a dull crump, muffled by the pressure of his shoulder on the gun muzzles. In a stark instant, a spout of energy lifted skyward something that resolved itself into a blue and red blur — blue from his old serge jacket, and red from his shoulder, consisting mainly of muscle and tendons from the front half of it, and, luckily for him, not much bone.

It was only a moment till his mate appeared at his side, and, the unfired cartridge taken out of the gun, he wadded up a clean handkerchief to jam into the hole in Donnie's shoulder before he ran to his tired black Buick to bring it as close to him as he could to carry him out.

Yes, Donnie's mate told me all this a long time ago when I was just a bit of a kid. Used to having lessons drawn for me from tales of people's misdemeanours, I listened. I had to, really. He was my father, after all.

With the passage of time, he didn't remember some of the details. He did say that he was amazed how well they stitched up the wound in the local hospital, and in due course Donnie at least regained enough use of his arm to be able to successfully ride his motorbike into the side of an unsuspecting horse.

"You know," he said, and I made ready for the moral, which I suspected to be fast approaching, "Donnie saved himself a cartridge, not shooting at that rabbit.... but the way it turned out, well, it wasn't a hell of a bargain, was it?"

I remember I thought of saying that I'd take the hint and never take chances with a hammergun, because I thought that was the inference I was supposed to draw. For one reason or another, I must have picked up some notion that there was more on the way, and so I said nothing till the rest came out. "Do you know...?" he said, and I waited.

".... Half his shoulder and most of the muscle of his arm had just got blown to kingdom come, and while I ran about a mile and picked my way in with the car — yeah, the whole time, Donnie stayed wide-eyed and bolt upright on his feet. When I got back, that was the way I found him. I loaded him into the car and he went in like a piece of four-by-two, stiff as a board along the back seat. I could've propped him in the corner. He stayed there, just the same, all the way into town, never moved, and nothing much'd bend. Just as well it was a big car."

There's a good argument for trying to isolate the moral of any story, and teaching it to a youngster. It was before my time and I wasn't there to witness it, but he drew me a good picture, and decades later I'm still not likely to take too many risks with exposed hammers on a shotgun. Whenever I think of Donnie, I can see him standing there in a sea of green grass as he waited for help to arrive, gun discarded, forgotten, left lying on the soft and sludgy winter ground, with a gaping hole in his shoulder, plainly in shock, and looking into the middle distance. For some reason, as I see him, his mouth is hanging wide open. And that's the particular part of it all that my wandering imagination focuses on.

I suppose it could hardly be any other way.

Only a Rabbit Dog

Despite his ungainly name, he wasn't just a dog; he was one of the best, the kind that any master would walk on hot coals for. Poor Boof; he made the mistake of being born and then named in the days when there was a comic strip character called Boofhead, and I suppose his owner saw some kind of similarity there when he stood back a bit. I never could, but then I didn't own the dog.

It wouldn't be surprising if he hadn't known about Boof's gifts when he named him, because he was a late starter and all his multiple talents were scheduled to come in their season, rather than being evident from the beginning. Anyway, if he objected to his name, he never showed it, not from the first, and not even when Les referred to him offhandedly as just his rabbit dog.

He was self contained, even a bit aloof, and had that innate obedience that so endears a dog to an owner trying to train it. I doubt there's anything more pleasing in a dog than the constant belief that his dog is working for him and not pulling the other way. Anyone who's trained a few dogs knows how that goes.

Les wasn't a demanding man, which could be one of the reasons Boof turned out the way he did. With a name like that, you'd hardly think he had the respect of his owner, but he did, as I came to know. I saw them together often enough to be sure.

His dog training methods weren't spectacular, either, just fairly ordinary, though it should be said he expected prompt obedience and he always said to me that before a dog was any good, he had to know who owned whom, and that was something I never forgot when I started with my own. Every now and again, mostly in his early years, Boof received a sharp reminder about who was top dog and who was bottom dog.

In daily affairs, Les loved a rabbit any time he could get his hands on one — rolled in flour and fried, the younger the better, and the front legs were his speciality. Sometimes he'd go out in the early morning and he'd walk with the shotgun to where he could find a warren. He was never greedy, and looking back on it I don't think he much liked shooting, something that would never have occurred to me at the time, because I was so young, and I did like it.

But he always took the dog, and Boof turned out to be a natural; I suppose I never paid any attention to that, either, more's the pity, and when he went about his business, I should've been attentive and tried to learn from the things I saw. I didn't, though, but treated my exposure to both of them as being just another opportunity to shoot. The young are like that.

When I did observe the uncanny obedience of the dog, and the rapport he had with his master, it wasn't so much in a shooting context as in a social one. Les would take the dog in the big river, in the midday heat; he'd been a swimmer in his youth, and he'd glide through the water with the dog behind him, the two of them barely making a ripple, neither dampening the hair on his head, with some unsuspecting civilian churning up foam in the rear and following along.

Then Les would turn backwards, and tread water, and wait till the audience caught up; he'd adopt a look of mock outrage, and when he had enough attention, he'd glare down his nose and focus theatrically on the dog.

"What the hell are you doing here?" he'd thunder. "You can't swim with people! Get out and go downstream."

And, so help me, that's what Boof would do. He'd swim straight back to the bank the way he came, then once out he'd look back and forth along the river, to work out which way was upstream and which was down. When he'd made up his mind, he'd meander twenty or thirty yards downstream, as he'd been told, and then he'd plunge in and swim by himself, as though nothing had happened.

He could be quite a crowd pleaser. There are plenty of dogs that will run for pleasure, but not many that will swim for it. He was one of the few dogs I've seen that would, and the fact wasn't lost on the observer.

No wonder Boof knew what to do when he saw a rabbit.

He was a big dog, thick coated, floppy eared, deliberate in all his movements, no energy waster. That's another trait not often seen in a dog. His shaggy coat could almost have come out of it thatched after he'd traipsed around some of that bad New South Wales back country. Dogs like that can be a nightmare, but he even seemed to have enough sense, or maybe dignity, not to need much keeping clean. He gave the impression that it would've been an affront to his considerable aplomb to take a curry-comb to him.

When he worked out what to do to make rabbit shooting better for his boss, he did it like he'd been doing it all his life. He could sense them as they sat in their squats, and he seldom surprised them. Somehow, he'd let Les know they were there. I don't know how he communicated the benefit of his knowledge to his owner; the truth is, Les wasn't all that much of a shot, but he loved his rabbit to eat and the urgency of the need to find a few seemed to be something that was known to the dog, and he performed flawlessly in an unorchestrated kind of way.

He didn't work rabbits like a good dog will, not with style, not in a rhythm, not even pointing them, not flushing them like a good springer, either; he just used his power of communication with his master when he sensed them near. Maybe something changed about his walk. Probably that's it, his gait altered slightly, and his master could see it because he'd grown sensitive to it. It's hard to say. I did find out that when I went and tried to walk up rabbits on my own I had a lot less success than Les did with the dog working for him.

Gun or rifle, the dog did well for him, no doubt about it. I'd have to say he was more clever than pretty to watch, though, with just the curious near-shuffle of a big, slow-moving bitser, but one that always seemed to know where to be.

It's not hard to see why Les liked it better and better. He ended up with all the rabbit legs he wanted. He had absolute obedience from the dog, and he didn't have to work all that hard for it. It was as though he and the dog were a mind-reading partnership.

He used to go out to work in the morning, these being the days when he was still on his own property, and sometimes when Boof had to stay home, which wasn't all that often, he'd take some household item like a broom and he'd put the dog at drop, and tell him that whatever the item was, it belonged to him and so the dog had better look after it till he came in to claim it.

Very amusing, his wife used to say later on, because for as long as Les was gone, then he'd be on guard, and nobody could get anywhere near to that broom. When he arrived back home, his first move would be to check on the dog and his charge, and invariably the two would be where Les last saw them. He'd chuckle and lift the dog's big paw off it, give him a pat and take the broom or whatever it was away to its rightful place, to restore domestic harmony, and the big dog would amble off outside into the sun where he thought fewer demands would be made on his time.

That was typical of the way the dog was. He loved his master and was secure in that, and with a stolidness that always appealed to me, he gave him unqualified mateship. And it was returned.

It seemed in time that Les didn't have to call Boof, but by virtue of that communication they shared he just had to think his name, and there he was.

The first time I tried to take Boof alone to walk up a rabbit it was a disaster. He wouldn't work for me. I used all the same commands Les used and I even tried to imitate the tones of voice, but it had no effect and the big dog didn't pay any attention to me.

I took him home and went over his head to the management. In my aggrieved state, I reported him to Les, who was my uncle, incidentally, and so had some sense of the proprietary toward me. I remember he looked up from his paper, called the dog over, and had a word to him. It was a quiet and conversational word, too, like the kind he'd have with the dog in the river, for a joke, and he did no more than explain to big Boof that he was expected to do what I said. Then he told me to go out again straight away, and bring him back three or four young rabbits for a fry-up that night.

I might have been the living equivalent of that business of theirs in the river, a joke, shared between the dog and his master.

Anyway, Boof behaved perfectly, then. I was back in half an hour with the rabbits, so I wondered what more Les could ask of an animal, but perhaps more to the point, I pondered the nature of the communication that had been apportioned out to man and dog. I wondered where it stemmed from — whether from the man, as a gift he perhaps had of dog training, or whether from the dog, with its own antennae, those nebulous receptors of information that somehow escapes us clumsy humans with all our computers and cars and complexities, and our abysmal lack of instinct.

That's the way it appeared to me, this communication, an intangible in the form of an instinct, read perhaps by the dog as though it was a breath of breeze on the neck or a pull in the forehead, a faint wisp of meaning that only he knew how to read on the blank page of a day.

It'd be too much to suggest that Boof didn't have any faults. He did. He was a freethinker, no other way to put it, and when the time came for him to go about his business, he did, and it took a lot to dissuade him.

Les eventually moved off the property, no doubt locked into his own struggle against the unkind fates, and, taking a little place on the outskirts of town, he started to work for a local tradesman. In the morning he'd go off to his job, under somebody else's instruction; in retrospect, it must have been a cruel blow.

His forays after a rabbit or two in the early morning became fewer, but when I visited him I provided that rabbit meat myself, mostly walking them up alone; still I was struck by the uncommon bond between the two. If the dog's life was restricted by their new circumstances, he didn't hold it against the man, and he was by his side all the daylight hours.

Boof's real fault, which I find I've been putting off stating, was to be a wanderer. He didn't do it often, but once every six months he'd pick up his big bones and when nobody was looking, he'd ease himself quietly over the hill. When he came home he'd be less than popular, but he'd look sheepish and his big mouth would seem almost to manage a half-smile as he sat and took his rollicking, laid onto his rough hide by Les with whatever was handy, and as dogs do he used to accept that it was his lot in life.

Les didn't hold this wandering habit against Boof; he didn't do it all that often, and I suppose he knew a dog had to be a dog, after all, but in one respect he drew a firm line. He wouldn't brook it at night, because his owner knew the score if the dog didn't. It became a serious matter, then. A dog loose in the country at night is likely either to kill sheep or at least get the blame for it, and as a man who lived in the bush he knew that he owed it to both his neighbours and his dog not to stand for either eventuality.

So one morning, when he was on his way to his new day job, driving the little way into town down the rough red track, it gave him a jolt when he saw the big, rough-coated dog coming towards him. He was nearly there, having reached the outskirts, and the side of the road was fairly clear of undergrowth, so he saw him a good way off.

If he lost his temper, it's understandable. The dog, with his broad instinct and his native good sense, knew what the rules were. This was an act of defiance, and the dog must have known he was caught at it. He'd been out all night, must've broken out of the back porch where he slept, gone roving after a bitch somewhere, and here he was, not long after dawn on a winter's morning, going home — and tired, too, worn out, even, Les thought, and later told me, because he saw him stumble, his big, loose gait worn and disconnected.

Les stopped the car well in advance of the approaching dog, which gave him time to find a heavy and pliable switch, and the dog came to him, as he always had, without calling, accepting.

He thrashed him soundly, no words spoken. He laid it on. It was one of the rules, and the job had to be done.

****

Sometimes, when I was staying with Les later, and I was lying in bed hearing the rain coming down on the iron roof, I'd think of the way his tight shoulders would've worked when he delivered that hiding to the dog. He was compact and strong, a natural athlete, and he knew how to move. Knew how to hit, too.

I couldn't find it in me to blame him, though I can't say he didn't blame himself. I'm certain he never hunted a rabbit again for the table, and to my knowledge he was very reluctant to pick up a gun at all. He never owned another dog, either, so perhaps the two, the dog and the gun, were locked up together in his view of the world, the way that they've come to be in mine today.

I never saw Les cry about anything, not even that. Perhaps it would have been better if I had. But I saw him come close, and that was when he told me about what had happened that day.

When he was found coming along the bush track, Boof's shaggy coat had hidden a secret that Les was fated only to find out when he arrived home later on that night.

No wonder he never had another dog. I think he was afraid that if he did it might have that same instinct, that same close communication that he'd had — or perhaps I should say he thought he had — with Boof.

That early morning on the road, Boof hadn't been tired. His rough thatch of hair hid the secret of a bullet's entrance hole.

He just couldn't see it, Les told me later, his mouth tight and his words squeezed as though with pain, he just couldn't see it.

When Boof was struggling back along the track and met his master, he'd been shot during the night by some property owner, caught out roving, and he was going home to die; that's what he did, that winter's day, on the doorstep under the shelter of the porch, home, with his head on Les's slipper, where he'd left it when he changed into his work boots and set off for the day.

I think Les nearly died, too, that evening, when he came home and found him, and he saw what he had done.

To Cuff the Pup

They seemed to me like hard men, these folk who walked through my childhood. All the relationships between the players in memory's grand scenes are bound to change as the days turn into the months and then into the years that put grey into beards. Nevertheless, droplets of distillation form.

They reserved a special kind of distrust that bordered on contempt for a man who didn't do the right thing with a gun. It wasn't something that I saw often, so I don't find it easy to quantify it. Someone who failed to use a gun properly was the cause of more than just uneasiness, perhaps along the same lines as a man who neglected to feed his family, or who wouldn't take responsibility for his dogs, or perhaps was always drunk when he was most needed.

They handled guns as tools, always with respect, nearly always with skill, but more as a matter of expediency than through a conscious decision. The pleasure that gave them was matter-of-fact; the game that they put on the table showed shooting to be a practical concern, not a matter of idealism. All the same, it offered a backdrop for a set of values.

****

With me, when I joined him in the red country in New South Wales, Les always insisted on gun safety, a fact that might not have been picked up by a casual observer. A gun was never far out of reach, and there would often be talk of a fox that found himself bowled over as a result of carelessly straying too close to the fowlyard, or of a hare now slowly making soup, spied sitting, as they may often be, not far from a single lonely tree in a grass paddock.

Nothing much was made of this. It was a part of life. It was what people did. A new rabbit warren was a topographical fact that was noted and stored away for the next time somebody felt it was time to have a rabbit casserole. The arrival of a half dozen wood duck on the house dam would cause a flurry of activity one evening, late in the week, usually, so the Sunday roast might have a different flavour from the usual one of lamb. But woe betide whoever brought a gun unbroken into the house afterwards.

This is all tied up with respect, with acceptance, with having a sense of place in the natural world. Life comes and goes, but it must never be wasted.

Sometimes, to a youngster looking on, this knowledge of self, of what's right to do and of what kind of role to play in the doing, was an almost mystical affair, a quality worthy of note, mistaken only early for adulthood, but soon recognized as more than just that.

It was Les's fate to be a role model for me. There were numerous things that made him worth looking up to. The way he shared an uneasy intimacy with his ancient Chev truck, for instance; held together with wire and good luck, it would start for nobody else in the world, though I'd seen others try to fire it up. He'd climb in and turn the motor over, and he'd start up his own low growl, deep in the throat, pitched to match the metallic clatter of the rattly old engine.

"C'mon, c'mon, c'mON," he'd say to it, hoping to get away to a patch of cover where he'd seen a dozen rabbits, and the sun going down all too fast. "C'mon, c'mON, C'MON!" — and to a boy's delight, he'd burst into a torrent of immaculate, unrepetitive and colourful bad language that went up two tones as he and the truck seemed to get worked up together. As the old galvanized iron shed would ring with the combining roar, the motor would hack its way disconsolately from inertia to usefulness and with the smoke billowing back into the cabin Les would smile happily as though he and the old Chev had just shared a secret.

Maybe they had, but when I tried to explain it to one of my straitlaced aunts, who knew only too well the larrikin in Les, I gave it up as a bad job.

Often I saw his grin, and it was reserved for me, I just knew. I once went across the little houseyard in a raging, teeming black thunderstorm, drenched in the first tropical seconds of it, coming back from doing an errand for him. He was sitting idly inside the open door, the light on inside, watching me approach.

A look of starkest horror suddenly clapped itself over his features. I remember his mouth, the instant slackness in his usually tight chin, the convulsive start of his body. As I recall it, the grin that followed seemed to come in an instant, even before I was airborne, but on reflection I doubt that it could have. It surely came before I landed in the kitchen, white and speechless, and about to enter a fit of shaking that was due to last for half an hour.

Lightning had struck in the yard just behind me, and he thought I'd been hit. But in the blink of an eye he'd seen that it had missed, and he knew full well that behind the lightning bolt there came the thunderclap; it was so close and so loud that if he thought I'd been killed, I was sure of it, and I doubt anything could've amused him more. No sympathy there.

Yet, next day, he took me out and showed me a gum tree he knew that had been split and felled by a lightning strike. He directed my eye to the rich colours etched into the wood, and in his quiet voice there was nothing but respect for nature. This is surely the way it ought to be.

Perhaps, I've thought from time to time, this was what he was guilty of, a sense of balance that was practical and took no nonsense. To see it from his point of view, a boy not killed but only frightened by a lightning strike is no worse for it — in fact, all the better, having learnt not to take liberties with the weather, and in that way there was no problem in smiling at his discomfort, not that the womenfolk would've seen it that way.

I didn't tell them a lot of what he did, the womenfolk. He used to sneak me out with him in the early morning in the car, to shoot rabbits, because he said I had a better success rate, and he'd sell them without telling his wife, so he could keep the money, often to spend on me.

There was the time he was in the local waterhole, its radio blaring the Sydney races, running a book on a Saturday afternoon as he always had, when the flying squad came out from the city to see how many bookmakers they could catch. The two plainclothes policemen stood in the corner, wonderfully conspicuous, gravely ignored by the locals, drinking beer they didn't want, and after half an hour one of them sidled up to him and very, very quietly asked out of the side of his mouth, "Know where I could put on a bet, mate?"

Pokerfaced, pointing to the little station over the road, he solemnly said, "No worries, mate. The local copper's the district bookie."

I thought this was the kind of behaviour that induced fondness in him from the locals, though it wasn't altogether that. It would've been enough to endear him to me, but there was more.

When I came to be growing up, Les was soon to lapse. He was a sixty-a-day man, and carried a carton of cigarettes under the seat of all the vehicles he used on the farm. He ran cheerfully ahead of the inevitable for a long time, to be overtaken all too soon at fifty, but before it happened he had a spell when his normally good humour was sometimes not up to the task of containing the sadness of his decline.

He was a small man, under average height, and had a slightly podgy look about him. He wore thick glasses, and he played useful trumpet. Years before, when I was just a bit of a kid, I'd asked him what he was afraid of. The water and spiders, he told me. So I asked him what he did about it. Became state butterfly swimming champion, came the answer, and started a spider collection.

If he took a serious line about his fears, he had an irreverent attitude to a lot else. In his trumpet case, as we later went around the district in a two-hundred-mile radius, playing for old-time dances, he kept a neutrally coloured carpet snake. They're not poisonous, but a quick look wasn't enough to make that clear to most. He'd long since grown tired of drunks and busybodies sticking their noses into his trumpet, because other than his dog it was his only valued possession. There'd be shrieks of fright, sometimes big shrieks of fright if it comes to that, when some unsuspecting victim lifted the lid of the trumpet case to mess around with what didn't belong to him. When the snake put its head up, the interest would fall into a sharp decline. There'd be a yell and a bang as something was dropped or bumped, and Les'd grin. "Ah, yeah, someone's checking on my trumpet for me."

These days, I recall Les with considerable fondness, and I've tried to work out why. Now I'm of an age for objective reflection, the skeins of memory are beginning to untangle. What was he blessed with, this man? Or what was he guilty of?

I look back on his easy acceptance of others, and his close engagement with natural things, his love of the bush and the practicality of his wisdom.

There was a day when we ran over a king brown snake. It was well over seven feet long and it spanned the whole of the road we were driving down. It was right outside the house, where the dogs and the house cow were free to roam. It's a breed that's deadly, not afraid, big enough to pump a lot of poison into a bite. He'd run two wheels over it and it was already stirred up and writhing before he'd finished braking.

He picked up the .22 rifle that belonged in the vehicle, gave it to me, and said "Shoot it". I did what I was told, but it didn't improve matters. There was a lot of snake and not much bullet. Its temper worsened, and I scuttled backwards.

He rolled his eyes to the clouds, probably imploring the silent witnesses to observe the ineptitude and inexperience of youth, and he quickly cast about on the roadside for a stick. My mind went to the plantation a hundred yards off, where there'd be fallen branches. Great was my dismay when he picked up a piece of stovewood that had fallen from a truck. It was ten inches long and two inches thick.

The little dance they did, the two of them, remains one of the firmest etched memories of my early life. As they played out a swift and urgent drama, the fine dust swirled up around them, and I can remember thinking that it'd be a long drive to town to try to find the doctor, with Les full of puncture marks.

He moved quickly, irregularly, in a roughly circular fashion, and the snake hissed and thrashed, writhed and flashed as they both jockeyed for position; yet when it struck, he'd always gone.

Perhaps ten or fifteen seconds after the match began, he went in and down like a fencer, his right leg bent almost double, the left trailing behind, his right arm extended, the left held high, for balance, and to my horror he used not the front end of the stove wood, but the rear, gripped tightly in his hand, to strike the snake once at the back of the head. The blow delivered, he came out backwards along the same line that he'd gone in on. There was genuine puzzlement across his brow when he saw the snake was still on the attack.

I thought he'd gone entirely mad. I couldn't believe that in the manoeuvre he hadn't been struck. And there it was again, the same circling, the same whipping of the huge reptile, now extending, then coiling, and the unforgettable hiss of its strikes, too fast for even a young eye to follow. Perhaps ten more seconds passed, and suddenly he lunged again, this time twice, thud-thud, came back out over his bent right knee the same way he'd gone in, tossed the stovewood over his right shoulder and made his way to the vehicle, leaving the distinct impression the job was done.

The snake had departed this life, no doubt about it, and in a stupor of wonder I sat beside him and watched him sideways all the way back to the house, annoyed with himself because he'd missed the first time. A day later, when his temper wasn't so bad, I asked him how he did it, and he told me that it was easier than it looked, the secret being in the way the snake lay. With a little experience, he said, it's not hard to tell what the position was that it could strike from, a snake being nothing more than a long muscle that could only expand and contract, and anyone reading it right could comfortably defend himself against the deadliest with something no bigger than a piece of stovewood. I suppose I believed him, but I had no wish to try it to see if it was true.

I thought for a long while as a young adult that this was it, his facility with his environment, that made me admire Les. Slowly I've come to doubt it was that.

There came the time when I joined him to play at a dance in a town not all that far from where he lived. I'd never been there before, and knew nobody. It came as a surprise when a wild-eyed young man I'd never clapped eyes on came and sat down beside me and started to tell me how much he admired Les. He'd seen us arrive together, marked me down and singled me out as soon as he could.

I listened till about the eighth time he told me that he always did what Les told him to do and then I moved away, but it didn't matter, because he followed, and sat with me to start up the record again, in his voice the sing-song urgency of the unbalanced.

He spoke with almost religious fervency, saying how much he liked him, how much he admired him, how good it was to see him. He was a couple of sandwiches short of a picnic, I could see that, and I tried not to be rude as I shook him off yet again and went about my business. Some time later, I found out from a local what had happened.

One night a year or two before, this young man had been drunk in some hired men's quarters on a big property nearby where he'd been working. He'd passed quickly through the objectionable stage, where it would be most likely someone would sort him out, and I don't know what led him to break the usual boundaries of behaviour, but I do know that before the evening was out he'd collected a rifle from somewhere and had everybody in the long hut bailed up in a frightened bunch at the other end. He raved and stormed and they thought they were for it. Maybe they were.

Nobody knew what to do. Those outside couldn't get in as he raged and yelled about life's injustices. Needless to say, those inside couldn't get out, either.

After some hours of stalemate, somebody sent for Les. I've often puzzled over why. In the first place, he was nobody special in the district; in the second, he was asleep, because by then it was the early hours of the morning and he was half an hour's drive away. They pounded on his door till he appeared and when he asked why they'd come, they told him what was going on and said that they just thought he might be able to work out what to do.

I'd guess he was annoyed when they woke him up, and he declined to be driven out by whoever it was who came for him. He took his own truck, and the lonely, pre-dawn drive would've given him more time to work up an appropriate temper. I doubt he was a happy man when he pulled up.

While the others hung back, he walked straight up to the door of the hut, and called out by name to the young man, who opened the door and stuck the rifle in his face. The muzzle of a rifle, it'd seem to me, would likely have an attention-focusing effect on most. Les simply asked him a question.

"That rifle — is it yours?"

Nobody expected that. Certainly not the young man, anyway, and, puzzled, he squinted at Les, and replied, "No. Why?"

And Les, God rest him, said "Because you can't shoot blokes with rifles that don't belong to you. Didn't you know that? Give it here."

With lamblike obedience, he did. Les took out the bolt — yes, the rifle had been loaded — and handed it to the first man he saw. He reached inside the door, finding the switch for the big, powerful light that served the beaten, flat patch of ground in front of the hut. By then he'd decided he'd need to see what he was doing.

Perhaps if that long, rangy youth had been smarter, he'd have looked more closely at Les's eyebrows. On the outside edge of them, the left one particularly, there was the little telltale lacework of fine white scars. Les had done this kind of thing before. Because he was short, he told me, he'd always believed in getting inside.

So in a few steps, he took the troublesome young man out into the yellow light, an encouraging word or two in his ear along the way to help him there without a fuss, and when he was in position he deftly and coldly thrashed him. They told me he didn't even take off his glasses. In barely five minutes he was on his way home, back to bed to pick up his night's sleep where he'd left it before.

****

He's one I remember often, Les. I'm done with thinking he snagged in my memory on account of his ease with both the men and the animals around him.

More often these days it occurs to me that to cope well with life is as much a gift as anything else. Les had problems, the same as we all have; but his weren't caused by a bureaucrat, and they weren't solved by one, either. So much is said by a man's attitude to firearms, and to Les there came a day when, for reasons we can only guess at, a young man used one to create deep offence. He dealt with it simply and effectively by making him answerable on the spot. When it was dealt with, it was over. The pup had been cuffed, and a long time afterwards he still remembered the lesson.

In a tempestuous world, as a hunter I look for simplicity. In a time when complexity in society was just beginning to compound on complexity, Les gilded no lilies, and was guilty of putting the horse before the cart. There are times when I long for more of that.

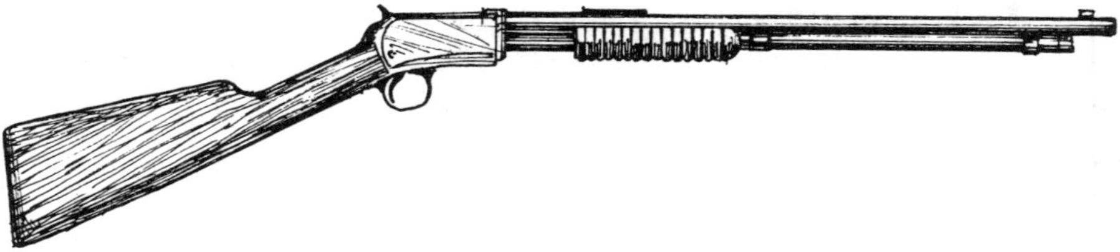

Alvin's Stammer

The reasons I remember Alvin are not the ones, perhaps, that Alvin himself would have chosen to be remembered for if he could have looked forward into the life and times of his travelling mate, my father, and seen how he would finally come to be viewed when his rapid footfall had gone quiet down the corridor of years.

I never met Alvin, never saw a picture of him, either, and though I sense it to be apocryphal, the significance of what happened to him still largely escapes me. All this notwithstanding, he nevertheless managed to open wide the door of my family folklore, and let himself in unexpectedly. Alvin ran into my father's life, and then in due course he ran out of it, too. He ran a few times in between, as well.

****

I think of him with his swag, like my father's, wrapped in the single blanket that most bagmen carried in the Depression days. In it, there was a takedown Winchester '06, with its slick little slide action and exposed hammer. When they could afford it, which wasn't often, they used to buy a packet of bullets for it and hope they'd last. I'd like to say it was an immaculately cared for piece of superior engineering that they carted with them through good times and bad, and somehow managed to keep in near new condition. The fact is that by the time I first saw it there was no bluing left on it to speak of, and the barrel was shot out, its chamber corroded from using dusty .22 Shorts instead of the Long Rifles it was made for. Shorts were cheaper.

It went to my father, in time, as this story will tell, and surely that was enough to make Alvin significant.

I came to understand later, and had reason to be glad of the fact, that Alvin had been a fine runner, one who had entered and placed in the Stawell Gift, even then this country's most prestigious foot race. He'd stopped entering competitions for the same reason that my father had chosen to immigrate, on account of the grinding poverty of the day. He was an inspiration to watch, my father had told me, but I learned he had cause to be biased.

Alvin had a bad stammer and a spare frame. Deliberate with his words, as is often the case with the speech-impaired, he took my father in hand and taught him the ways of the road as best he could. They boarded trains, jumping the rattler, my father always called it, going from one place to the next, and then back, in the long and demanding search for work that was so seldom rewarded. They saw there was hope in the world — but they doubted it was for them.

They'd met because my father was new to the train-jumping business when he arrived in this country from Scotland in 1929. He and his brother were in a small group outside a town somewhere, not welcome; to even the load, the two of them divided up their goods, which didn't amount to much. My uncle took the food and the utensils. My father took his mandolin, the only possession he'd brought with him on the six-week boat journey, and the blankets.

They lay on a hill beside the railway track, and waited for the old coal-burner to slow as it tackled the long uphill slope; they, the old hands, had instructed him, the new chum. Near the top, when it was at its slowest, they were to rise to their feet, every man for himself, the engine long past, and make their run, catching hold and then swinging up onto the freight carriages, then together make a nest for themselves on the canvas covers, with a bit of luck in a spot where the cargo was a little more soft than hard. If he waited and watched, he'd see how the others did it, and he could follow. There was nothing to it, they said.

So it came about that my father was the last up. He never did run well, a stayer, not a sprinter, and he'd always disliked it. The others had all made their move and had clambered aboard, and by this time the train was starting to get away from him. He'd paused and watched too long. He realized he had to make his run, and so he did.

Holding his swag in his right hand, he dashed to the side, found the rhythm of the run, and in a moment had swung his left hand up and under a leather thong dangling from a triangular fixture on the canvas tarpaulin covering the load.

He was on, and the train quickly gathered speed as it breasted the hill and started down the other side. Still holding his swag in his outside hand, and still gripping the leather thong in his inside one, he couldn't swing up any higher, and was conscious that his feet were feeling insecure. He observed they only had a slippery grip on the steel frame, the edge of the box that made up the freight truck itself.

Well and good, he told me as I listened in my teens, many years later, patiently milking him of all the information he'd give about those days, well and good, until he heard rather than felt the troubles unfolding beneath his left hand. Under his nose, almost too close to see at first, he saw his handhold giving way. Stitch by stitch, he heard and then saw that the leather thong that supported him was losing its mooring, and his eyes followed the popping threads, fascinated, as one at a time they gave way around the supporting triangular patch holding the thong that was keeping him above the grinding train wheels and the speeding gravel around the track.

One by one they gave way, he said, just on the end of his nose, the quiet popping like a metronome spelling out the last minute of his life, heard with clarity over the clatter of the steam train.

He suspected he was in trouble, all right, until he looked ahead, and found to his dismay that a tunnel was coming up, and he was about to be plastered over the side of it, and at that point he knew he was.

He didn't want to let go and jump off the accelerating train, he said, because his brother had the food. He was instantly aware of the prospect of starvation, one he'd felt before and not appreciated. However silly it sounds, he simply felt there wasn't a lot of future in taking a risk on surviving a jump onto the rocks beside the line. If it did nothing else, it would smash his mandolin, his only important possession.

It didn't look good, till Alvin ran into his life.

It was his head he saw first, as he stared wide-eyed in the direction of the tunnel. Alvin had suddenly become aware they were a body short, and had thrown a glance over the side of the carriage, there to see him hanging on. He didn't know the stitches on his handhold were popping, of course, but he could see him stalled. He looked forward in the direction the train was travelling, and saw the tunnel. In a moment's calculation, he reckoned his chances, and decided he could do it. My father said he was like a stork, all legs as he charged toward him along the top of the train, racing against the tunnel.

When he arrived, he brought with him no ceremony. It was a handful of hair he reached for, and that was what he wrenched upwards. My father followed, his bellow of pain drowned out. The two of them, the hair of the one still in the hand of the other, fell flat on the top of the freight car in a tangled heap just as the train roared into the tunnel. And that was how they met.

****

He always said he was glad Alvin could run. He had other uses, too. They kept company on the track, throwing their lot in together as my father's brother found work on a farm somewhere and stayed awhile.

One of Alvin's advantages hinged on what went on in his mouth. When he turned twenty-one, his father had given him a trip to the dentist as a present, and he had all his teeth out. Teeth were thought by many to offer more of a drawback than an advantage, and Dad had reason to agree. He was one of the very few Scots I ever knew who completely lost his accent, and it was all because of his mate; his stammer notwithstanding, he observed the way Alvin's tongue flew about in his mouth when he spoke, and it wasn't all that hard to see because no teeth impeded the view. A little comparative study indicated that Scotsmen tended to keep their tongues still in the middle of their mouths when they spoke, while Australians let theirs flop around. He followed suit, and the back of his accent was soon broken.

****

It's strange that two men who went on the track in the fellowship of their hunger throughout the first half of 1930 should share so much while sharing so little. My father told me later that they were mates, not friends, as though that explained everything. It didn't, to me as a boy, but I hadn't suffered what they did.

Alvin had his little Winchester .22 in his swag, but mostly no bullets. When he had some, he'd take two or three, load the rifle and prowl the flats, looking for the eye in the tussock. One time they ran a rabbit down. They hadn't eaten for three days, and they took it in turns to put the pressure on the bounding rabbit.

Even Alvin the sprinter couldn't catch it in a burst of speed. It can be done by two, though, if a steady pace is kept up and one person stays well out, heading it off from wherever a burrow might be, rounding it up, driving it back towards the other runner, who must then pick up the pace. Running not together but taking it in turns, they kept it out on a flat and away from its burrow until it eventually gave them best.

They had a fire going back at camp. Alvin knew how to do it, he said, and they scooped out the coals, skinned the rabbit, slopped heavy mud over it from the river, and dropped it in the hole, then covered it with the coals. This, he said, was how the natives did it.

They hadn't reckoned with their hunger. Three days must be a long time, and the thought of the meat cooking under the little mound was too much for them. They didn't have a coin to spin for it, but they picked up a small piece of wood, and spat on one side. They tossed that instead, wet or dry. My father won, so he chose the carcass half that had been lying uppermost, nearer the coals, and Alvin was to take the lower half.

They dug it out to eat without looking too carefully at it for fear of what they'd find. They deftly cut it up the centre and divided it as they'd arranged. The side nearest the fire was cooked. As they ate, the blood ran down either side of Alvin's chin. Never once, my father said, did he complain.

As it happens, this was not the way Alvin made his mark in my family's folkore, though. Neither did he make it by the way that he span out of the paternal orbit, though that's worth recounting, as well.

They'd had a hard journey, down into New South Wales. My father learned how fast he could run, which wasn't as fast as Alvin, when they stopped at an apple orchard that nobody was showing an obvious interest in. They were shot at there by a farmer with a shotgun loaded with saltpetre and soon found it a local sport.

They were shot at again, this time by police, when they tried to jump a train and were spotted. He told me later they carried .32 handguns, so he must have been close enough to them to identify them. That the police did this was never printed in the papers of the day, he said.

It seemed that Alvin was always running, and that was the way it ended. As their journey lengthened and they drew closer to the Victorian border, going south, they detoured from the main line whenever an opportunity offered, so they could look for work.

One cloudless night they made camp after climbing a six-feet fence, noisily, late, one holding the swags while the other clambered over. They walked a while until they found themselves coming up against a bit of a bank, and because it was out of the wind, they decided to sleep there rather than walk further in the near black.

My father told me that just by coincidence they both woke together, at about the first full light. There was a half squawk, half scream from Alvin, and he leaped to his feet in a full run. It seems he cleared that fence by express, and my father never saw him again. He left his swag behind, and that's the simple explanation of how my family came to be the owner of the '06 Winchester which in time I came to grow up with. They'd just spent the night, it transpired, lying in the lee of a huge marble slab, in a cemetery. Evidently this was too much for him.

But no, it was not his running that earned Alvin his place in my family mythology. This he cemented for himself outside a town in New South Wales called Molong.

However erratic might have been his coming and his going, however little equilibrium the manner of his departure might have suggested, he seemed in a way never to have lost his sense of proportion. Shot at just trying to survive, living in fear of arrest which would lead to lice-ridden clothes from the dirty prisons, risking their lives just to get by, he and many of his peers had a good humoured opportunism about them that it could be tempting to think of as almost transcendant.

On this day, he and my father were not travelling on a box car with the freight, but instead they'd taken the unusual step of making their way into a passenger carriage, where they paid attention to the sound of anyone approaching, half-expecting a ticket collector at any moment.

It was a dapper little man in patent leather shoes and carrying a matching briefcase who appeared in the doorway of their carriage, blinking when he saw the two bagmen as they sat dustily, feet up in unaccustomed leather-upholstered comfort, with the compartment to themselves.

His upper lip sported a very carefully tended affectation of a hairbrush moustache, and this in the days well before Hitler.

His head came inside the doorway, and he carefully eyed them up and down somewhat disdainfully before he condescended to speak.

"I say there," he said without ceremony, in tones as clipped as his upper lip, just as the train began slowing for its run into the station. "Is this Molong?"

"Ahh, y-y-yes," said Alvin wisely, " b-b-but it c-c-could be longer!"

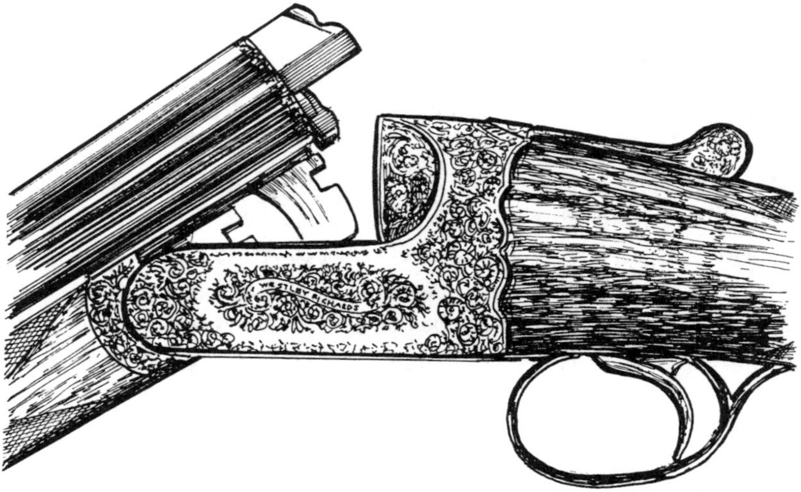

The Auctioneer

Part One - A Good Killer

It used to be such a common term, but nowadays it's hardly ever heard. It goes to show how much times change.

In the days when there was a firearm in every home, any shooter was likely to have a pride in his gun bordering on ferocity. Woe betide the man who went into a country hotel and threw mullock at the gun of someone who was said to be able to shoot a bit. In a shooting town, the person receiving the criticism was likely to take it just a little less kindly than ridiculing his choice of wife.

Guns were proudly handed down from one generation to the next, and the magical qualities of the names of certain makers were often passed along like secret family recipes for haggis in Scotland. Many's the old Greener I've been shown with a wink and some blanket assurance — "Ah, but Dad always said she was the best killer on the swamp this side of Gitchiwarrah."

"A good killer." It was the duck shooter's accolade, the only definition that counted. Some guns were just thought to hit harder than others. If the gun wouldn't put meat in the pot, then what was the good of it? Collectors didn't collect in those days. There weren't any; instead of that, shooters shot.

A good killer might have come by its reputation for any one of a hundred reasons. Maybe it had been in the hands of a good shot, who used it to better effect than most. For this he'd be rewarded by people telling each other it must have been the gun. Folk are like that.

Perhaps it was a gun that was lent a lot. In this way it would go through many hands, and so it would be sure to fit someone, and that someone would probably shoot it well, and so it would move on with a good reputation. As often as not, I've always believed, a good killer was often just a gun that had at least one barrel open in the choke (when people usually believed that it was very tight, too), and the result of this was that it was more amenable to hitting moving game with.

So it was, for one reason or another, the fame of some guns seemed fated to spread. A gun so named was always sold at a premium in any community. I've seen it, and old timers will remember it; if a fellow was trying to sell a gun, and someone was prepared to step forward and pronounce it to be a good killer, then its price slid up on the strength of it, just how far it moved being perhaps influenced by the reputation of whoever was speaking on behalf of it. No gun ever suffered from having a good champion.

The auctioneer had seen them all, good guns and bad, expensive and cheap, famous and unheard of; they all went through his rooms and at the fall of the hammer they left old owners and went in new directions.

One day a young fellow came in with a Westley Richards, and it had two sets of barrels. It was that special action type that today has come to be known as a droplock, but it was not called that then. The metal of the action was gracefully scalloped where it met the wood, and the engraving was full coverage.

It was cased, as it ought to be, and it had the look of class about it, the glow, that any auctioneer and all his patrons love to see. It was arranged that it should go into the weekly sale on the Saturday coming, and a reserve price was agreed. It was obviously an heirloom of significance, and the young man representing the family was unhappy about his errand, but the times were hard, and in the manner of the day he said little of what he thought and gave away even less of what he felt. In a few minutes he'd turned his back on the gun and he was gone from the rooms.

He came back in good time for the sale, though, and on the day he stood at the back of the hall, watching intently, dressed formally, hair slicked down, alone. The gun failed to make the reserve and so was passed in; by the time the sale had finished, he'd slipped outside and was gone again.

This happens, sometimes unaccountably; it's the way auctions are, and the auctioneer didn't think twice about it, but just scheduled the gun again for the next week's sale and carried on with his business.

When the time came, the whole process was repeated. The second auction was better attended than the first, but no bid was received for the gun, and casting his eye around the floor, spotting several keen shooters who should have been interested, the auctioneer saw no sign of the young man.

At the end of the second sale he did stop and think about it, though. In a quiet moment he repaired to his office and took it out of the case, to focus his attention and to check it even more carefully. Perhaps the local shooters knew something about it that he didn't.

Both sets of barrels fitted properly. It wasn't loose in the action. The engraving was sharp, there were no dents in the metal or bruises in the wood, and he concluded it had obviously been looked after because it was properly oiled. The signs of neglect weren't there to be found.

It wasn't much of a step from there for him to throw it to his shoulder and test the balance. He liked it; he fitted the second set of tubes and he tried again. It balanced just as well with those, and this only confirmed what he had known all along, that he was holding in his hands some very fine quality. It wasn't lost on him that it fitted him, too, even though he took a long stock.

A thought entered his head sideways.

In those days, he wasn't a very wealthy auctioneer, but he did like to shoot, and his own experience with guns was known around the town, which was why so many of them went through his rooms. But relatively speaking, guns were no less expensive then than they are now. This one had been through his respectable rooms twice, and attracted no attention at all. Perhaps it would be in his interests, to say nothing of the interests of those whose custom he relied on, if he made entirely sure that there was nothing wrong with it.

The moment he thought it, the idea was there to stay, and he couldn't shake it. It did more than appeal to him. It stayed in his head after he put the gun back in its case. He took them both, idea and gun, home to his young wife, and her first thought was that he'd bought the gun for himself with money they couldn't afford. He was able to assuage her doubts with the assurance that she didn't have to worry — it owed them nothing. He was just testing it, a free service to the integrity of his auction rooms.

She understood. He put it to a trial, indeed. There were a lot of rabbits around in those times, and he spent a day every weekend right in the thick of them. The first test was a bit inconclusive, of course, and so he felt he ought to take it out a second time; he wasn't too terribly disturbed to note that it went through the third auction once again without attracting a bid.

Just to be sure, he was meticulous about using not the first but the second set of barrels when he went out the following week — and, yes, they functioned perfectly, too, and he shot very well with it.

The gun once more went through the auction without attracting a bid, and once again he was forced to consider this. There was usually a fairly brisk trade in guns, and those in fine oak and leather cases with good makers' names were seldom given to sitting around gathering dust on the auction room floor.

He did like it, there was no denying it. It soon turned into something of a ritual. He'd take it out to shoot, he'd roll a big pile of rabbits with it, he'd return it to the rooms none the worse for wear all cleaned and oiled, and it would go through the next sale with not a flicker of interest being shown in it.

One Saturday morning as the usual sale was about to start, he looked up to find not the young man, who'd gone unseen for several weeks and several sales, but the whole family: at the forefront there was a big, domineering woman of an obviously matriarchal bent — it occurred to him she was the driving force in the events. Then there was the young man, next, and all his brothers, of whom there were many, and his sisters, and a young friend or two of theirs, and by the look of it quite a few in-laws...they'd turned out in force. Strength in numbers. They were all of them wearing their best clothes, and they were less than frivolous about the proceedings, too.

Grim. That was the word that came to him. They looked grim. Evidently he wasn't the only one who had been having misgivings about the gun.

It didn't take long for an up and coming young auctioneer to work out that he was suddenly under heavy scrutiny. Events were turning serious. Perhaps his reputation for fair dealing throughout the town hinged on his performance that day; if they thought that he was doing something fishy, that he hadn't been offering the gun for sale as he ought, then their hostility would be quite understandable. After all, they were the ones who stood to lose, and none of them had been there to see that it had in fact gone through, week after week, with no interest being shown in it.

He resolved that the only way out of this was to ensure that the gun and its virtues went under the hammer with nothing but his very best spiel, so his fairness in dealing would remain unimpeached, and his reputation unharmed. Carrying on with the sale as he thought this through, he glanced at the program and saw to his chagrin that as it happened the gun had been scheduled to be almost the last item for the morning; his hammer thumped and lot after lot came up, the gun still undealt with, and the faces of the row of relatives grew colder and more implacable as he failed to announce the Westley Richards.

He worked methodically through his card, conscious of the hardness of their stares the whole while. There was nothing he could do except let it wait its turn, and, of course, at last it came.

With a gusto that was designed to allay all their unspoken hostility and put to rest any doubts they could have about his good intentions, he launched vigorously into the task of selling a perfectly good shotgun. He stepped down and took the action out of the case, and held it up.

"Now, ladies and gentlemen, what am I bid for this beautifully scroll engraved highest quality boxlock ejector twelve gauge shotgun by the famous London and Birmingham maker, Westley Richards, complete with single trigger, two sets of barrels, the famous Model C bolting arrangement, and the equally famous detachable locks?"

As though to confirm his worst fears, the silence of the crowd established the relatives in their angry phalanx at the back: no bid.

What could be worse? Perhaps his whole future hung here — no bid! Again! After weeks and weeks, still nobody in the fairly considerable number of people in the city was interested in what was obviously a fine piece of gunmaking. His eyes flicked up to the unforgiving back row, taken up by all those forbidding expressions.

He put down the gun. It was time to reach this crowd, time for a straight talk with them.

"Ladies and gentlemen," he said, staring straight at the back row taken up by his silent critics, and trying not to flinch, "I can't work it out.

"Week after week I've offered you this fine gun, and nobody among you is interested in it."

And then, even as he spoke, it came to him, that country phrase, that highest form of praise, and he blessed his own silver tongue.

"Ladies and gentlemen, and all the many shooters among you, I have to give this gun my very highest endorsement; I have to say to you...." he went on, this time unbendingly looking straight into the matriarchal eyes, and being won over by his own eloquence: "....again, I say I give it my very highest endorsement, ladies and gentlemen, I know, I am absolutely certain...." Just for an instant, as his voice rose, he wondered — there was the matriarch, not all that old, either, but where was her husband?

"....Am personally convinced, ladies and gentleman, and I can assure you all with absolute certainty that *this gun is a good killer!"*

It's a wonderful thing, he mulled over it later, the way the tongue races on, like a trigger finger committed to a shot even after the brain has lit up all the red lights and sent out the signals telling it to stop.

Still staring into her eyes, he knew as he said it, long, or so it seemed, before he saw her start, and then blanch, long before his ears had closed and failed him, and the noise in the room had grown dim and very far away. It had come to him in an instant, long, or so it felt, before the expressions of shock had crossed the faces of all the rest of the family, and then spread like a stain to the faces of all the others, who knew, every one of them, he was convinced, later on, every single one of them in the town except him — and nobody had told him! — that, yes, the patriarch himself, God rest him, apparently couldn't stand them all another day longer, and when he did himself in, it had been the Westley Richards, the good killer, that he'd used....

The Auctioneer

Part Two - Just Small, not Little

As well as seeing all the guns, the auctioneer saw a lot of human nature, too, as people acted out their parts on the stage of the auction room floor. He told me, in his measured and reflective way, about the day of the small man.

He came from the Coorong in South Australia, and he lived somewhere beside its long, game-filled expanse; he shot ducks in the autumn and the winter, and he caught fish in the bad winds that blew there, winds that needed strength to cope with, and endurance as well.

It must have been a hard life. It's unlikely that he would have chosen it if he hadn't needed to. In those days during and just after the war, nobody had anything much in the line of comforts, and for a man with a relatively young family it was surely a struggle. Yet, like a lot of other folk who had nothing himself, he took part in community activity and was well thought of. He was known as an association man, and he had connections with a local youth club. He didn't spend all his time on the Coorong. He was able to attend the auctions because he never failed to go up to the city for his club commitments on the weekends.

It's appealing to believe that people somehow had a bigger sense of duty in those days. There are those who deplore its loss. Maybe that's what made him give service to the community when he could well have been excused for giving nothing but bitterness in exchange for his circumstances.

He used to come to the auction regularly for the things he needed. He'd buy secondhand fishing gear or a cheap single-barrelled gun every now and then, and other outdoor equipment related to the kind of living he had to earn.

He dearly wanted another motor, to power the craft he used to take himself out onto the Coorong where the fish were, and to cross over from the land side to where the ducks could be seen in the great rafts that still existed in those days, before the barrages were put into the Murray, those man-made barriers of death to ducks.

Engines were at a pegged price at that time. They were very scarce after the hard, troubled days of the war. It wasn't possible to sell one for just any figure. The auctioneer had to offer one in the usual way when it came up, which was rarely; then, instead of its being auctioned, it was drawn for by lot. Anybody with an interest in it had to submit a tender for it, but it would be at the government-appointed price. The successful bidder would be chosen not through the value of his bid, but through having his name drawn out of a hat.

The fact was that the small man had need of a good working engine to support himself and his family. That didn't mean that he was down and out, not by any means. He'd turn up at any auction when a motor was advertised, and he'd dutifully submit his tender and wait for the draw.

His shoes were always polished; perhaps it's forgotten these days, but when times are tough enough to make it difficult to afford shoe polish, the skin of a banana will do a pretty fair job, and it was a point of pride to him not to have dirty shoes. The blue suit he wore, complete with waistcoat, could easily have belonged to his father, and for that matter it probably had. In those days, men's fashions didn't change from one decade to another, any more than their sense of duty did.

With his tidy clothes he wore also a tidy hope; at every auction when a motor came up, he was there to be found, but he was never lucky in the draw, and he never complained. Those who knew what was going on, and it was most people there, wouldn't have blamed him if he had. He never did win the engine because he was never allowed to.

His competition took the form of a very blustery seventeen stone and six feet two, a man who had a big business in the city, a large family and a lot of workers. He also had the firm intention that the small man would never buy a motor in the auction.

Every time one was presented for sale, he'd bring down his entire workforce, his relatives, and anybody else he had something over, and they'd all come in and tender for it. With all those names in the hat, what hope was there for a small man with a simple living to earn? No engine came his way, but it never stopped him from trying. Time after time, he'd turn up on Saturday morning, dressed as always, making it his business to be there, and knowing full well what was happening.

What could he do? It was legal to tender for engines, and his foe could be accused of all sorts of things, but whatever his behaviour might have been called it was still within the letter of the law. The auctioneer couldn't help him. To fiddle the sale would mean he could lose his licence. He watched on, as the unfairness continued over many months.

One day, quite early in the sale, which was inevitably going to be played out the way it always had, the auctioneer was in the middle of a call when suddenly the small man appeared in the middle of the auction ring with a startling flurry of limbs, as though he'd been propelled there.

He didn't lose his rhythm, and carried on with the sale while the man rearranged himself on the other side of the ring. But from his vantage point above the crowd, he watched, puzzled about what could have happened.

It was only a minute or two later that once again the small man almost flew into the middle of the ring; this time, the auctioneer saw why. He'd been pushed hard from behind. In the place where he had been standing before he was so inelegantly shoved, the auctioneer plainly saw one of the sons of the small man's opposition.

He looked closely as he found a third place to stand, back in the crowd, and this time, he saw it plainly for himself. Another son came smoothly up behind him and shoved him violently in the back as he faced the front.

The third time he turned around and shoved back, with the heel of his hand, and in a moment he was faced by the father of the boy, who towered over him, and heated words were being exchanged. The auction was forgotten, and to try to retrieve some semblance of procedure, as well as to save the neck of the small man, the auctioneer publicly announced that he was closing the sale. He thought to give him time to make his escape, because the odds were all against him, but then he saw him slide backwards as the big man dropped his shoulder and tried to position himself to king hit his victim, and maybe get him out of the auction rooms for good and all.

The small man was white behind his bluish chin, and it surprised everyone when he moved quickly back, eyes round him for the three sons, locating them, making sure that none of them cornered him, his left hand doing up a button on his jacket to stop it flapping in case he was caught and had to fight in a confined space; he was going not to the street, but deeper in, to the door leading into the auction room's yard.

He went through it first. That way, he couldn't walk into a punch from someone who'd beaten him to it. Once outside in the open, he flicked a look over his shoulder, and seeing nobody within ten paces of his heels, he unbuttoned it and slipped it off, the blue jacket that matched his chin, but he didn't bother with the vest.

The big man couldn't believe his luck. He barged outside, everybody with a taste for it following, and the hostilities were soon under way.

The auctioneer admitted it was only about then that he recalled he'd already noticed one or two of the signs, never thinking much of them, the loose joints, the two or three little white facial scars, and most of all, the slope of the shoulders. The oldtimers knew, it's seldom the big square shoulders that are built to punch, because they get musclebound; it's the narrower, sloping ones, the kind that stop just short of being round, they're the ones with the real sting.

The big man and his sons didn't know all this, though, not till later. He has a good turn of phrase, the auctioneer; he said the small man didn't even lose the part in his hair.

He stayed well out till the bigger man had no wind left, and no sons left, either; they'd caught the drift of the way things were unravelling and called discretion the better part of valour. The auctioneer hadn't even seen them go, which was no doubt the idea. Their father couldn't have cared less. He was busy. As his arms got heavier, his feet dragged in the dirt of the yard, and the small man's moved too fast to see, the same way his hands did.

The auctioneer reckoned long before it was over, the big bloke wanted to lie down, but he was never allowed. The small man just worked around him and took little strips off, one at a time, nothing ambitious, until there wasn't a piece of skin left on the knuckles of his left hand. He slid and he moved, under the haymakers and never inside until there was nothing left to fear. By and by the big man couldn't even see.

When he could hit him at will, he gradually upped the ante until rather than being knocked down, his aggressor, the cause of his frustration for so many months, just tottered and fell over on his back with a thud that passed along the ground and through their feet to the crowd.

He'd evidently seen the sons leave, or else he just knew that by the time of this scene in a two-act drama he had no more to fear from their kind.

He must have done it to some extent for his own satisfaction; maybe he did it because they left him no choice. Living as we do today, could we ever really know how he felt, not being able to get among the fish and the ducks that he required to do justice to the way he supported his family? No, we couldn't — but I suspect he also did it because he thought it needed to be done.

In a minute or so, when the big man more or less came to again, and his eyes were still looking in the direction of the stars he'd just been seeing, the small man walked over and actually stood astride him, looking down at him. And then he said in tight, clipped tones the only words he spoke throughout. The auctioneer remembers it well, and he quoted them to me.

"Well," he said, "I suppose you and your boys might like to continue this discussion some other time.

"I'm busy through the week, but I always make time for the club on Saturday, when I come up to town." And at this, he reached into the fob pocket on the vest he hadn't taken off, and he took out a small, white card. He dropped it on the big man's reddened shirt.

"If you ever feel you'd like to see me again, you'll find me any Saturday afternoon without fail, at the Adelaide Police Boys' Club, where I'm the instructor in boxing."

Water Enough

We pick up a pup from the kennel; we take it home and the bond is there, somehow, in a few days or weeks, unobserved at first, perhaps, but growing and eventually almost tangible.

They don't come with a guarantee, though, dogs.

****

They were together more often than apart. She had the run of the house — the way she should, a lot of us would say. She was supposed to be a gun dog, but we've all heard that one before.

They hunted rabbits together, on the flats, with gun and rifle both. Sometimes he'd wonder how she knew she had to work close in, for the gun, or a long way out, for the rifle. She knew, all the same, and to fetch them in was her pleasure, night or day.

She was a german shorthair, tick, with a liver saddle, and in the matter of work it's hard to say what her first preference was. She took rabbits in her stride, sometimes too much to ask of a lively dog of that breed, and yet she didn't get overawed and distracted by their bobbing tails when there were quail she was supposed to be sniffing out. She had a sense of what she was meant to be doing.

She loved to retrieve, and she went courageously into cold rivers, pounding through the rock pools, when ducks were soon to be on the menu. There came a day when the water was nearly the end of her. Not for a long time, though, not till after they had the partnership confirmed.

They went everywhere together, over the years, and that was to include the property of a relative of his, quite a few hours' drive away, with irrigation. Where they grew lucerne and had a good water supply, it was fair to expect ducks. He took her there early one summer, before the duck season opened, and as they drove up along the house track, though she'd never been there before, Anna knew, and she quivered. He wasn't the only one to look across the acres of green and see standing pools, leading back across a wide expanse to the tree line that he knew tracked the river.

Not only that, he discovered, driving in, but there was a wide, inviting lagoon, with a boat standing on its edge, and a little outboard in place to make it go. This swamp was fed by the river, and even as they drove up, a pair of teal rose from their safe haven in the kumbungi and flew out over the lagoon's wide expanse. He thought it was a good thing, to have a lagoon for a front yard. Going by the twitching nose, so did the dog.

It was the middle of the afternoon when they pulled up, man and dog, and they were treated to the usual country hospitality. Related the two men might have been, but they didn't see each other often and so they had a lot to catch up on. There was always plenty to talk about, farming matters, country things, the state of the machinery and the economy, the crops and the family.

He'd put the station wagon under a tree for her, and opened its back door, leaving a breeze blowing through, so she'd be comfortable. It was there he left her and gave her a pat as he took himself up onto the front veranda and settled down inside to chat away the latter part of the afternoon.

They filled each other in, just the two of them, in the absence of their womenfolk, and they took a couple of hours or more to do it. During the conversation he learned that there were things about the property he'd never heard about. He'd never seen the back yard, and, until he was told, he had no idea how far the lagoon stretched, and where the ducks gathered.

It was out of season, so there'd be no shooting. He needed to go and look, all the same, because that's the way he is, and in a while he started to find himself a bit edgy, and thought he'd better be getting along out in the boat to see what there was to see. When it was polite, he suggested it, said he'd like to go and poke around the swamp in the little boat, and so he and his cousin walked out to the car together. When they did, they found no dog.

Nothing much to it, this being the country, where there were no passing cars to cut a dog down. Shouldn't be a problem, they both said at first, both quietly thinking it was possible snakes could be a worry. They searched, after he called, and there was still no Anna. They walked up one side of the swamp, then back again, and along the other. In a few minutes, they did begin to be concerned. It wasn't like her, and there seemed to be nowhere for her to have gone, other than back towards the house....

To the house! Suddenly his cousin took fright and without a word he made a run for it, not the front and its veranda leading to the living area that they'd been sitting in, overlooking the swamp; he ran to the rear, crashed his way through the back gate, and there she was, two ears and a nose, circling, failing, floundering, going down, in the tiled in-ground swimming pool, with only minutes, perhaps seconds, left.

Both men dived in simultaneously, clothes and all, and they lifted her out, to place her on the ground beside it. She was limp under their hands.

Yet her tail wagged, as she leaked water at both ends. They saw her claws, ground back to the quick, bleeding, where she'd been scrambling, frantic, at the unfamiliar hard blue side of the pool, trying to get out of the uncharacteristically blue water. Round and round she must have swum, all four feet finding those tiles, slippery, unyielding, to the point where she was exhausted, sliding beneath the water, then rising with yet another effort, each one closer to her last, till just before she must give in they burst into the yard and found her.

Exhausted, she lay quite unmoving in the sun, soaking up the warmth, feeling herself dry. How long? Over two hours he'd been in the house. They tried to reconstruct the events, the way she must've found entry under the fence into the house yard, jumped into water as she often had, and suddenly found herself battling against it with no bank to climb out by, swimming for a time that could only have seemed endless, thrashing for her life, going in circles, finding only the hard surface of the sides to scratch against in a vain effort to win free. They couldn't work out how long she'd been in it, and gave up, just grateful that she was there with life still to be found under her saturated hide.

For half an hour they stayed with her. Dried with old towels, but still shivering, she appeared cold to her core. He was sitting beside her and along about the hundredth time he looked at her he saw the funny side of things, and he laughed a bit, relieved beyond relief that she was there to laugh at. So he picked her up, and he carried her out to the back of the wagon, and put her in it, still limp. There she could lie in the blanket they'd found for her, and get some strength back.

He took himself inside again, after the hundred-and-first look at her, and said he'd like to take the little boat out for a run round the swamp, look at the lie of it, perhaps give it some thought for a visit when the duck opening came round in a few months. His own clothes would dry on him in the late sun, he said.

No worries, his cousin told him, fuel in the boat, she'll be all right now, go and have a look around while I put some tucker on... And he did.

He checked on her, and she registered him the way she often did, with that tiny wag of the stumpy tail. He looked again at her feet, and winced. They were oozing blood, the claws so far gone. The front ones had worked so hard and so long against the tiles of the pool wall that there was no skin left on the front of the feet at all, and no claws left. They were worn right off, down beneath the quick. Even the back toes had the claws blunted off square to the centre of the foot and were abraded to bleeding.

The last he saw of her at that point she was played out and cold as wax, stretched out in the back of the wagon, but he knew that the light was coming back into her eyes.

He walked the fifty or sixty yards down to the boat, clambered in, kicked it off, started it, quickly found that the edge fell away into deeper water, and let the little motor chug away and carry him gently out into the wide lagoon, where he could forget the events of the previous hour and perhaps find a few birds to watch and remind him of the coming season.

After he'd gone a hundred yards, he scanned the horizon, right to left, turned back to see the way he'd come... and in the wake of the boat, he gave a start as he saw a nose, two ears on the water, and there she was, paddling after him, faithfulness with bloodied feet and a determination no human would be likely ever to match.

****

"'Wait for me, Boss', that was what she was saying," he told me later. "She couldn't see me go off alone," and there was no mistaking the quiet pride in his voice. At the time, I was at his house looking down with him at her ruined feet, healing only slowly, and she gave her dog-smile to him, under his stroking hand.

"Yeah," he went on as he remembered the sight of her, paddling, "you'd reckon she'd've had enough water by then, eh?"

True. And one more thing. He's lost her now. On an evening not long ago she quietly slipped away. But I said to him that every day he'd had with her from that time on was the purest bonus, a gift to him, made of her loyalty and tenacity of life.

They bring no guarantees.

The Day They Took the Boss

In the bush there are some things that are done and some that aren't. We all have different standards, but most of us who've grown up with a gun or a fishing rod know a sportsman when we see one, and even if we don't warm to him entirely, we still acknowledge his way of life and we tend to help him where we can.

So, in the event of someone living in an area where he has some quail shooting, it isn't out of the question that other folk might hear of it. He could even have his hospitality imposed on by those who aren't as fortunate as he is. If he happens to have a way of being a bit handy with dogs, then that could compound the problem and invite even more interest from others less fortunate. This is the way it was in the matter of the big boss.

Often enough, the shooting men who live in the wide expanses of the wheat country don't bother with quail. But there are still those who do, of course, and they're inclined to work hard, covering lots of ground, and to follow the little birds as relentlessly as the shooters of game with bigger feathers. For them, when the birds are in, it's a serious business.

They came in one year, and Keith was out and amongst them. Everyone in town knew that they'd arrived, and in roughly what numbers, because of the size of the crease in his face, which was a kind of district quail register: a big grin meant lots of birds.

It was Keith's friend from the city who phoned. The telegraph goes further than just through the bush. He knew when his old mates were finding birds, so there was no escape.

His city friend was a boss and a shooter, and a pal first of all. He'd done his share of what they call getting on in the world, and he was more of a boss than a shooter by then, so he did a lot of his own hunting in board rooms and in meetings, sometimes with his eyes closed, watching shadows in his past as the talk ran on, at other times maybe searching out the line of a curling pigeon dropping between rooftops, his gaze lifted out towards a cloud somewhere in the blue.

This didn't mean he'd lost the will — just the time. His values were still in place and he knew how to commit a kindness. This was why he rang Keith.

It seems the boss was being visited by the big boss, from England. Instead of letting terror strike him, charity did. He knew the big boss, knew that he could shoot, that he did plenty of it at home, and that he'd make a day free. How could Keith refuse his friend? The big boss had a good advocate, and before a few minutes had passed, he was booked in to shoot on the following Saturday.

When the time came, he appeared promptly at the appointed meeting place, the post office in the little town, which was a good sign to the slightly suspicious local, Keith the quail shooter. Sad though it is to say, for all his patience he sometimes received less than courtesy, even from bird hunters, who should have been taught manners by their pointing dogs, which as we all know tend to have them naturally.

Not only did the big boss come on time, but he had the right gear. He didn't have to 'borrow' cartridges, like some guests before him had done. He didn't say a lot, either, and that was another good sign. With few formalities to worry over, they drove to the current hotspot and made themselves ready; with the lending of a game bag and quail pins and the hollow clunking as barrels were slotted into a borrowed break-action gun, the eagerness of the big boss was plain. When the two of them set foot in the paddock, the big boss released a few more surprises from the cards that he held close to his chest.

In the first place, he wasn't one of those fat and breathless bosses. He was more of a lean and limber one. His corduroy'd legs were not for decoration. They propelled him through the stubble at a respectable clip, and they kept him up with the pointer.

At the first set of the dog, they had arrived at the part Keith continually dreaded. Always in the back of his mind there was a doubt about the credentials of a hunter newly met, whether he'd be safe and considerate of the dog and other shooters, or whether he'd learnt his gun handling recently and badly, the way some latecomers to shooting have. Sometimes he felt he took an unnecessary risk when he went afield with an unknown quantity as a favour to a friend. Still it seemed to keep on happening, because there was no shortage of those who knew that he was inclined to find his share of birds.

The big boss, at a nod from the owner of the pointing dog, stepped confidently in front of the shorthair, and flushed the bird the right way, on the leeward side and with his head up.

When it took to the air, his left foot moved in the direction the bird was flying; the butt of his gun just flowed into his shoulder pocket. The stock met his face and as it did the bird fell neatly dead at thirty yards.

The big boss did instead of said. He went on, and he seemed to sense the way the bird would rise; from the start, he seemed to know to take the curling one as it began to straighten up, and the straight one before it hit the wind and curled. He knew where the dog was, and he showed himself mindful of the handler. When the first pair rose, he took the harder front bird first and left a reachable second, as though he'd been doing it all his life, which he hadn't; in fact, he'd never shot quail before, because there aren't any to speak of in England.

Keith began to relax and even to enjoy the day, seeing his dog twist herself round backwards on some pretty points, watching a good shot at work. To his host, the big boss began to show signs of turning into a fellow traveller, a man of the open spaces and the clear air.

Not long after they'd settled into a routine, from his preoccupied position it occurred to the big boss that he was the only one shooting. And when he turned back as he walked in on a point, it dawned on him — Keith was carrying no gun.

Why should he be? If the shooter was a menace, he'd want nothing to distract him while he watched and assessed whether or not to continue. If the shooter was in order, then he could do exactly what he'd been doing; he could show him the courtesy of a shoot, watch his elegant little dog at work, and enjoy the walk and someone else's success. If all went well, perhaps a little later in the day, he could break out his own gun and pop a few caps himself.

Perhaps we can excuse the visitor. Perhaps, coming from the boardroom, he'd forgotten the manners he once had; perhaps other things were on his mind. Also, and sadly, there is another, more likely possibility: nothing was on his mind at all. Or in it.

He finished his walk in and shot the quail in proper style, and then with a smile that covered all his face, he broke protocol. He breached the law of the paddock and the field. He patronized his host.

He picked up his birds, looked at Keith, man without gun, and he forgot to see a treble clef in the pretzel shape of the pointing dog, and to recognize the consideration extended to him by the brotherhood of seekers after game who follow it to the place where they hear a sonata in the whirr of rising wings.

He turned on Keith as on someone he'd seen often but only just recognized, and he called out triumphantly to him.

"You aren't shooting, are you, old boy! By Jove, you know! We have a name for fellows like you back home. We call them *gillies*!"

Even the dog swallowed hard. The gentle quail shooting breeze stopped as the air turned chill and cloudy. Fellowship froze as the lean bird hunter in brown corduroys with a wisp of quail feather stuck on his cheekbone grinned inanely and turned back before Keith's eyes into the big boss, and crushed their camaraderie.

"Yeah, mate," said Keith sadly. "We've got a name for 'em, too. We call 'em bloody idiots. I reckon I'll shoot tomorrow, when you've gone."

The Day They Took the Doctor

They'd seldom seen a quail season like it. By the time they were well into it, Keith and his shooting mate had a regular Saturday afternoon appointment, and it was widely known. Naturally, then, they weren't all that surprised when the doctor from a larger neighbouring town telephoned one Sunday to see how well they'd done the day before. Keith assumed he just wanted to try his luck at getting a few shots in, or maybe cadging a free feed of quail. There were plenty of people who did one or the other.

This one soon showed that he wasn't just half inclined. He telephoned again on the Monday, and then the Tuesday, and on the Wednesday as well, by which time there was a note of pleading in his voice. On Thursday and Friday it had moved on more towards desperation. On Saturday there was nobody to phone, because Keith was out shooting, but he was on the line again on Sunday, and by midway through the following week he'd won, and been invited to go shooting with them. The lilt in his voice changed to excitement.

He called again on the Thursday and Friday of the second week, as well, but that was probably just out of habit.

On Saturday afternoon he met them at the place where they asked him to wait for them. Keith wanted to be behind the wheel, so that when he took his visitor it would be by the longest and most confusing route, just in case he tried to go back uninvited. After a fifty-minute drive to one of the larger cereal farming holdings in the district, in due course they went in by a back gate, so as to bypass the front entrance with the big property name written on it.

Suddenly it appeared that the doctor was no longer a slightly pitiful figure, begging to be taken by the expert to where he might find a quail to shoot at. No. The doctor instead had suddenly become a man imbued with purpose. When he stepped out to do business with these birds, it was no other way than grandly.

He swept into the paddock in full regalia; the many badges on his jacket said he'd been on the state skeet and trap teams, and gone overseas to shoot sporting clays. The boots were new, but worn in. The shooting glasses set off the colour of the shooting cap which had been imported at great expense, and which matched the game bag, which in its turn had been hand-stitched.

The sun fell sharply onto the coin finish of the elegant English sidelock double gun that Keith, knowing a little of these things, roughly estimated would've cost half the price of his house and four times as much as his car. He was almost moved to ask if he could have a look at it, gazing at the Prince of Wales stock as he stood sadly fingering his own worn, third-hand and mass-produced under and over. Somehow, he gulped back his curiosity about the doctor's desirable gun, because he sensed that it wouldn't be welcome. The small-town doctor may be a man worthy of respect; perhaps Keith shouldn't pry. There had come over this medical man quite suddenly an air that betrayed his unmistakable intention to get down to tin tacks and take some birds that afternoon.

Naturally, as a matter of policy, and as with any guest, they deferred to the doctor for the first bird as the dog held it in a perfect point. It made a classic sight. He stepped out gravely in the six hundred acre stubble paddock, right by the other six hundred acre paddock standing alongside it, and he saw the little bird on its way.

As it rose and clattered off, the doctor looked over the stock of his graceful, best-name English double and focused on the ground, so that he could check the proper positioning of his feet. Then he disengaged his right hand from its graceful timber, and he pushed his expensive glasses back carefully on his nose; he pulled his exotic shooting cap forward just a fraction further, too, so no errant ray of the sun could fall on his watchful shooting eye. Then his hand moved to adjust the hand-wrought game bag....

Keith whipped up his gun and shot the bird a couple of yards before it was out of range. The doctor's face registered shock — even pain. He turned and confronted his host.

"I say — " he said, "my bird."

Keith apologized profusely. "Sorry, Doctor. I thought you must've had a misfire."

But the doctor had already pushed back his exotic shooting cap, and moved away, following the lead of the dog, already looking birdy as it came up to another point.

Naturally, the aggrieved doctor moved in to take the shot, and as the bird flushed, he checked his feet, adjusted his glasses, pulled forward his cap, and, satisfied with that, he ran his hand to his game bag and pushed it further behind him so it wouldn't interfere with his gun-mounting. He raised his side by side, and waved it hopefully in the direction the bird was last seen travelling in. No shot was fired, because the bird was no longer in sight, let alone in range.

Neither was there a shot when the next ten quail were flushed. His hosts quickly came to learn the routine, and they'd grit their teeth as he adjusted feet, glasses, cap, and game bag, and they'd look the other way, to avoid having to watch a wasted opportunity.

At about the twelfth, Keith's mate broke. The strain was too much. The doctor had progressed as far as the cap part of the drill when he heard the shot. Like Keith, his mate seldom missed. The bird, although a long way out, crumpled before the doctor's astonished gaze.

"I *say*!" he cried. "*My* bird!"

Nobody moved. Keith's mate said, kind of half heartedly, "Sorry, Doctor — thought the sun might've been.... in .... your...." But his voice trailed off to nothing as the doctor, with his jaw set, was already moving in on the next point of the obliging dog.

At somewhere around the fifteenth bird, neither local could stand it any longer. When it rose, they looked at the doctor simultaneously. It was as though each was the measure of the other's despair. They both snapped at the same time. Feet...glasses... and when he got to cap, without communication or warning they both swung their guns and shot the bird — twice, two barrels each, in unison, almost as a mark of desperate defiance.

Before the quail had hit the stubble, the doctor moved with a speed they wished they'd seen him capable of before. His features became contorted with humiliation and rage. With a violent motion he broke his gun, the understated English gem of best workmanship, still unfired, and he flung it in a burst of temper on the ground where he stood.

Then he looked straight ahead, never back, and he stormed off a very long way to where the vehicle stood, the only landmark in the expanse of stubble. If there'd been a door to the paddock, he'd surely have slammed it.

The two hosts were amazed at first, and then when it was obvious he wasn't stopping and this was serious, they followed him in confusion, a little ashamed, to try to make amends. His driving stride displayed the measure of his anger. They felt as though they hadn't shown him the hospitality of the field, somehow. So they trotted after him and they spluttered and spoke half-sentences in his wake, but it was all to no avail.

Perhaps they suffered some confusion about what their obligations really were, and lost heart in stumbling through the stubble after him, because in his cold rage he beat them back to the car, all that distance off. They saw him fling the back door open and haul out his imported vacuum flask and sit on his patent folding seat to drink coffee and mull on his misfortunes.

When they caught up to him, their excuses sounded lame, even to them, and deep down they weren't any more convinced by them than he was. Having begun in the role of the offended, he kept it up, and for their part, though obligation niggled at them, their apology at best was faltering, and at worst it was insincere.

The remonstrations and the confusion of the mismatched little group faded out, eventually. But the day by then was over, and they walked back out into the reaches of the stubble, though they couldn't undo what had been done.

At least there was a happy ending, though, as sometimes there must be, the god of the hunt giving a wink and getting his own back on those who deserve it.

They have enormous paddocks of wheat in that country. When eventually the autumn sun came down on the six hundred featureless acres of stubble beside the other six hundred acre paddock that was just like it, and turned them both golden pink, every acre still looked the way it had looked before: just, in fact, like the other eleven hundred and ninety-nine.

They searched everywhere, the three of them, batting around and stumbling against this clod and that stone in the half light, and finally in no light at all, but from that day till this, and despite the fact that Keith went back four times, they never did find the doctor's gun.

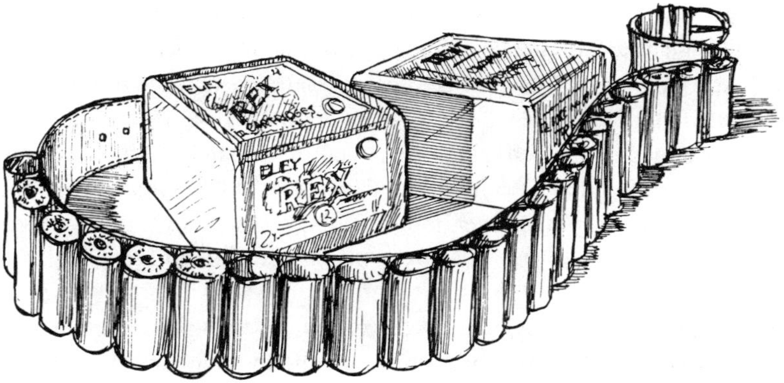

How to Treat a Cartridge Belt

When I was a fifteen I looked at my old .22 and wished for a shotgun the way a man in worn-out sandals thinks about owning a pair of Florsheims.

The great day did come eventually, of course, and I owned a twelve gauge. Just what chicanery was called for so I could come by it is best left undisclosed, in case this story falls into the hands of children. From time to time, when the right star was in the ascendancy, and when I hadn't stepped on too many cracks in the pavement, I even owned some ammunition for it.

Such a state of affairs unfailingly made me very happy. Those old cartridges came in all sorts of colours and configurations, and I ought to know because I became a great scrounger of them. In postwar days, up through the fifties, it's amazing how many junk drawers and back sheds yielded up a couple of mouldy looking old paper cased Rexes or Trents of dubious effectiveness. A lot of them made loud, harmless noises in the general direction of startled rabbits, after they'd been carefully dried on the brick hearth in front of an open fire, when all the family looked sideways at them, silently expecting that there'd be a time when I did that once too often.

One wet day I was ratting around in the enormous back shed at home when I came across a leather cartridge belt.

Up until then, when I was rabbit shooting, most of the time I'd carried Grand

Prix sixes in my right-hand pants pocket and fours in the left, and looked bulgy when I walked. But with this new discovery in my hand, the world looked like a friendlier place as I bolted down the stairs to find my father for a full explanation about exactly why I'd never been told about the existence of this treasure.

It was simple enough; the fact was he'd forgotten it was there. Interestingly, though, he'd made it himself, many years before, by hand. He'd cast around for the best piece of leather he could find, and he'd stitched the twenty-five loops by hand. He did it in the winter over a few evenings, always the night owl looking for a practical task to do, up till all hours to make something functional with his hands.

Suddenly the loose collection of cartridges under the bed came into order. The sixes went into the right-hand end, to go into the right barrel of the double, and the fours went into the middle, with a couple of loops kept ready at the left end for some twos to be called on in the event of running into an obliging fox, expected to stand still while I changed the loads in the gun so as to be correctly set up for the encounter.

The old hammergun dated from before the turn of the century, and the belt must've been made in the early thirties. They seemed to me like a good pair. In no time at all, I'd learnt to wear the buckle in the middle of my back, allowing an uninterrupted view of the brass heads. This, I thought, was progress.

It wasn't surprising when the stitching started to fail. The passage of time had to have its way. It was from then that I started to wonder how to treat a cartridge belt and I went on to spend a lot of time thinking about it.

Somewhere I found some Dubbin, and started applying it liberally to everything in the house that was leather. Boots and old gladstone bags alike came in for their fair share of treatment, but this wasn't in time to save the cartridge belt, of course.

I bought a new one, with money hard-won, and thought some more about how to treat a cartridge belt. Neatsfoot oil — that'd be the answer. Very nourishing. So I begged some of that from somebody, Dubbin forgotten, and applied it to everything else I could find with the same vigour I'd been using before.

Meanwhile, more of those tell-tale little crescent-shaped marks kept on appearing on the stock of my old hammergun. But I loved the feel of neatsfoot oil, and I told all those who'd stand still long enough that it was wonderful stuff, would penetrate anything.

Now I'm older. I'm not under any illusions about having time to change my loads for foxes. I can live without being drenched in neatsfoot oil. My shotguns may not be glorious antiques or best London sidelocks, but they also don't have little dents up and down their stocks, because the fact is I've learnt how to treat cartridge belts.

What's needed is a large, smooth, white stone, set up at comfortable working height. Take the belt, and carefully wrap it around the stone; then, fasten the buckle. Place the stone and belt in a suitable conveyance, and proceed to the nearest body of standing water.

This for preference should be boiling with piranha activity. Take the belt, wrapped securely round the rock, and toss the ruddy thing in. Then go and buy a shooting vest, and for the remainder of your days there'll be no more unaccountable scratches up and down the side of your gun stocks, where the brass heads of cartridges bruise the wood.

That's the secret. This is how to treat a cartridge belt.

Choosing Your Enemies

On a small bay with the splashing lake water clear beneath his hip boots, a market hunter put out decoys in a wind from the south southwest.

He had finished rebuilding his hide, using reeds from the site. The structure he preferred was entirely built in, its roof a thatch of reeds, so that it could not be seen into from above. This took more work, but it paid a dividend or he would not have bothered with it. He would shoot from one or two holes he'd make in front, depending on whether he was alone in it or not.

The decoys he used were made of cork, shaped by hand. He could move the necks and make them look even more lifelike. They were plumed and not painted, using the skin and feathers of real birds. This he had learnt to do himself.

He had markers placed in the water at forty yards, beyond which he tried not to shoot. He also had his set of forty-five decoys put out with a seven-yard gap in between the two distinct lots, to invite the birds to land in the middle. This space he always provided for incoming ducks, but exactly where it was to lie was something he would adjust in accordance with the angle of the prevailing wind.

When he called, he did it by mouth. The effect of this on ducks within ear-shot was eerie, as though he was working an unseen magnet. They spiralled in towards his decoys — ironically, as though their lives depended on it.

Unlike the hunters of today, he shot at them when they landed. He used a double-barrelled gun, full-choked because it's harder to anchor a bird sitting on the water. This was another reason he needed his decoys well divided into two groups, so that his shooting low across the water wouldn't in time cut up his own handiwork.

He used number five shot, specially ordered and bagged for him, and six if he expected teal. If he had a secret weapon, it was the place itself. The vegetation underfoot was lush and green, without slime on the water. Ducks want to be where they want to be. He was well enough experienced to recognize and go to the place that was attractive to them. More importantly, he only ever went there when the wind was exactly from the south southwest, because he was fully aware that this was the best time to intercept them pulling in there rather than to a bay somewhere else.

The day in question he shot forty-eight black duck, and his labrador retriever worked steadily all morning.

****

There's a lot to be gained from thinking about Grandfather. Those without one of their own could perhaps think about somebody else's.

I was moved the other day when I stood looking across a swamp, and saw it the way it used to be. There were a couple of hundred hectares of water, laced with fallen logs, standing gums, and vegetation to attract ducks in swarms to match the mosquitoes. I'd stood on the hill and looked down at it after the shoot, and even though it was getting on for noon there was still the occasional flash of a wingbeat far out into the depths of it.

I thought of how it must've been for our forebears, who had this all round them. There would've been waterfowl like we today could never imagine. The city I live in stands on what was a huge flood plain, and the hundreds of thousands of people who live here all take up space that was once alive with every kind of waterbird.

I imagined throwing the gun into the car, and driving out to the nearest swamp like this one, twenty or thirty kilometres from town. I imagined selecting roll crimped sixes for teal, or fours for black duck, out of an old wooden cartridge crate marked ICIANZ — Imperial Chemical Industries, Australia and New Zealand.

I could see myself wading out to stand under a tree, shooting enough ducks to make a gift to the neighbours, and maybe the neighbours' neighbours as well. I thought of the sidelock English double I'd have had, and just possibly appreciated, too, even though everyone else had one like it.

That all goes to show how silly I am, doesn't it?

Yes, there were undrained swamps, ducks, motor cars, sidelocks, and roll crimped cartridges, but what a mistake to think they could all get together.

Twenty or thirty kilometres today takes maybe fifteen or twenty minutes to cover, but our roads are good, even at their worst, compared to those of the early part of the century. We have mechanical reliability. The places where I shoot my ducks I can drive to, across paddocks that are smooth enough almost to be called landscaped.

But my grandfather? Why should I assume he owned a car? Even if he did, I wonder if he could afford the fuel to go on forays to where the birds were reported to be any more often than today's equivalent hunter can afford to go not to Buloke or the Riverina or the Coorong, but to Spain or South America.

When he did manage to arrive where ducks were congregating, why should I assume that the paddocks were flat enough to drive over? The fact is, they weren't even cleared. To gain access to them he'd have needed to drive and then walk as well. What a walk it would be. My guess is that to reach good swamps, after the drives, it would have been treks sometimes of several kilometres, bashing solidly through the stuff we see these days just around the edges of our clean, modern low lying waters.

More than likely he had no car at all. He rode a bicycle at best. He worked longer hours, and at more physically demanding jobs. I rather doubt whether a man who'd spent all day in a boilermaker's shop would choose to nip out ten miles by bicycle after work with all his gear, shoot a mess of ducks, clean them, carry them home, and be up bright and early at six for the ride to work next morning.

If we consider prices today, because the numbers are big, we think they're expensive. Yet ammunition in this last couple of decades, minor fluctuations aside, is becoming relatively cheaper. Grandfather probably had to make every shot count, when he could afford to shoot at all. He didn't shoot a best sidelock, either, any more than I've got a gold-engraved K-grade Browning with two sets of barrels under the bed.

No, if he wanted to shoot, anybody's grandfather had his share of problems to overcome. Like everybody else in the world, then and now, he found if it was worth doing it was probably hard, one way or another.

He had bitter, harsh enemies: transport, costs, and probably simple fatigue. Ours are different. They're misguided preservationists, the media delirium about gun ownership, the difficulty of giving an account of a country pursuit like shooting to a highly urban population, justifying its validity.

But they're bitter and harsh enemies, too, and they'll stop us just as effectively as they can, all questions of right aside. Grandfather must have fought his enemies — that's why we've got the legacy of his shooting tradition alive in Australia today.

We should always remember that it's a rare luxury for a person to choose his enemies. They do the choosing, and we have to take them as they come. I ask myself: what am I doing to overcome what I'm up against? It's a question worthy of someone's grandfather, with just a bit of a change of subject, that's all. Is life hard today? — yes, as it was then, but hard differently.

****

When the professional used to leave his house in the town and head down to his beat north of the Coorong on South Australia's big water, he'd be setting out for a week of fishing and duck shooting. Mainly set up for fishing, he had an eighteen-foot sailing boat, and behind it he towed his working fifteen-foot dinghy, which was made for rowing. All week he'd fish, mainly for cod, and he'd shoot when he could, any time the big rafts of teal and mountain duck were to be found coming into the little freshwater soaks he knew so well on the salty Coorong. The ducks would be sewn up in wheat bags and sent to the market by rail.

Friday night was the one he used to set aside to make the trip, so he could convey his week's work to the landing, where it could be unloaded for transport to the city. He didn't like to use the motor on his boat, because it took too much expensive fuel, so instead he rowed himself and his entire catch.

In the evening, after he'd spent the Friday afternoon killing his fish, when the sun was low he'd set off alone to ply his oar across the big water. All night he'd put his back into it, building a rhythm, one that he could stay with through the long black hours as he steered by the stars. He never knew what a gun law was, and he never saw an animal liberationist. Did he think his life was hard?

The distance he covered was from Wellington up to Milang, roughly sixteen miles of rowing.

When he used to pull into the little town on the Saturday morning, well after the sun was up, he'd had a night of backbreaking work, alone, in which of course there'd been no sleep. He needed to arrive in time to secure the transport to the city he needed for his catch, and that was the main thing, because it was his only source of income, and the result of a week's work.

After his night at the oars, he'd dock the boat and unload it. Then, while he was there, he said, as a very old man, he used to play football with the local Milang team on the Saturday, because he couldn't bear to waste the effort of his trip into town.

When I think of him, for some reason the picture that comes to me is of the calluses on his hands.

Clarrie's Tree

It was a lone tree, and not particularly memorable, not to anyone who didn't already know about it, and most didn't, that morning, when Rex drove out through his white farm gates.

He drove along the road into town in the big utility truck, pleased with its humming engine which he'd not long run in after replacing, and he half noticed two magpies ahead on the road, one standing tall, flashes of black and brilliant white. He eased his foot off the accelerator because he knew how fearless they are and he didn't want to hit them.

As he drew closer, he saw why one was tall and the other was not. The second was dead.

The usual flash of regret went through his mind when he saw that common but sad spectacle on the roadside, the kind that animal liberationists make so much of. One of the pair was dead, and the other wouldn't leave its side. It was determined to stand there alongside its mate, unmoving, even though the vehicle was bearing down towards it. It stood up proudly, illustrating what the new-age philosophers would have us all believe, that birds and animals are just people in feathers and fur. This could be a lesson in steadfastness, an example of all the best that nature had to offer.

He drove past carefully, the V8 burbling, and quickly picked up the picture of the two birds, living and dead, in the rearview mirror.

It was then that he saw what was keeping them together. The live one was eating the other.

****

Clarrie had been a shooter of some renown in the district and Rex had been tutored by him in his earliest days, so that when he grew up he came to know that old gum tree from every angle. Clarrie had more or less adopted him when his father died, and without anything much being said about it, had let it be known that the boy with the shy smile and the courteous demeanour was his to position when they took themselves out to the swamp where they all shot.

This Clarrie would do, before retiring to his place, which was the gum tree, standing as it did at the edge of a natural point that extended out into the water. It was just as unspoken but even more fully understood that this was Clarrie's to shoot from, because he was the oldest in the district and he'd found it for himself when none of the others were old enough to hold an argument, let alone a gun.

This was common, once. There was a sense of place and order amongst the shooting community. It seemed to function by itself without the need for external policing. It ran on dignity and common sense.

It extended from there. When the boy had gone with Clarrie, he'd made sure he had taken his manners with him. He never took another man's shot and he helped pick up for whoever might have been shooting nearby. He took the good-natured banter and responded as befitted one of his age.

The tree and the little complex of flight paths around it were a source of a lot of game for many people in the district. In the hard times there were families within earshot who'd hear Clarrie's old gun whump in the evening, either from his tree or from the small backwaters near it, and in the morning they'd step out to find a half a dozen gutted but unplucked ducks strung up in a bunch by their necks, put anonymously on their back verandas, so that their children's bellies would be filled.

Rex had benefited a lot from what Clarrie taught him. He'd asked his advice, and in many ways had modelled himself on the patterns the old man traced in the world.

Clarrie had since passed on, and in a way Rex had thought it was just as well. In the year after he died, the plans for the proposed new highway had been approved, and two years after that the road was a reality. They were scything paths through Clarrie's ways.

It was onto just this road that Rex had turned during his journey into town to collect his mail and complete the one or two items of business that had to be done each week. It took him around the edge of the swamp, now dried back, drained by the improvements the shire had seemed so happy about implementing and so brash to boast of.

It took him, in fact, when he was just at the half way mark, directly past Clarrie's tree, after which the road unbent and ran straight for the rest of the way into town. It came to him as something of a shock, some days, because it stood as a kind of parody of Clarrie, a man he'd respected and learned from. It was bereft, now, that tree, a measure of the change we all know is inevitable, but the change we nevertheless don't believe will happen to us. It was bare and it was dead, its branches falling. Under some compulsion that he never questioned, he would always look for the single six-inch nail that Clarrie had driven into it, just a whisker below the fork, where he'd hang his old army bag holding his spare cartridges and sandwich. He was on the pension at the end so there weren't all that many cartridges for it to have to hold up. Sometimes when he'd see it in winter, it would be because it had glinted, a gleam through the rusty red, the sun being lower in the sky at that time of year. Then, in summer, it would stand out more sharply anyway. When he glimpsed it, this made him feel better, as though there was indeed something to rescue from the past, all the good associations of the place, memories of red mornings of the duck opening, the grey, misty ones of later in the season, the full bags and the empty ones, Clarrie's billy tea and his quiet advice. These were the memories provoked by Clarrie's tree, and they helped, they helped with the sadness.

****

This morning of the magpies he was lost in thought about the stark lesson that they conveyed, and as he drew level with the tree it occurred to him that he didn't have the bearing that he needed with him. It was going out on the bus that day and he had to have it there because the tractor was old and there'd been a renumbering of the parts that had caused some confusion. Without it, he couldn't make the repair, so there was nothing for it. He turned the wheel and did a U-turn to go back to the farm.

As he did, there, under the shadow cast by Clarrie's tree and its outline broken by the saltbush, he saw the police radar, angled towards the town and waiting for some unsuspecting speedster. If it was anything, he thought, glancing vainly in the direction of the fork, it was just another modern misuse of what had been a fine tree, once. He drove back to the farm with his thoughts locked onto the picture of the two magpies on the road, the live and the dead.

****

After he picked up the tractor part, he drove without incident through to the town and went up the main street, where he attended to his errands and wondered at the rash of out-of-town cars in it. He looked at all the people driving them and though he didn't know them, he thought they looked familiar. Most common among them all were the obviously youthful. Many looked like students, the kinds with young beards and a lot of show.

Then it dawned on him. The duck season was to open on Saturday and he'd heard that a protest was scheduled for the area. Here it was, unfolding in front of his eyes. Many of the cars were obviously owned by their parents, because they were new and expensive. He glanced into a few of them and he wasn't all that impressed with what he saw inside, but he mentally shrugged and decided that might be his own prejudice, so he ignored them all as best he could.

At least he tried. He went up the road and there he saw the first lot drinking in the car, and a bit further up another crowd was gathering on the footpath, and what they were smoking might get them into trouble if the local policeman turned up. He could overlook most of what he saw, but as he passed the group he saw the litter they'd dropped and he thought that was another matter.

Maybe his eyes narrowed. A couple of the louder ones followed him as he went back to his vehicle, and they climbed into theirs as well. One was carrying beer.

He'd seen enough of the stupidity of the duck-hunting protesters on the water in the last couple of years, running unharmed moulting non-quarry birds to a standstill, so they could be 'saved' from the shooters in time to die of shock in the 'rescue' tent for the television cameras. Like all other country people he understood how little they knew of what they were meddling in. He remembered in his childhood the work put in by Clarrie, who'd insisted that if he wanted to shoot with him at the opening in the coming year, then Rex had to join him while he repaired one of the levy banks on a little lagoon set back from the big water, near the tree. Clarrie knew, and he made sure Rex understood, that a few months from then there'd be at least one clutch of teal that came off that little swamp. It was only possible if the water was preserved, and so the two of them had put in half a day with a couple of shovels, working out of Clarrie's decrepit T-model, the last one in the district. It had worked, too, Rex remembered, and Clarrie had taken him down twice to spy on the young birds as they grew through early summer, result of the handiwork of the two in repairing the breach.

When he climbed into his truck in town and rolled out the way he'd come, it wasn't long till he had the same two faces alongside his. He realized that they'd pulled up behind him, and seen the sticker on his bumper bar — "Gun Control is not Crime Control" — and they'd identified him as one of the enemy.

He did what he could to ignore them. There were a couple of girls in the back of the car, and the two young men in the front; he wouldn't have time to go out to the opening shoot in the morning, but he could already lament the misguided effort that would be going into the protest.

As the two vehicles set out onto the straight run from town, they made themselves more obvious to him and there was nothing he could do about it. They came up alongside him in their sleek sedan and made to pass, but then dropped back, and they were a mass of hand gestures.

The windows came down as they drew level again. "Do you murder ducks?" They began to shout, and then to screech. "Whaddya need a gun for, big man?"

He accelerated. Suddenly he was angry.

They sped up, too, and they stayed with him. That big motor in his vehicle, only burbling before, then started to roar as it sucked in air, and suddenly the two vehicles lurched forward as though tied. The road out of town was clear and straight.

Why him? He didn't know. He did know that this was suddenly unpleasant. He could look after himself, he had no doubt, but he was more than offended by the behaviour of these young fools who'd come to his town to tell him how to live, their only basis for doing so the fact that they didn't have enough sense to find out the realities in the first place.

His own anger began to increase to a matching hostility. He looked sideways to see the same leering faces, the same lewd gestures. As the speed picked up he felt rather than heard their hostility and so he put down his foot. Both vehicles lurched into a second, higher bracket of speed.

He thought of Clarrie; what would he say if he'd known this was what his district had come to? What would he think if he'd known that his ways had been so misunderstood, his beliefs and his integrity so questioned that this kind of behaviour could suddenly be found to be chewing its way into the normally mild and steady young Rex he knew those many years ago?

The very thought sent his foot to the floor in an angry spasm, and the two engines screamed. He flicked a look at the speedometer and he didn't believe what he saw, but he kept his foot down all the same, the road still straight, the half way mark to town soon upon him, and the voice of Clarrie coming to him; yes, he knew what he'd say.

"Don't risk yourself, son. They're not worth it. Slow down." But the car stayed with him, and both engines thundered.

He was reminded of where he was by the fast-approaching stark outline of Clarrie's tree as it stood tall on the edge of the swamp in the distance, and again he could imagine the measured tones of his old mentor's voice: not worth it.

He slammed his brakes on, hard, sustaining the pressure, grinding his boot floorwards, squarely on the tiny rise that only a local would see, just a hundred yards or a bit more before the gnarled gum outline that suddenly assumed the silent, moderating role of his dead mentor.

So he was under full braking, and they didn't hear him roar with glee. The greenies blasted past him, car horn blaring, claiming best, all open mouths and beer cans and derision, at what he later described as more than a smidgin over double the highway speed limit, and on, past the old swamp, past Clarrie's tree, and past the police radar that stood under it. The tattoo he played on the car horn when he passed their stationary vehicle a couple of minutes later, and saw their glum faces, was a little message strictly from him, and not Clarrie.

Duck Camp, Moonlight

It was the second opening, so it must've been later than the end of summer, and the night was clear and cold. It wasn't dark, though, because the lack of cloud cover ensured that what moonlight there was must fall on us all. Picture that duck camp with me, as I remember it.

****

We weren't so much a group that year, more an agglomeration of whoever turned up. There was the usual collection, but one or two ring-ins, blokes we'd had to feed because they'd smelt our stew and come into the firelight. We didn't mind. There was plenty to share around.

I remember old Ernie was there, tooth-stained, gap-mouthed. He lived in a colourless van, mostly on the Murray, and there were few regular duck shooters in Northern Victoria who hadn't passed the time of day with him or at least seen him. He knew the bush and he fished and shot in subsistence, living mostly off the land. Seasons didn't worry him all that much, not the government-set kind, not in those days, but all the same the declared opening must've been a bit of a relief to him, so for a while he could be on the side of the law, and probably, in truth, he liked the exclusiveness of his own company no more than most of us do, because he always found something to say when he'd rolled the paint-faded Bedford to a stop and brought out his folding chair.

He was there, and I remember that, but there were many others, too, and the camp stretched out a way. Soon there was a big fire, too big for comfort, and it grew warm enough for one or two of the fellows to have to light smaller ones nearby to do some serious billy-boiling on.

Some came into the firelight, and moved out again later. One quiet, fairly abrupt man, taciturn, even, sat not far from me on a low stump, and his big retriever was with him, not too close, but watching his every move, too, in the manner of the dog that belongs.

That was a magnificent animal, calm, almost stately in the way he moved, and he had character. One or two fellows wanted to pat him but it was as though they had to ask permission not only from the man but from the dog as well, and they couldn't quite bring it off. I watched that dog, and saw royalty in him.

His owner certainly had little to say. The men around him seemed to have nothing much to ask of him, either, and the conversation kept shifting away from him. Like his dog, he was big, but he had an air of inviting no engagement. There was an element of the solitary about him, a difference. He listened well enough, but he didn't seem part of the company all that much. He just wasn't comfortable and I felt almost sorry for him. He didn't let anyone in, and I wondered if he knew how to.

So we sat around and talked, and when at last the camp fell silent that night, most of us had gone to tents, two or three to hammocks, a few to the backs of their vehicles. The dogs were tied, the fire burned down, the occasional clank of a tin mug or a pannikin fell away, and only the bright moon and the dying fire were left over, the remnants of the hospitable activity of evening.

I was restless. I've never been all that good at sleeping, and the night before a good shoot is as luckless a time as any to settle down.

I dozed; there'll be those who know what it's like. I half-dreamed and half-saw ducks, perhaps prompted to it by the chuckle of the hen teal as they fed somewhere across the water. More than once I gave up trying to sleep, and spent a while looking straight across my feet, out the flap of the tent, and into the red of the huge campfire's remains.

The big dog had slipped in front of it; unlike most of the others he wasn't tied up. Perhaps his manners had been thought too good to need it. On the other hand, perhaps nobody had wanted to have been the one to ask his owner if he'd mind doing it.

He was free, anyhow, and at some point he'd taken his big, curly coat down to the fire to lie by it and soak up its warmth.

The moon showed it all to me. It must've been past two in the morning, getting on to three, with not a sound in the camp, when I discovered that I wasn't the only one who'd been having trouble sleeping. The big dog's quiet owner, the one who'd seemed a bit churlish, came from his own swag into the firelight, where nothing stirred, and where only an occasional shadow rose from the fire to match the bird-phantoms as they flicked across the big water that had drawn us all there together in our common expectation.

He appeared almost suddenly in my view, went quietly, purposefully to his dog, and looked around. I didn't feel like an intruder, but only because there wasn't time.

He bent from the waist and put down his hand, and I sensed an instant communion. After a couple of strokes of the broad head, and receiving a couple of responsive if sleepy wags of the tail, he dropped suddenly to his knees beside that dog, the two of them clear to me in the combined light of moon and fire, and in a simple gesture that he must've felt nobody could understand should they see it in the light of day he bent again, low, from the waist, and buried his face long in the dog's woolly coat, as though to breathe him in. Then he was gone.

I hope he slept better afterwards. I know I did.

Four Hunters

In the early sixties, there was a place that could be like thousands of others on this continent. It was at the foot of a mountain range, in an area desirable as a hunting spot.

It was cool, flat land, not too heavily worked by the local landholders, and so it carried its share of game. It was also scenic, like so much of the country we all love to roam in, regardless of what our particular kind of hunting interest may be.

The fellows who owned the properties adjoining it might have been a bit rough around the edges, but they were what we all know so many farmers to be like. They worked and lived in the district as farmers everywhere do, giving a hand in the community, minding their own business, carrying on with making a living out of their properties.

On this particular day, there happened to be a group of the local landowners sitting together. That in itself isn't all that common a thing, considering the workload of the average farmer. On this day, they were together because a couple of them had been in the same vehicle on their way to some shared task. As well as that, the place where they were all sitting was a corner that formed a junction of three of the properties, and that brought another two of the neighbours, working on a fence, into the picture.

They were sitting down having a yarn, and as they talked, four figures came into sight, a large one and three smaller, all different in size, and all carrying rifles.

As they drew closer, it became evident to all the farmers that the man at one end of the line was the father, and the other three were likely to be his sons; and as they came closer still, it seemed the eldest of the three was no more than twelve. To one of the farmers at least, that was too young to be carrying a rifle. If he was too young then the youngest was even more so, and to a shameful degree.

As the father brought his small assemblage up the slope towards the group for the obligatory g'day, the biggest farmer's curt comment, directed against the father, floated to him through the clear morning air.

"Bloody fool."

But a second farmer's quiet comment also drifted across to him.

"I wouldn't be so sure of that."

The second farmer hailed the father, asked him how the shoot went, calling him over to the gathering. As soon as he was within clear hearing, the first farmer, loud, perhaps a bully, called out with more than just a bit of mockery in his voice to the smallest of the boys, who seemed no more than nine years old.

"Hey, show us your gun, son."

He might have been the youngest there, but he was no fool. He looked up. "Can I show him, Dad?"

The father had remained impassive despite the thinly masked attempt to do some stirring. "Yeah. You know what to do. Go ahead."

So the small boy stepped into the centre of the group, and did as he was asked.

He looked the smug adult right in the eye, and with the muzzle of the rifle pointed away and to the ground, he calmly went through the drill that it soon became obvious he had learnt singularly well.

He started with the already open bolt, which he pointed to with his free hand, and he said, "I opened that as soon as we came across the top of the hill and I saw you sitting here."

He took it and disengaged it as far as it would go from the action without leaving it, and he handed the rifle over for inspection, muzzle still pointed safely away, and he went on. He didn't have to say much.

"There aren't any bullets in it. In my brothers' rifles, either. We go with Dad. We have to pretend they're loaded, but we aren't allowed to have any bullets, 'cause we're still doing our safety training."

The second farmer spoke up quietly, mostly to the first farmer, but probably to everybody there, a little proud of his own judgement, and with just a trace of a chuckle in his voice at the discomfiture of his neighbour: "Y'see," he said, "they've always shot on my place."

One of the other farmers smiled and looked away. The one next to him avoided his eye. Perhaps the premature speaker had been loudmouthed once too often.

The now completely embarrassed farmer who realized he had spoken out of turn didn't have a lot of room to move. He coughed, and half turned away to the hills. Then he made a good fist of it and said, "Well, I suppose they'd better shoot on mine as well, then."

Today, over thirty years later, they still do, all of them, and on the other adjoining places, too, four safe hunters who know a little discipline and have some respect. And they're all good mates with a wiser farmer, older now, who noted just a month or two ago that the eldest one of them has just started his youngest lad shooting, with an air gun, because he's too small to lug around a rifle.

He didn't need to ask; yes, that's right, it's an empty air gun.

The Full Choke Man

I have nothing against full chokes. I am a tolerant person.

Over the years I've encountered many strident full choke proponents. They tend to have a vision of what shotguns should do which is not necessarily shared by those who are not as fortunate as they are.

I was talking to a fellow just the other day who was trying to sell a mate of mine an old Greener. When he ran out of superlatives to describe its extraordinary qualities, after exhausting what seemed to me a pretty impressive supply, he explained that it was almost as good as the best gun he ever owned, but which was sadly no more, owing to an unfortunate accident involving a trailer, a dog, two neighbours, a missed appointment, a successful — no, a very successful, or even an extremely successful — duck hunt, and Lord only knows what else.

This gun of by now legendary capacities was a sixteen gauge. Full choke, of course. It would kill from here to the other side of the road and back again. This feat left me in no doubt about the quality of the piece concerned, although I confess to being a little intrigued by the getting-back-again bit. But anyway, that's what he said.

These types of full choke men tend to come out once a year, often after the shooting is finished, I've noticed. But nothing shakes their ferocious faith in having the maximum constriction at the ends of shotgun tubes. Or at least not their public faith.

I don't say Lou was one of these folk. Maybe his belief in such guns was justified. Perhaps he brought down his game with awesome efficiency. I don't know. All I can say is that fixed firmly in his mind was a yardstick by which everything related to shotguns would have to be measured. He had a vision of how far it was between two points — not just any points, it must be understood, but two very specific ones. Against this he measured all his shotguns.

Many of us do this. I know people who judge distances in terms of cricket pitches. Ask a few folk. It's surprising what they carry around in their heads related to odd little bits of the here and there of the planet, and use to measure things with for their own purposes.

Lou's little bit was how far it was from the front gate to the church steeple.

He came from a village overseas, and nobody was in a position to know whether from the front gate he'd ever actually shot anything that happened to be flying past the steeple at the time. But did it matter? Lou referred to it so often in the company of his shooting mates that a few of them began to pick up for themselves some rough idea of what this distance looked like. In this respect he became something of a neighbourhood expert.

He swore that this is what his guns back home would do, and he insisted that any gun worthy of rack space had to do it now, too. Any shotgun shooter will understand. It's possible to have the dickens of a time getting past the illusions of distance and actually pinning judgements to realities.

Perhaps his mates grew to be quietly grateful to Lou. How far is too far? What's the point at which the bird is a fair target? Anybody who can teach us a method for quick analysis of this to expedite a good decision does us a favour, and is not someone who should be derided.

Lou's mates never spurned him. They tried to apply his yardstick as best they could. In the matter of shotgun range he was well enough thought of as to have become a guru. He seemed to have it down so pat that his words carried weight. From the front gate to the church steeple — that was how far shotguns had to kill at. Transmission ends.

One day it happened in a set of those strange agglomerations of circumstances we all see from time to time that one of his more youthful cronies had to leave these shores and go to a place very near to Lou's old village.

He was a man of an inquiring mind, which is usually a pleasant trait; he thought about many things, including his shooting, and he was always pleased to work out how best to derive value from another's experience.

Before he left, he hadn't intended to let it be widely known where he was going, but the word did escape, and nobody asked him to take a tape measure and some surveying gear to do some triangulation so he could come back with accurate figures.... at least, not outright, anyway. But one or two of his circle did happen to mention that they'd be interested to hear just how far up in the blue they really did fasten old-fashioned church steeples, and he soon had the message.

When he arrived at his destination he threw himself into discharging his responsibilities, and freed himself as quickly as he could for the trip to the neighbouring village.

When he undertook this, he was soon tired of what he'd been doing, as it was only mundane business for his more remote family, and he finished it briskly. After a short bus trip to Lou's old locale he set out by walking to the outskirts of what was in fact a far-flung and tiny outpost. It dawned on him that he truly might have to do some triangulation to determine the exact distance from the gate of the old family villa to the steeple of the church. They were so far out in the sticks that Lou could have fired a howitzer there without too much interference from the local gendarmerie. He hoped his mathematics would be up to the job.

He thought again of Lou's gun rack, well stocked with full-choked twelve gauges.... The fellows were all interested, so he'd better do it all properly. Just how far a shotgun is supposed to kill game consistently and reliably has always been a matter of interest and debate. Forty yards? Forty-five? Fifty?

So he applied himself, methodically and carefully, as was his habit. He went to the villa, introduced himself, and was well received, though it had of course changed hands. But such hospitality is customary in the Mediterranean countries, and the current owners remembered Lou's family well, and Lou himself, too, though as a much younger man than more lately he'd become.

They weren't put out when he made entirely sure that the villa, and, more importantly, the fence, had never been shifted in all those decades since Lou had tamped the dust there with his bare feet and gazed skywards, cradling his full choke gun. No, no, no, it had been placed centuries ago exactly where it now stood; they even showed him some repairs, and were able to date them.

The priest was also charming and helpful. They didn't receive many visitors round that way, and he was more than able to give him the church history — and, of course, in this too the inquiring young man had to be most specific with his questions.

Indeed, there were certainly not two churches of the same name; there was not the remotest possibility that the church had ever undergone extensive renovations or any movement, as all the plans were still there, and he was just looking at them the other day; and yes, he, too remembered the younger Lou, the beginning hunter, and remembered his attendance at that very church, with his whole family — the only church, there, exactly where it stood now, underneath the same steeple it had always borne.

He covered all the bases, the earnest and inquiring young man, because he knew how important a few extra metres could be in a discussion like this one; he wanted to have it indisputably right, not just for his sake, but for the sake of his whole group. He sensed that they were relying on him. If a good gun really could kill from the front gate to the church steeple, this was a concrete matter that inquiring folk ought to look into closely, now that the opportunity had arisen.

So when at last he travelled home and met his mates again, it happened to be in a duck camp, where they kept a place for him, after his trip. The plane was to come in while he was still on leave, allowing him a few days before going back to work, so they left a message for him at home that they'd keep a spot warm for him if he wanted to drive out the day he arrived, so he could sleep off his jetlag and shoot with them the following morning.

Naturally, he took up the offer, and had no sooner driven in, stowed his gear and tied up his dog than they called him to the fire, dispensed with brief formalities, and asked him outright — they'd obviously been debating Lou's full chokes, their thoughts now turning to duck shooting — how far it was from the front fence to the church steeple.

Because he was a meticulous young man who paid attention to detail, and because it was a community effort, relying on all the goodwill he received from those helpful people at the villa and the equally obliging priest, he was in the happy position to give them a fairly exact answer, and he did: not counting whatever difference might have been made by the slight undulation of the ground, and by the nearest to possible means of effecting a straight line, he was able to say with confidence that the distance between the fence and the steeple.... was no more than a smidgin off four and a half kilometres.

Fox Fur

Foxes bring out the worst in people.

For years they were the scourge of the farmer's life. They had a thoroughly well deserved reputation for thinking evilly, being able to hide under a match-box, and for being everywhere at once, except where the man holding the gun expected them to be.

I have followed a fox into a patch of bracken that I could spit across, and I am not very good at spitting. This bracken stood up alone in a bald paddock. All around it was nothing but a hundred bare yards of well eaten grass.

There was no way the fox could get out, and there was no way I could avoid finding him, and after ten minutes of going round in circles I concluded he could stay in there till pigs have straight tails for all I cared because I was going home. I'm not usually a quitter, but a fox in ten metres by ten of bracken was enough to bring out the worst in me.

I'm not alone in this.

In a little country town in the red dust well inland there was a hotel, and the blokes in it on most Saturdays were an unambiguously hard-bitten bunch. From time to time there was something of an argument that developed there, and some-one would go home with a bruise or two, or occasionally be carried out on a door.

It was also a very hot country town, and in summer it was only natural that there would be more people in the pub on a Saturday when the temperature rose. In a community whose livestock was plagued by foxes, it would follow that there'd be a bit of activity on many a Friday night as the spotlighters went out to try to reduce the number of the sons of Reynard that were intruding into their fowlhouses and causing havoc amongst their lambing ewes.

One hot Saturday there was a local in the pub who wasn't going through a phase of being notable for his popularity, on account of one or two episodes of nastiness that he'd been involved in around the district. For some reason he didn't stop to think of, there was a surprising number of people who were keen to shout him a drink that day. It seemed like he couldn't get away, and every time he'd make a try for the door, he'd be called back for another beer by someone else. So naturally enough he stayed on.

He finally made his way out when the worst of the heat had cooled out of the long day and the sun was sinking. As he weaved his way closer to the car, he was hazily surprised to notice its windows were up. He thought he'd left them down, to let some air through it.

When he opened the door, the upholstery was steaming; so was the big, dead dog fox somebody had put in the car five minutes after he'd gone into the hotel earlier that day. Nobody who has never had a good whiff of a dog fox up close can understand this story. He had to sell the car.

There was a West Country Englishman, too, who knew about foxes. He came from a place where they kept a lot of poultry, and he understood them on that score. But when he immigrated and moved to a country town, he found they had another value altogether. Over here, people sell their pelts for money! This put a completely different complexion on things. It made the pursuit of them a much more practical affair, less of a service to mankind. He became quite fanatical in his pursuit of them for their skins.

One day he drove around a bend and he found a dead one on the side of the road. He wasn't in a tearing hurry, and if the truth were known, it wouldn't have made a lot of difference if he had been. This fox had a skin, and a skin was money. Dollars. Coin of the realm. It had been there two days, but he wasn't hugely bothered by this fact. He stopped, unsheathed his large knife, and took to it. No go.

Later on he lamented his bad luck. It seems he did everything a man might reasonably be expected to do in the pursuit of a pelt that was lawfully and morally his. He tugged and he pulled and he sliced and he hacked. It was all to no avail, so he did what also came to mind as a last resort. He took the fox home and into the laundry where he filled up the copper with hot water and he tried giving it a good soaking. Eventually he was forced to capitulate in the matter of that skin, and he shook his head, complaining about the fox, saying that despite his best efforts it still wouldn't give it up.

It won in the end. They're persistent, foxes.

They even corrupt the law. There's a policeman in a country town who went driving on one of his nights off and filled a large bag with the red reflectors he liberated from the white posts on the side of the road. He then went out and laid poison baits in long, tubular holes he dug with a posthole digger; the idea was that the strychnine was put in fat, and the fat poured down the hole, so that as a fox came and dug it up, he had to work to dig the fat, which had by then of course solidified. As he dug, he'd send the poison through his system, and he'd die on the job and be easy to find.

When the policeman was out ostensibly on his rounds at night, and in accordance with the time he reckoned he could crib from work, he'd take in one of his baited roads. The reflectors he'd simply used to put on bushes as markers, fifty or eighty yards back from the roadside beside where the column of fat had been put down, and he could confidently walk out to the spot in the low-lying, same-looking saltbush with the help of his service torch, and pick up his newly-dead foxes for later skinning in the small hours when he'd finished duty. He was a policeman who fell asleep a lot at his desk in the daylight hours.

To the surprise of many, though, foxes are not only cunning but they're notably silly, too, sometimes, in an unaccountable way.

I knew a man who shot a slide action Browning .22, and he could hit things with it that I needed a shotgun to deal with. He went after foxes often, and I suppose he made the mistake of thinking that he knew the way their minds worked. The place where he lived was hard, dry clay, in country that saw rain in big lots when it was lucky enough to see it at all. That accounted for the deep watercourses, and he'd go out and walk and whistle, walk and whistle, until he brought Reynard into the range of his little rifle. He'd pull off a head shot every time.

He'd practised as a boy, he told me once, by sitting with a takedown Browning semi-auto chambered for .22 Shorts on the back doorstep of the family farm on Saturday mornings. What he did was unorthodox, but it must've taught him a thing or two, because the lesson stayed with him. He'd been given the regular job of killing and plucking the chicken for Sunday dinner each week, and so he asked his father if he could do it his way. Yes, he was given permission. He'd sit there with his box of bullets thirty yards back from where the hens ranged, and he'd watch their bobbing beaks and head-shoot the one he wanted. With enough practice at this, his reflexes came to be well and truly in his favour.

I once saw him kick two rabbits out of winter seats in tussocks, and as they raced off in a winding run at ninety degrees to each other, he bagged them both with three shots. So he could shoot a bit, and I could understand his confidence.

On this day in the watercourse, he walked down one side and into it, then along a way, turning and twisting, watching carefully in the early morning light, hoping he'd find a fox walking through it on its way back to its den from feeding overnight.

As he turned a bend, he was rewarded by the flashing fur and sleek brush he'd hoped for, and as Reynard reached the top of the gully he whipped up the little rifle and flung in a running shot.

He knew it was a good one, he told me next day, the Sunday when we met, and he followed it confidently out of the watercourse and up to the flat, only to find that the gully snaked around in a semi-circle to appear forty yards away in front of him again, slicing its way through the dry earth. He walked straight to it, taking the line the fox had been on, not doubting that he'd soon be picking it up.

No sooner had he reached the new turn in the little gully, the pleasant early sun shining down, than his first look into it showed the prone fox form he'd expected. He slipped over the top, and bent over it, putting out his hand to pick it up, motionless. And that explained all the bandages on his hands and arms, because it was the wrong fox, sunning itself.

Duck Oil

A carton of milk is a very tidy item, not like the udder of the cow that gives it. I don't have a lot against milk cartons, but sometimes it's hard to get a grasp on how far we've come in the battle to forget the earth that we derive our living from. There's no shortage of packages, and they do quite a job of helping us to forget or ignore the source of the food or whatever it is inside. This is called progress.

Then I think of the benefit the outdoorsman knows, the pleasure of making a fishing net, or of lovingly and carefully making a blade that will become a skinning knife, crafted to requirements out of a piece of selected steel. We aren't big on that sort of thing any more, in this age of the prepackaged and the plastic.

****

I found myself in the house of a man who has spent just about all of his life outside the confines of the city, fishing, shooting. He has come back here now in his retirement. He used to love to shoot on the big salt a way off from here, and when we discovered we had it in common we took a wander in our minds around dogs and ducks and guns. When we arrived at the guns, he naturally showed me his, as anybody would, and I marvelled at the condition they were in. They were not new, the old hammergun from his father's day, the American guns perhaps from the time of his father before him. I knew how hard they had been worked, and the salt is not easy on guns. But the steel had the patina of use, and not the roughness too often visited on it by the unkind salt spray.

I didn't exactly ask him the secret, in case that's what it was. I did think it was a real achievement to be able to look after gear like that, and said there must be a lot of pride wrapped up in it.

Nothing to it, he told me, as he set about describing his discovery, learnt in the bush from an Aborigine he worked with.

First, shoot a couple of fat black ducks, or some others that take your fancy, just as long as they're in good condition. When it comes to the cleaning, around the vent there's a fair supply of bright yellow fat. This is cut away with a sharp knife, and put in a glass jar.

The jar then goes into a warm place, in open air and sunlight. There are half a dozen spots around the house that will do. A good one could be some seldom-used bench space in a garden shed, a place that catches some afternoon sun through a window. There has to be some give and take here. It's one thing to have the fun of the end result, but the innocent passerby doesn't deserve to have to put up with the ripe aroma that unfortunately accompanies this part of the procedure. In a word, leave it where there's a bit of room for unwitting civilians to steer clear and walk well around it. Be warned about this. In the initial days, it will set a brown dog coughing and it will cause passing pussycats to faint. Approach it cautiously and only from the windward side. Preferably in a gale.

That fat will melt, though, and gradually turn into an oil of the same yellow colour. To carry the process out correctly, put it into one jar and prop that one up at an angle just above the horizontal so that as the fat dissolves it will run down and fall into the open mouth of a second similar one underneath it.

The residue left behind in the first jar is the dried out tissue that contains the fat. What runs into the second may be bright yellow at first, but it won't stay that way for long.

Having decided that's enough, it's just necessary to put the top on this second jar, now full of a surprising amount of oil, and to leave it in the direct light, as before, perhaps standing on a window ledge in the same garage. It might take a week or two, or even a bit longer, but that oil will become clear.

Not only that. After it has stood for a while, and after the discarding of the first jar and the smelly tissue it came from, and after the bad memory of how potent it was at first, there comes the discovery that it has lost every trace of its violent smell.

What those ducks will have given, as well as some good dinners, is a sizable bottle of clear, neutral-smelling oil.... and that oil just begs to be put carefully onto the exterior surfaces of any gun to protect it entirely against the worst and most insidious moisture waiting to work into it.

It doesn't take much reflection to understand why this works. Ducks tend to be on the waterproof side.

****

We might have to buy our milk in cartons, but we don't have to like it. We can fight back.

It was by just this method that a quietly observant and humble man who might not have had a lot of money for gun oil kept hardworking firearms in spotless condition for thirty years. His children will enjoy them in time to come, and they will remember him and a hundred black ducks by it.

Duck oil. Make some, and try it.

An Overseas Trip

If some folk live for football and others for their work, Red was a man who existed only to shoot quail over a dog. All his life he'd done it. He grew up that way. He favoured english pointers, in the days when the german shorthairs hadn't made it here.

He was a salesman in a time when there was a market for what he sold, and it meant he made money. He did well at his work so that he could do better at his play. He had above average success in both, the result at least in part of his unusual degree of energy. He bought a fast car so that he could cover ground and not waste time, and he shot quail wherever they were to be found through his state, so that there were few parts of it that in time he didn't come to know.

When he'd seen them all, he found they weren't far enough spread to suit him. He shot stubble quail through the lower south-eastern reaches of the country, and then the fit came on him to shoot the big brown ones in the north, so he organized a trip up there and he did that as well. When he'd travelled far enough, he'd seen all the places in between and it came to be time for him to run out of country.

Everybody understood the way he was, and his family didn't mind. It wasn't thought of as a certifiably pitiable condition in those days. He and his dog, Sledge, were a familiar sight in many a district wherever there might be a few quail to find. If anything, the biggest emotion that followed them was envy.

One day he heard casual mention that there is such a bird as a californian quail. This piece of information was a parasite that bored a hole in his brain. He went to a library, asked for some help with the encyclopaedia, and before long he'd not only discovered that but he'd learned of Gambel's quail as well. That was two, and they were different types. They could be found in the United States. They were hard fliers and both were game birds. He had to go. It was that simple. He'd discovered the months of the open seasons there before he'd left the library.

A man not lacking in organization, it wasn't long till he ran up a telephone bill. Even though these were the days when people didn't fly as often or as effortlessly as they do now, he rang the customs people to see about organizing his quail gun overseas with him. The telephone operator in his small town soon became used to him. He made inquiries of startled American locals he telephoned at random to ask about quail in their districts, he tracked down a guide, and under his capable application a plan fell into place in no time. He had a travel company lined up to give him the air ticket he needed, and he was getting set.

Not for a moment had he ever forgotten Sledge. The dog was so much a part of his quail shooting that he'd just automatically incorporated him into the equation and it never occurred to him that his dog might have to stay home. When someone suggested it could be the case, the idea was nearly too much for him. He went straight to the telephone again with the customs number, and it was a question he asked through clenched teeth: what about the dog? Can he go, too?

If the answer had been no, that would've been all about it. Mates are mates. A trip of a lifetime, but a man wouldn't go without his dog, and that'd be that.

Wonder of wonders. The answer from the laconic customs officer was yes. Nothing to stop him. Nothing to say you can't take a dog to America. He asked him to double-check, not trusting. Nope. Dogs can go to the United States, no worries. No hidden charges, no taxes. Away you go. She'll be right.

He had a padded crate especially built. Nothing would be too good. He made the travelling arrangements, even took some of Sledge's favoured tucker, and cast around till he'd found veterinary insurance. He lovingly packed his gun, said his goodbyes and went to America where he spent six weeks shooting quail in more ways than either of them had ever imagined. Red and Sledge had the time of their lives. Four species, they shot, in every kind of cover imaginable, from desert to thicket. Bobwhites left Sledge near ecstasy, and Red beside himself. The overseas dog's performance was the talk of the little bands of quail specialists he found in two or three small towns. Both man and dog found themselves among friends, people who understood them.

****

When they arrived home on the plane to Australia, customs wouldn't let him bring the dog back in. He protested that they hadn't told him there was a law against it, but they said he couldn't have asked.

The dog went into a quarantine kennel for the nine longest months of Red's life, and when he went to pick it up, it bit him; it didn't recognize him any more.

Getting Something Back

It's often a pleasure to be able to say "I know a fellow who...." and then carry on to say something that brings order and makes sense out of what we do, we hunters, and what we think it's all about.

I think it revolves around getting back a thing or two from the land without the interference of the tax man, the greengrocer, the neighbours, the building society, the butcher, the unsympathetic spouse, the less sympathetic boss, or any other of the thousand worthies who all lay some kind of claim to our time, the ones who play the middle man in the great transaction of life when we know deep inside that we ought to be buying direct, if the metaphor will just sustain itself.

Perhaps life used to be a do-it-yourself operation; if so, it's surely changed into a string of dependencies, and sometimes we're bound to feel like we're on the blighted and distant tail end of them.

When I feel like that, I do know a fellow who....

....In the worst of sporting traditions lets the first few of his early morning ducks land in the water in the pale light, so he positively won't miss and have to go home empty-handed. Coming in from the field without something to show for it is a shame to him, a greater smirch than any breach of commonly held sporting ethics, like never shooting ducks on the water. To him there is an older, deeper article of faith than one imposed by tradition. It's the law of the growling belly whose dictates he minds.

I suppose it could be harmful in some ways, if he were a game hog, but he's not. He often shoots under the limit when the birds are flying and there's opportunity to shoot over it. I've heard him say that to sit over a pool at dusk and pick up two or three black duck satisfies him entirely. His bigger bag comes about by the weight of days — a few birds today, a few tomorrow, and a few more the day after that.

Even though his own children are no longer young, his extended family's big, and his pocket is not. Perhaps that could amount to cause for him to take more game than he ought. Yet he spurns repeating guns, and uses a single-barrelled workhorse he bought new some decades ago. It's probably fairly clear by now that he doesn't miss all that often.

He and his sons rigged up a scoring system of great complexity and they had a competition, once, to see who could put the most wild fodder together in a weekend. It only had to be edible, and points were allocated according to taste and desirability. Game birds carried high point values, rabbits lower ones, and of course the fish species available were all represented. He won. The reason for this was that he could see game where others couldn't; the pile of yabbies he caught, for instance, he took from a little stream that still runs through the centre of the big city he lives in. The rabbits came from burrows in several spots around the edge of town, ones that he'd mentally marked when he was driving. The trout came from the local reservoir, its fences high and overgrown, not even seen by most. There was much more. His sons and other family contestants, meanwhile, being young and impressionable, were making the mistake of leaping into their vehicles and fleeing unknown distances to the bush to shoot their bags there. No doubt they wanted to astonish all other participants with a sambar and a dozen wild pigs each. He stayed close by, and won because he has the gift of being able to see past the buildings to where the game is, which is often closer than most of us think.

He lives in a humble house, and he drives a humble car. A lot of the time he's out of them both, in a paddock somewhere, on the search for feather or fur.

All this being the case, I wasn't surprised when I ran into him the other day and he told me about his latest game-finding scheme, not in boast, but almost a bit reluctantly, as though breaking a long silence.

He was taking his duck punt and a red spotlight run off a small battery, and floating at night down the quiet, meandering path of a little river, not much more than a creek, that crosses the outskirts of the city.

It's pitch black there on any moonless night, of course, and he's no longer a young man. The water's cold, so he rugs up. Naturally, it's a lonely route to travel, and there's some discomfort involved, as there often is in hunting. When he floats underneath the main traffic arteries, he stops the boat, and with an air rifle he calmly picks off the feral pigeons that roost under the bridges, trying to angle it so they fall into the boat. If they land in the water he scoops them up with a little fishing net. They make good soup and stew for winter.

I asked him what he thought, on an excursion like this, when it was midnight and cold, and he was hours from his bed, picking up a couple of damp and feather-ruffled pigeons out of the icy black water, the plucking yet to come, and the heavy trucks thundering all the while across the bridge overhead.

It stopped him for a moment, that question, but it must have been a vision of his full freezer that crossed his mind.

"I wonder," he said, "what the poor people are doing."

Gregor the Snipe Shooter

He was a quick, intense man who could talk at length about matters of the church. He always knew what the sermon was, and there were some of the locals he'd engage in conversation about it any time he'd run into them. Because the town was fairly big, it seemed that not many of them wondered about why they didn't see him in church in person, and they didn't ever work out that in fact he was never actually there himself.

He knew a lot about the local court, too, was aware of who was being prosecuted for what and why. People thought that this was a very upstanding citizen.

If he wasn't, there were certainly worse ones. He kept himself fully aware of church matters because he had a continuing interest in who went to it. Church time for the worthies in the town was poaching time for Gregor. When they were in church, he was walking the depressions in their back paddocks, flushing snipe.

Only the ones who for their own reasons wouldn't let him in to shoot, of course. It was the same with the court. His interest there was in the movements of the local wildlife officer. Any time he was in court prosecuting, then Gregor would once again be about his poaching.

He particularly liked the mid-sized properties, the ones too small to afford a manager, but big enough to have the ground to get lost in. He knew every drain, every pool by every gate, every dip that caught every puddle in every storm, because where there stood shallow water there may be snipe. He knew every dairy, with its effluent line, because he understood full well that if he took up a position near one of these by the light of the first full moon in September, he'd hear the harsh cry and the rustle of wings as the first birds of the season came in. Not everybody liked having shooters around their cow sheds, though, or around the pools in the front yard. But this is how the snipe shooter may have to operate, finding two birds here, four there, always the same water bringing back the same number of birds, year after year and down the decades.

His mates used to turn him round in the street when they met him, so they could look for holes in the underside of the legs of his jeans. They joked that they could recognize the different barbed wire tears as he jumped his neighbours' fences.

It wasn't true, of course, but they all enjoyed it. He said little, and kept doing it. They enjoyed the fruit of his labours as well, because a lot of people dined on the game that Gregor shot. He wasted nothing, and his energy was prodigious.

He lived alone in one dwelling, and his mother cooked for him out of her own kitchen in another house beside it. They were of Eastern European extraction; she wasn't thought to be kind to him. She lived independently in her own cottage, entirely bare of ornaments, except for a stuffed snipe that was placed on a small log on an occasional table, perhaps a reminder of the Siberian variety that she knew from her own domain of years ago. Her house stood sixty yards from his, and she walked across the way and took his food to him hot in the evenings. They said she muttered a lot about him, and resented him; people asked why she lived where she did, but nobody knew. It was said there was no love lost between them. This might have been true. There was also no overt argument, but then neither of them mixed much, socially, so how would anyone know?

In due course Gregor's old mother sickened. Nothing changed at the time. Then she went briefly to a nursing home. In a while, she died.

Only a day or two afterwards, not long after twilight, the red of the sunset was rekindled. There came an emergency call to the fire service, and the truck roared out to what was said to be a big fire at Gregor's place. When the crew thundered in the gate, they found to their horror that it was the old woman's house that was heavily ablaze. Before they could start work in their practised hurry, someone noticed Gregor, sitting off to one side on a broken farm implement and neutrally watching the fire burn.

One of them asked him if he was going to help them fight the blaze, now fully under way. Couldn't see why he should bother, he told them laconically, because he was the one who lit it.

This was in the order of a bombshell, not taken well by one whose biggest role in life was the fighting of fires. It didn't seem right that a man should stand and watch one burn, let alone say that he was the cause of it. None of this fazed Gregor in the least. No, he said again, he didn't believe he'd be fighting it, because he lit it. It was on his property, it was freehold, and there was no law against it. He appreciated the fact that they'd all come out in such a hurry, but they could all turn around and leave now and there'd be no harm done.

With that, he turned and devoted his full attention to the flames, which seemed to be pleasing him.

It was the time of year for the grass to be green, and there was no danger of the fire spreading, so not knowing what else to do, the fire crew did nothing. In a few minutes they'd trooped back to the vehicle and were gone in a cloud of their own bewilderment.

The game supply to his friends and neighbours stopped abruptly. His mates reported that Gregor never poached snipe again. A few quail he did still shoot, largely, he said, to keep his dog working, but only ever with permission.

Make Me a Fox Whistle

It was a sleepy town, not a sizable one, but big enough to have a railway station and a main street full of farmers' cars on Saturday as they came in to break the routine. It was also big enough to have a few men working on the railways, so that when they were posted to it some of their children thought that they were in seventh heaven, being in the bush.

Young Colin was one such. He's not now, because he must be nudging sixty, but he was then, and for him the joy of the bush was boundless, because it meant foxes.

Colin's father took his country railway posting with the same stoicism that was common to the age. He didn't like it, but he was not going to lose his job over it, so he went, and it was just a small side benefit that made his son so ecstatic at being able to do what he developed a real skill in — and this was coming to grips with Reynard.

Colin's father in his younger days had been prone to shooting a fox or two himself. He'd made a fox whistle for his son even before they'd moved out of the city and on to the country town where this all happened. Even though still a boy, he used it in style. There came to be a modest bounty on a fox scalp because foxes are incompatible with sheep. It wasn't a bad thing to have a son who could take the old Harrington Richardson and a couple of cartridges, all the budget could stand for a single outing, and come back after dark, tired, with two pelts.

One day Colin had his fox whistle at school. He couldn't remember why. It was probably an accident. When he took it out of his pocket, one of the boys asked what it was. He told him. It was made out of a jam tin lid, bent over, with a hole punched in the middle.

This was a town dweller who asked, not a bushie. There was sometimes quite a difference to be noticed between those children who'd been brought up in the town, and those who'd always lived in the bush. The kids themselves somehow perpetuated it, even in the country school. Colin explained to an interested audience that the skilful whistle blower could just about do 'Swannee' on it, and Brer Fox would come at a run, enticed by what his sharp ear heard as the pitiful squeals of a dying rabbit, a free feed.

Human beings are like foxes, inclined to read what they want into the things they hear.

He asked for a demonstration. What boy would refuse to give it? Another schoolfellow joined the party, and soon Colin had an audience. Without much effort he could run up and down the scale, varying both pitch and intensity, making the whistle yelp, then scream, a thin, dry, piping note that could almost split an eardrum. Taken in, a couple of them asked how he came by the whistle, and were told how his father made it in the shed, the work of just a few minutes, but the holes had to be placed accurately in the tin and the sharp edges had to be dulled and rounded to make it safe to carry and use.

They all seemed impressed, and the boy who'd inquired originally said Colin ought to show the school inspector when he turned up in a week or two. Colin had forgotten about his coming; it seemed to be important to some. He said he wouldn't bother, but he was surprised because once again it was a townie who suggested that, not one of the country boys.

He left at the end of the day, and when he arrived home he was puzzled to find one of his classmates observing his house from over the road. He waved a bit too casually as Colin went in. Two hours later, his father came back from work. Before he was inside, still mounting the back steps, the boy was at his heels.

"Mr Porter, would you please make me a fox whistle?"

He was surprised, but he did it. He told him to hang on, scrounged a bit of tin from off the floor in the back shed, and did the job, the work of a few minutes. That was on Monday.

On Tuesday, at the same time, there was another boy, but the question was the same. He ended up with one, too.

On Wednesday, there were two boys, not one. Mr Porter was a busy man. On Thursday, there were four. He ran out of jam tin lids, but it turned out all right, because two of the kids had fished in the pockets of their oversized shorts and come up with their own, the jagged edges not seeming to bother them in their enthusiasm.

Colin heard of all this from his mystified father, and thought he was surrounded by beginning fox hunters; he started to worry about the competition. He pondered on how he'd have to ride his bike further out, carrying the gun by some hayband looped over his back, instead of just walking out to the scrub from the edge of the town. To his credit, it never occurred to him that he'd bag fewer foxes.

His father drew the line on the Friday.

"Mr Porter, could you please make me a fox whistle?" He answered the plea, this time at the end of a long week, and thankfully from a single voice, by saying yep, he would, but it'd cost threepence.

This didn't cause his young patron the slightest setback. He held out a skinny hand with a penny in it, and bolted. On Saturday morning, he knocked on the door, and thrust a second one into Mr Porter's hand and again ran off before any words could be exchanged. On Sunday afternoon, he came back with the third penny.

Mr Porter, ruefully ready for the exchange, solemnly took the third penny, and handed over the whistle, and a shiny threepenny bit with it. He told its buyer that there were now enough fox whistles in the district, and the mayhem that could be committed against the fox population would be nothing compared to the destruction he'd wreak on any small boy who asked for another whistle that side of Christmas three years away. It's doubtful whether the boy was even listening.

On the following Wednesday, the school inspector was to arrive, important, feared, powerful, and if it was the way it had been in the past, his presence would dominate the school, hushing it, with even the teacher being more carefully dressed than usual.

On his way to assembly that morning, Colin had wondered whether he'd be asked about his fox shooting exploits, all the mornings when the grass broke underfoot from the frost that crisped it, or the day when he took the big vixen off Taylors' after they'd had three drives in an attempt to get her and missed her every time. He wondered whether the other, pretend fox shooters who seemed to be springing up all around him had between them managed to get even a single pair of ears.

He was worrying over nothing.

The school band ushered in all the children, in front of the inspector, playing a stirring march, ten boys and girls, with the bass drum for keeping time. Fife, flute, recorder, and the great man looked on benignly, smiling, his hands clasped proprietorially behind his back in the manner of school officials everywhere. They marched past proudly, to the shrill tones of 'The British Grenadiers', played with a penetrating sharpness and a level of clarity better than he'd ever heard from them before. "Hell," Colin thought, "they must've been practising..."

Colin was in the front row of the assembly. And as the band went past him, the drummer and nine other kids all in short pants, one of them turned his head and winked at Colin, and flicked up his lip. Held between his teeth, while his fingers did the mime of a shuffle on his flute, there was a disc shape that gave the unmistakable flash of silver, just the colour that would be reflected off a jam tin lid, or a fox whistle.

The Letter in the Gun Case

It was in the lining of the oak and leather case, the kind with brass corners that were moulded and fitted to protect the edges. Inside, the lining was worn, because the metal parts of the gun had been lifted out a thousand times in the dawns before the ducks had started to fly, and put back a thousand times in the dusks after the quail had stopped.

The bluing was worn thin, in parts gone altogether, but it hung on tenaciously to those surfaces that hadn't suffered a lot of contact. There was a film of oil that had done its job of preserving the metal, and on all the gun, from the locks to the underside of the trigger guard to the crown of the muzzles, there was no trace of pitting from rust.

On the inside of the lid there was a label, yellowed and stained from oil and age. It was in looking at the green baize of this lid one day, as he cleaned the gun in preparation for the duck opening, that he discovered the corner of the yellowed envelope pushed well back into the space between the lining and the leather of the case lid. Being careful not to tear the material any further, he pulled out the paper. It had his name on it, but no address, and was written in a firm hand that he didn't recognize.

"Dear Charlie,

"We've barely met, but I think we probably know each other well.

"In this case, as I believe by the time you read this you will well know, is a Boswell sidelock, and it was made in 1903. It served me well for thirty years, and it would have done for longer but it took me my first fifteen shooting years to save enough money to buy it.

"It has two sets of barrels, and this was what I wanted when I wrote the first of my letters to England and ordered it. The money I gave for it, a hundred and ten pounds, was a small fortune in those days and I wanted it to be right. It turned out to be just what I asked for and in all my life, even in the hard years of the Depression, I never regretted buying it. I thought of it as a single lifelong investment in pleasure, a companion to sit with in the sunset, when I needed someone to complain to about the midges when they bit me. I thought of it as a tool, the finest of its kind, a piece of craftsmanship that would outlast me, and serve someone else, as I hope it is doing for you.

"You'll notice the two sets of barrels are the same length. At the live bird club they thought I was all wrong when I ordered it that way, but I was never sorry because that was what my experience told me I ought to do. Over the years it helped to teach me what value there is in following one's own judgement. That was one of the gun's many lessons to me. Never reverse a good decision for no better reason than self doubt.

"It also taught me to extend myself in buying workmanship and quality, because in all those years it never let me down. Never.

"It taught me to take care of what I own, because every second year I sent it to the best gunsmith I could afford so I could have it looked over, and it might have been a strain but it was money well spent.

"I used it to train your father in gun handling and the manners of the shooting world, and I am sorry to say that I think I see in these a decline, because in those years with him at my side, years that would have been different if there had been no gun, I had my happiest moments. Perhaps you'll use it in your turn to train your son. I hope so, because respect and perspective have to be taught to us all, and a gun or a fishing rod is as good a way as any to start, and better than most.

"In my lifetime I carried this gun in countless places in many states, and if I could have afforded it I would have carried it overseas and shot it there as well. I could not, but though never crossing the sea I have nevertheless had the same experiences as the wealthiest Indian rajah.

"I gave it to your father when my eyes started to fail, but after his sickness he could not walk a lot and I knew he would have better use from my fishing tackle. I know he will care for it after I have gone, and from what he tells me it is to be passed to you. I am sure it will find good use in your hands.

"It is not just a gun that I leave you. I leave you an expanse of twilight across the duck decoys which is not open to description, but only to experience, a vacancy of air that holds a beauty and a privilege matched only by a responsibility to appreciate it and to preserve it and its conventions for others to come...."

****

It was signed by his grandfather, of whom he had only the haziest childhood memories. And I see I haven't quoted from the ending, which was probably the best part of the letter.

"....I am putting this letter into the tear in the fabric inside the case lid for good reason. If you are to read it at all, you will have to care enough about the gun to look closely at it many a time, perhaps take the case to a craftsman to have it repaired, and in that event he will find it, and give it to you. Even better, you could repair it yourself. If it is not important to you, then you will never see this letter.

A good place to buy the best quality baize such as lines this case is from a place where they make or repair billiard tables...."

Shooting Snakes

A bit over half a century ago, a father took his son rabbit shooting in autumn, hardly a very remarkable occasion. Of course, in those days it was seen more widely as a family excursion than it is today. Permission wasn't hard to come by and there was often no need to bother with it at all. Distances to travel were shorter and in most areas rabbits were easier to find. They were used by mindful shotgunning fathers to exercise their children on. Many a father trained up a son in the ways of the bush with a fortnightly course of rabbit shooting.

So it came about that on this particular afternoon, the son in question was at the side of his attentive father, carrying a .410, a double barrel Stevens, I believe, while the father had his twelve gauge, and a watchful eye on the behaviour of the boy, whose gun handling, incidentally, was supposed to be by the book. And it was. As the father said, so the son did, which is as it ought to be.

They left the car on the side of the road, near a tiny dam in the corner of the paddock, and strolled into the bare-after-summer rolling hills. There they walked and shot rabbits, of which there were many, and the sun shone down on them in golden approval.

The son would probably have stayed out not only all that day but all the next as well. By and by, though, the father decreed that it was time to go home, and so they went, well pleased with the day and each other's company, back to their car, just beyond the dam.

At the end of their walk, they had to pass by the dam, as the road lay just beyond it. The boy was looking at the car and not the ground as he put down his tired feet. Suddenly he let out a piercing squeal of fright as an enormous black snake seemed to leap at him from under his feet, and slither up and across the yellow bank, into the shallow dam. The two didn't connect, to the relief of the father.

In those days, everybody routinely killed snakes when they encountered them, and that's one thing that makes the story's ending different from the one it might have had today. But the concerns of fathers for the education of their sons is timeless. He saw the boy was shaken, and wanted him to overcome the fright. Used to being carefully heard, he said to the boy what was obvious to him: it had gone into the water, the dam was a dwarf, the snake was big, and there was nowhere for it to turn but back up out of the water, the way it went in.

"We'll wait him out," he said. "We might even time him."

He took out his gold Waltham fob watch, the one on the chain, and he laid it on the dam bank between the two of them. They both sat down, gravely looking across a few yards of muddy water, the boy peering intently over its surface, trying to see every bit of it at once, and the gun was ready across his knees.

The minutes dragged on, and the boy thought the snake must surely drown. He flicked a glance sideways at his father, but he didn't look like moving, so the boy resolved to sit just as still, and only his eyes moved back to the open watch when he snatched quick looks at it.

Nineteen minutes after they'd sat down, another car pulled up, Saturday afternoon, and nowhere much to go. A local farmer had been passing when he saw the two figures perched on the dry clay dam bank. Nothing unusual about a bloke with a gun in a paddock — but on the bare edge of a pocket handkerchief dam, and right beside the road?

Twenty minutes.

A big, slow-moving man, he hauled himself out of the car and ambled over.

"G'day," he said, grinning happily. "And what're you blokes doing?"

"I'm teaching the lad to shoot," said the father, not looking round, still staring fixedly at the smooth water.

"Yeah, I can see that," the local said. "But shoot what?" He left off here to laugh happily at his own joke.

The father flicked a glance at the boy, and he kept a straight face, which ensured the boy did, too.

"We come here," he said, "when we want to shoot snakes."

The local's laugh died down a bit, and there was a pause while he digested what he'd heard. It didn't take long to start up again when he realized what a bright pair he had here.

Twenty-one minutes.

"Well," he came back cheerfully, amazed at his own wit, "d'you mind if I watch?"

"Not a bit," the father said, "as long as you keep quiet."

He promptly sat down beside the boy, grinning. He couldn't resist it, as he looked at the bare paddock, the empty horizon, and the puddle-stretch of water. So he chortled happily to himself, not expecting another answer, and said, "So you come here to shoot snakes, do you?"

In the son's opinion, and he's had sixty years to chew it over, he couldn't have timed it better if he tried. At twenty-two minutes by the gold watch, the water boiled up, and the huge black snake thrashed to the surface. Still as tense as a lockspring, the boy snapped up the whippy little .410 and shot its head off, and then after a few splashes there was silence over reddened water.

The local looked at the two. No faces, and not the farmer's now, were creased in smiles. He watched them as they stood up, and briskly dusted themselves off, and he looked back and forth from one to the other and then to the water, as the boy unloaded the unfired barrel and they started to move away, leaving him sitting.

For a final time he looked at their faces, and at the water, and all the bare landscape.

"Well, hell," he said, blankly, "I reckon you do, too."

Two Icil Sevens

In the morning, after the sun was up and the pale spring sky cast its white light over the swamp, the wing commander dozed in bed and thought about whether he could lie there awhile.

It was a weekend, and he deserved to sleep longer. Conscience was too strong, though, and he eased out of bed to sneak a quick breakfast. He hoped to do it undetected, so he could eat it in peace, but there was not much chance of that. The young ears were too sharp. The pup heard him moving and was straight away excited.

When he finished, he went out the back and picked up his favourite shooting coat from the peg on the door. It was well worn and had kept him warm in the chill of many a morning shoot, and as he lifted it down off the door he heard the bump of the weight in the pocket.

He put his hand in, and felt them, then pulled them out, two Icil sevens, left over from a shoot he couldn't remember. Must have been the year before — snipe shooting, maybe. Icils — paper cased, star crimped, maroon in colour, high brass, a fair dinkum second barrel used by blokes who were serious. He held them in his palm a moment, warm in colour and warm to the touch.

He dropped them back into the pocket and thought no more of them, because the pup was clamouring at the door. So he took the side by side from its slip, picked up the dummy, and headed for the door. Rubber boots'd do that morning. The grass was damp and the air sharp; it was southern Victoria, after all, and it can be cold early in the day.

He had a measured, steady stride that was a contrast to the ginger in the pup, knowing what he was heading off to do and loving every minute of it. He let him run it off, smiling despite himself, and then called him to heel, and together they made their way down to the swamp.

They didn't have to do much more than go to the water's edge. He hefted the dummy in his hand. It was shaped like a dumbell, to make sure the dog understood the idea of centring it accurately when he picked it up. It had four black ducks' wings bound around it with twine, wings carefully removed from birds at the end of the last season.

The dog enjoyed the feel of the dummy, and he loved going and finding things, though he still had to be taught that it wasn't only a game, but an honour, a job to do well, a role in life.

He made him sit. He threw the dummy, and raised the empty gun a few times in the direction of the throw. The dog twitched, but held steady. He took down the gun, and waited, and he looked across the water where he sensed rather than saw the flicker of wings. Letting his eye rove, he detected far away a pair of teal, and smiled, knowing it was out of season, but content to wait. They'd be there for the opening. They always were.

"Fetch!" Away he went, joy on four feet, splashing water high and wide, enthralled by the game. Back in no time, dummy found, he sat up straight to be told what a good fellow he was.

The previous lessons had gone in. The pup was beginning to think that it was a challenge, that he had a duty to find the dummy, whether he could see it, or whether it was stuck in the resinous reeds. His development was under way.

Out he ran again at the command — "Fetch!" — and back he bounced with a smile and a joyous dance that only a happy pup can produce. Then, growing all the time in confidence, out he went for the third time.

Suddenly the man heard a buzz in his ears, a whine. Then a howl. It didn't register at first, being so out of place in the quiet swamp, but then it split the air. The dog was exposed in the water, and out of the sky, revving like only a powerful model aircraft can, it dived at him, and frightened him into a witless canine terror.

The retrieve forgotten, he raced to shore as the model plane flicked aside and was gone, still screaming, quieter then, in the direction it had come from.

Pups aren't all that fond of model aircraft. He took some pacifying. The dummy was still there, so he called the pup to heel and they waded out into the shallow water and retrieved it together, and then he waved it around his nose and teased him with it to try to stimulate the pup's interest again. When he flung the dummy out, the little dog went to it at a trot, his surging enthusiasm gone.

Out of the sky it came again, screaming its hardest. The dog yelped in confusion, and floundered to the shore. The wing commander laid the gun down, and stood on a log. From there he could make out the operator, up at the other end of the swamp.

Still working on the dog, he calmed him down, settling him to heel, and with gun broken over his arm as it should be, his measured stride took him round the curving water's edge. He was very patient in his words: it's a big swamp. The dog's edgy, being young and all, and he needs the work. We come down here and go through the routine some Saturdays — that kind of thing. Not a lot of response, other than a silly grin.

Back again, to exactly the same spot, just to reinforce in the young dog's mind that it was safe to retrieve there, that the sky wouldn't always be full of confusing, whining devil-machines.

Out with the dummy, but before it hit the water, that noise filled the air, as the plane again bore down on the pup. The lesson went home, undoing all the work of before, and the dog retreated in near panic.

Gun broken, and again the measured tread: it's a big swamp. You can have your fun at your end, and I can have mine up the other. We aren't going to get in each other's way in the least. Now, I'm minding my business; couldn't you mind yours? — so it went.

Back again, with a problem to solve now, the dog jumpy and unwilling. He went in again in answer to the next throw, though only just.

Half way out into the water, the air was full of its manic shriek as yet again the model aircraft dived hard at the dog, and, with all it had learnt forgotten, it ran, this time in open terror.

The hand slid into the coat. The gun came up. As the plane, expertly manoeuvred, lifted out of its dive, he led it five feet and drove in the first barrel, and it exploded into matchwood. The engine, free of the weight, suddenly shied up higher, still screaming, and with a twitch of his moustache and a glint in his eye he swung out in front and poured his tight full choke left barrel into that, hammering it hard across the swamp, to fall with a dead splash into the water. And that was the part his eyes always sparkled at later, when he told the story, the part about hitting the engine with the second barrel.

The dog, stirred back into life by the reports, went out for the dummy. Meanwhile, out of the side by side pigeon gun, smoking in the still air, he pulled the two spent cartridge cases, Icil sevens, maroon, and warm to the touch.

Jack's Place

I've been on a few properties, I suppose, but there's only ever been one place like Jack's. I've shot a lot of quail there, a big and rambling station, not too far from where I live. Jack was quite a character in the district, an eccentric. He had a flag complete with flagpole the local larrikins had liberated from somewhere and put up in his yard. It was an Australian flag, and it happened that it was upside down, and flown habitually at half mast.

This was not a matter for a lot of concern to Jack. With other bits and pieces like a baby's carriage pinned unforgettably on the houseyard gate, and a dozen old wheels welded grotesquely into a bizarre statue by the door, a flag flying upside down above the house would hardly be worth a second look. I doubt he even noticed it as he passed. Inside, as out, the place was ramshackle. Jack was an alcoholic.

He was also a good bloke. Whenever I turned up to be polite and to ask permission to take the dog around a few of the sprawling grass paddocks, often run to seed, I'd always find a warm welcome, though it was never Jack who told me what I needed to know. The fact is he was often too far out of it to be able to. Whether I'd come at four in the afternoon or at ten in the morning, it didn't seem to make a lot of difference.

No, Jack always sent me to find Robbie, his hired man. Jack was about fifty, big, bloated, and not all that much use any more. The running of the farm was to all intents in the hands of Robbie. I had a lot of reason to think about Robbie from time to time and I grew to respect him. He was a youngish man, certainly under thirty, and he had plenty of work to do to manage a station the size of that one. It looked like Jack gave him a free hand, and he'd had to learn as he went.

Anyone wanting to shoot quail properly will know it's information that makes the difference, and I found I could always get it from Robbie. They're in the bottom paddock, he'd tell me, saw them there when I was feeding out yesterday. So I'd go, and there they'd be, and the dog and I would walk it and shoot a bag of birds. He never gave me the wrong idea. If he didn't know, he'd say so, and any time he could he'd make sure I didn't travel all the way out for nothing.

I discovered after a while that he'd been responsible for a lot of improvement in Jack. When he'd first gone to the job, he found Jack never ate. He had a dozen bottles of beer planted in a whole round of places on the farm, and he'd go out every month or so on a replenishment run, a big, winding loop around the property, passing all his drop sites and making up the dozen stored at each one. Local wisdom said he was meticulous enough to rotate them, old stock up the front, like a grocer. No matter where he had to go to attend to his work, there was a drink waiting for him and he'd down it before he went on to do the next chore.

After he'd been working there a while, Robbie discovered he liked salads, so when he came to work of a morning he started leaving a few tomatoes around the place, and maybe a head of lettuce. In a while he noticed it would sometimes disappear. Jack had begun to eat, something he'd apparently neglected for a long while before. He was still drinking his two dozen a day, though, but he was better for the food.

Then I came to hear some history of the man. He was talented, had been a fine sportsman in his day, and it seemed that when he was young he'd treated the only woman in his life so badly that she'd had to leave him. Everybody in the district knew about it at the time, and it was accepted that he never recovered from it. The story sounds so hackneyed that it could come from a soap opera, but that's the way it was. The steady decline he was in seemed to me to be so strong that it could never be reversed.

Robbie tried, nevertheless. In a while I learned a bit more of his background, too. He was a city boy, and he'd come up hard. His parents were relentless people who'd made impossible demands of him and still not been glad when he left them for the bush. It could have been that the force of their spite was what drove him away. It's been done often enough in the past. He drifted around the area he ended up in, and went from job to job, working casually for anyone who made him an offer, till at last he ended up with Jack, and in time he moved into the homestead to stay.

Some of the sourer townsfolk said he only stuck it out because Jack had no one, and he had his eye on the property; it was clear that nobody believed a drinker like Jack was going to make old bones. I didn't believe it, either.

Over the years I turned up for a while in most quail seasons and I watched the procedure. Jack's sense of humour, never entirely gone, improved, and in fact it grew ever more outrageous, and increasingly I discerned in him a ghosting of the man who might have been. The quail stayed on, some years; the little birds like a taste of wild native seed. I always enjoyed walking the paddocks, and I'll admit to being grateful that in my first few seasons they weren't always in the best of repair. Robbie tamed them and brought them back to good productivity as time went on.

Always he'd tell me how Jack was coming along. It was as though he was taking quiet pride in the help he gave him. I thought at the time that it was gently paradoxical that a man who had suffered bitterly from a lack of something could do everything in his power to ensure that someone else didn't go without it. And with Robbie, of course, the absent factor was what the sentimental might call a home.

On my way out from a shoot, I'd always pull up and thread my way through the empty oil drums and the clutter, the rotting wheat bags and the rusty engine blocks, round the riotous sheep dogs and through the defunct houseyard gate ("That's what you call a COD gate," Jack would always hoot if he saw me coming, "Carry or drag!") so I could drop in a few birds, cleaned and plucked, and I was pleased to know by that stage of Jack's re-education that they'd be bound for good use at Robbie's hands on the big wood stove.

It wasn't as the locals said. They were rough men, Jack and Robbie, undemonstrative, and they lived without refinement. At first I thought perhaps it could be a temptation to a young man like Robbie, coming with nothing and working his heart out on someone else's place for low wages. It would be understandable if he'd hoped to be left something. Then I thought it over, and I was sure that I could see that pride in his achievement for Jack was what motivated Robbie, not a mercenary interest directed towards inheriting his property.

I came to believe that the experience for him was altogether new in his life. A hand-to-mouth existence as a rouseabout and itinerant farm worker had provided him no comforts before, that's true, but neither did the rough station homestead he'd finished up in, with inside its bare and unswept floors, outside its sweeping winds and penetrating rains; I saw Robbie while he was doing the crutching, his back bent and his day long. I saw his tracks, deep into the property, fresh, from where he'd been up in the small hours, driving around the lambing ewes with the .22-250, and putting his keen pale blue eye into the telescopic sight to do business with the slinking fox while Jack snored in a chair by the dead fire.

He told me once that he had to pay for the ammunition himself, and he gave his hard smile and cold blink. None of this was comfortable for him. Far from it. I knew he'd often come home from a hard day when Jack would've gone bad on the job and left him to do it alone, whatever it might have been, heavy work, some of it, and when he finally came in after nightfall he'd find a man in a stupor and then have to cook for them both.

It didn't seem right to me, somehow, but just when I was coming to believe this, thinking Robbie must've wanted something for his sacrifices, I'd call in again and in the surprising astuteness of their humour and their hard men's raucousness I'd see no resentment, no restraint. They enjoyed each other's company, and so much for what the locals thought.

Despite what I heard, I believed I'd come to know better. I knew that what drove Robbie was some loss, some void in Jack that struck a chord in the younger man, and gave him a direction in life, a sense of place and perhaps even a grander purpose the like of which he'd never known before in his troubled city life. He'd willingly changed one set of problems for another, because the second set was problems with a human connection instead of just problems alone. Seen in that light, it seemed a good trade to me.

****

I often think of the conversations I had with Robbie about how a good man can ruin himself with a little practised neglect. I liked him. He always used to tell me sternly how bad the grog can be, as he lectured me about its evils, and I used to think he was glad to be a witness to what he lived through daily, and was hoping that the events he saw unfolding in his life might be a lesson for the good of those with eyes to see. Perhaps in his own way, it occurred to me one day, he was worried about me. It struck me that as he probably did with many folk, he gave me the benefit of his own life's experience to warn me of a danger he feared I might have missed seeing for myself.

Not much chance of missing it.

No, it wasn't just Robbie I had time for. I had a lot of time for them both. Always the optimist about the way things could turn out amongst good human beings, I thought that in a kitbag with not much in it, each had scrabbled about on the bottom and found something that the other lacked; Robbie wanted a family and a home, and however unlikely it might sound, he'd found it with Jack. Jack for his part had wanted — yes, a family and a home, as well, and if he perceived only dimly the role Robbie was actually playing in his life, it didn't matter, because some part that was still alive and well in what was left of him woke up, and it responded with a vigour that was strong enough to surprise. No, I thought, the hell with the locals.

****

I still shoot quail there, even these days, still drop in a feed when I'm finished, and often I see a hatful of tomatoes and a few onions around the place, the legacy of Robbie, not an imposing one, perhaps, but then, many of us leave not a lot behind us when we're gone — lucky to leave anything, sometimes.

Now and again, when the winter wind blows across the flats that have run more to seed than ever, and the cold quickens my step, a bird rises after a staunch point from the dog, and I might be lucky enough to get my feet right and shoot it on the curl.... It's at moments like that when I see I have no answers, but all the same it makes me ponder on what they're both missing, Jack and Robbie.

I telephoned as usual a year or two back. Jack answered. I asked him how he was, and he said fine. I asked him how Robbie was, and he said dead. I suppose I thought it was a bad line, though that's not something to expect in this age, either, so I asked him again, but it didn't make the answer change. I drove out to see Jack.

He carried his bottle of beer outside, and he propped himself on the gatepost. Under the flag, upside down, beside the baby's carriage on the gate, Jack told me how over a long period Robbie had written cheques, nineteen thousand dollars that they'd traced so far, forging Jack's signature, to buy heroin with. One day he'd overdosed and someone had found him dead in a car. Nobody knew whether it had been deliberate or not. He was just as dead either way.

Jack told me he was glad. His voice was flat. He hadn't appreciated being robbed. And when he said it, it was as though I'd seen a house of cards fall down in front of me.

Cause for Wonder

It isn't the biggest puzzle in the world, but it still bears thinking about.

One day I went with a farmer in his four-wheel drive utility. We took a look around his sheep, grazing out to the furthest reaches of his property, which was where the rabbits ought to be. That's why I went with him.

There were four dogs in the tray, and the back window made a partition in between us and them. We drove down through boggy country, and up onto drier ground before we found the mob of sheep, all grazing along quietly, and then we got behind them and he gave them a gentle nudge along, playing a bit of see-how-they-run just to make sure everything was in order.

There were a couple of thousand in the mob. Those not fully familiar with sheep always think there aren't as many as there actually are in a mob; I guessed a thousand, and he told me two, so that's how I know the number.

We were watching their rumps moving up and down in the peculiar way that sheep have of moving, and his eye was roving across them all, watching as they went forward and fell back, the whole mob flexing and changing; the dogs watched with the same intensity, but through the glass.

Suddenly something caught his attention, and I heard the engine note lift just a fraction as he accelerated more into the pack, perhaps trying to break them up and spread them out, but they stayed fairly well lumped together and wouldn't scatter. As we drove up onto a flat he turned and looked at one of the four dogs, all of which by that time had made themselves more than available, all excited, all ready to be called on.

When he selected the dog, I didn't know which one it was. No word was spoken. There was no movement of his arm, no pointing or gesturing. All that happened was that he swung his head back and he looked at the dog he wanted to do the work. This was the one that then jumped joyfully up and over the side of the vehicle, all on its own with a task to perform.

What they'd been looking for, of course, was flystrike. The patch of daggy wool on the rump can hide it, prevent it from being seen while the damage is done underneath, leading to the death of the sheep.

Neither the farmer nor his dog wanted that. The thing that reached me was not that the dog, like its master, seemed to have an eye for it as a possibility; nor was it that the dog had a way of knowing that it had been selected for the work, even though I, an outsider, couldn't tell how it knew. All that I could live with.

What I found hard to grasp was what I saw a minute or so later, after the dog had gone into the swelling and surging mob of sheep, and pulled out the one with the brown stain on its rump that in some indefinable way didn't look quite like all the others. The boss stopped the vehicle and walked over to the sheep, and then together he and the dog discovered that they'd both made a mistake, and the sheep wasn't flystruck after all.

There was a communication of some sort that had taken place there, and whatever it was I'm afraid the nature of it was beyond me entirely.

It's not the only time this has happened.

Another time, my mate and I were shooting ducks over decoys from an unusually elevated position, set back above the water on a big isthmus that ran away to our right as we faced the water. Well along there from where we sat, maybe eighty or ninety paces away, there was a fence that came in beside a little inlet, at right angles to the water. The land sat at our backs.

It was in the full light of morning, and we'd had some shooting. My dog sat behind us, and retrieved from our vantage point. He'd been out and brought back a good few birds, so he had the idea and his blood was up.

A teal crossed left to right along the big water in front, and I shot it twice before it had reached the decoy set. Perhaps I put the shot just a little far back, but I saw its wings set, and I knew it was hit hard and would soon pitch in to be safely gathered. It could easily turn into a long swim for the dog, though, and the water was cold, so I wasn't too keen on that.

When I looked around for the dog he'd gone, uncharacteristically left his position behind us and suddenly taken it upon himself to run back away from the water and inland from where we sat.

We both stood up, automatically, and the whole event was played out in front of us. The duck was planing down along the water's edge, now past the decoys, but the dog had bolted away at forty-five degrees from the water, inland behind us, over the brow of the little slope we could so plainly see down.

The teal reached the fence line where the water came in, wings still set, and the dog in his run had ignored its line of flight entirely; when the bird reached the fence, it swung to the right, off the main body of water and along the little inlet — but inland, along the fence line.

The dog by pelting backwards over the land had in effect taken a short cut, running hard in a straight line downhill, in the direction where he had somehow sensed that the bird was going to make a right angle turn. He extended himself, stretched to full gait, and while we gaped and the duck was still gliding shakily in on its set wings, we saw him use the speed he'd picked up from running down the hill and launch himself high into the air on an interception path and pluck it from its course, sweeping an arc with his big jaws open and set for the task.

He caught him in mid-air, and it was no accident.

There are deeper mysteries in the world, we can be sure of that, but sometimes when I'm sliding away at night and my thoughts drift in darkness, I wonder if just as I have to think about taxes and repairs to the car, under the same starlight a dog in a kennel somewhere is planning his next drafting of a sheep, or has begun to moan and twitch because he fears one day that with the onset of age a duck is going to escape him by flying up a fenceline to the left after he's taken a right-hand turn — and because in his decline he has come only to know as much as a human, and no more.

Just Looking Around

I like to shoot rabbits among the stones. Big stones, so I have plenty of good excuses for missing. If the rocks are too small, when the rabbit runs behind them there's still enough rabbit showing for me to have no defence when the gun goes off and the rabbit is still plainly hale and well.

Sadly, I have to report that more often than should be the case, the rabbit does keep running. But with any luck at all, it's okay, because I'm amongst big stones, with my ready made excuse.... *I was right on him. I'd just swung past him, and I had the lead worked out — then just as I pulled the trigger he swerved behind the rock. Yeah, that big one over there. Honest.*

I'm not silly, you know.

Some might say the stones have disadvantages. Too right they do, some of them quite severe. There are a lot of snakes in this stony country, and they hide under them, to appear unforgettably at the psychological moment, and there's positively nothing more likely to cause a pattern of sixes to go where it shouldn't than the sight of a four-foot brown snake with blood in his eye in full wriggle a boot-width away, making a slithery getaway through the tussocks where his head can't be seen.

There might be other slight disadvantages as well. There is, I allow, the occasional barked shin, raked down the face of a great lump of scoria. But this is not a common event, and it just serves as a reminder that it's a privilege to be there, and there should be no complaining about the odd bit of discomfort or some well meaning bunch of over-citified preservationists will no doubt make a concerted and well televised drive to have big stones barred from the countryside on account of their being enjoyed by hunters going about their lawful business.

Another small disadvantage is that when enough of these large stones lie together with sufficient of the smaller ones it makes a pretty big pile of rocks. Nature tends to go in for overkill and there are plenty of places where I walk myself to a standstill amongst great sweeping ridges of rocks, grey-brown and sprawling; if I can find a position up high enough to look down, it's as though some giant making a meal of green grass had left long lines of lumpy gravy smeared across the broad landscape. They run in ragged battalions across the flats in between for distances as far as the eye can see, and every rise of stones looks like the one the other side of it.

In and out of the rocks go the rabbits, and shooting them is an entirely absorbing task. When I do it, I don't do anything else at the same time. I'm too busy looking for a safe path among the rocks and around the thistles, all the while avoiding the snakes with the evil eyes.

As we all know, those who want to shoot rabbits have to put in the walking time. So I'm sure it's not going to come as too great a surprise if I say that recently I was accused of getting lost while I was out amongst the stones, walking intently from one rise to the next, in the warm late afternoon.

I can understand why somebody who didn't know me better could think I was lost. There were thirty or forty thousand acres of country in the equation, I'll admit that. Yes, it was getting a bit close to dark. That's true, too. I was very involved in shooting rabbits at the time; I could hardly deny that, either, seeing I was carrying half a dozen.

But I wasn't lost. Lost! Me?

I could see the setting sun quite plainly. I knew full well where I had to walk to arrive back at the farm where I was staying. Just to satisfy the cynics and establish it on record, it was due south. I think. Anyway, I could see the sun setting, so how could I be lost? West is west. And another thing, I still had the rabbits. It's well known that one of the first acts of a man who is lost is to abandon his six rabbits, with great reluctance, for the foxes and other scavengers with an interest in them, so that he can carry on with bravely walking his way out to his longsuffering and deeply worried loved ones, gathered fretfully round the hearth at home.

No, I still had the rabbits, and when I noticed the dog was limping and his foreleg was sore, I sat down under the tree with the last vestiges of liquid light draining from the great inverted cup of the rabbit hunter's sky, and had a word with him, told him we were just resting, that this was purely temporary, and that in a while we'd go ahead with the process of heading back. I distinctly remember the calm way he took this, which is even more evidence that there was no panic involved here. I point out that it was after his mealtime, too.

Now, seeing I knew which way I had to walk to find my way back to the farm, it can hardly be held against me, the minor criticism that I didn't appear to have much of an idea which was the way to the vehicle. I could have found my way to the farm; it was only the car that was temporarily misplaced, in amongst all those blasted rocks.

So about an hour and a half after dark, my friends from the farm all turned up with a light that they waved around in the air, rather showily, I thought, and making a lot of noise in the vehicle, under the impression that just because I hadn't come back on time I was actually lost. Did you ever hear anything so silly? I told them what it was really all about, though. They spend too much time playing around with livestock and feed and crops and other such foolishness, and they'd be far better off appreciating someone like me, with their interests at heart.

No, I wasn't lost. I was just out in those thirty thousand acres making sure everything was as it should have been — just having a good look around. If you happen to run into any of them, tell them to leave me alone, to recognize it and be grateful when somebody's doing them a good turn.

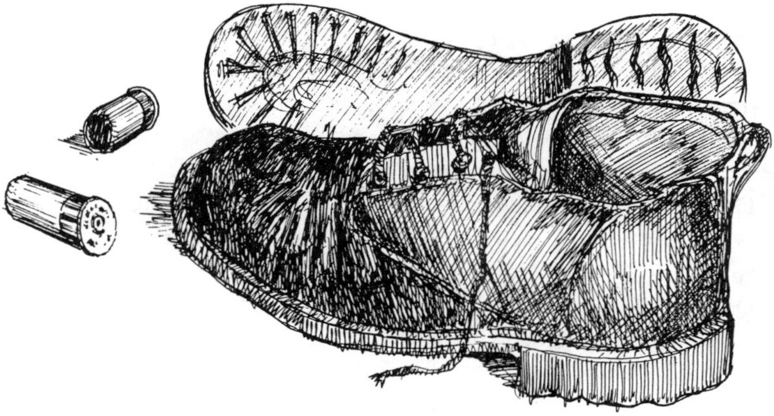

Under Attack

Mick was living in a little town down about the border, alongside the big expanse of state forest. He didn't have a lot of time for the city and the things that go with it. His biggest need was peace and quiet, and not far away a duck on a dam or a few rabbits to walk up after work. He had all that when he moved there, and it was the way he wanted it. Then things started changing.

Nobody much knew why they picked this particular town to adopt, seeing it was similar enough to many others not too far away. If anything, perhaps it was the proximity to the state forest.

This was the place where they grew their marijuana. A couple of teenagers who were out walking, innocently enough, Mick was sure, knowing the families, found themselves beaten up because they strayed too close to where yet another valuable row of plants stood.

The locals didn't like it, but there didn't seem to be too much to do about it. Nobody could work out where to start. When they told the district policeman, he protested that he already spent half his life racing into the forest to find yet another six plants to tear up by the roots and burn in a splash of petrol after he'd finished his inquiries, the ones that always seemed to come to nothing. He couldn't do much till he actually found somebody engaged in a crime.

They lived in a few of the houses that seem to be common around little country towns these days, on the outskirts and maybe a bit further out than that, too. But not too far for the fly-by-nighters to try for a little casual work here and there, get to know a few properties, and then suddenly walk off without notice, leaving the owner stuck half way through a job. And not far enough away to prevent his shed then being ransacked and cleaned out of tools in the middle of the very occasional night when he'd be off at a Rotary meeting somewhere.

Perhaps this is inevitable, part of the changing face of the country. That's not the way the townsfolk viewed it, of course, and particularly not the way Mick saw it.

One night he was home alone, living as he did near the main road, where it curved round the monument. He heard the squealing of the tyres, a noise becoming far too prevalent in the previously quiet town.

This Saturday night, there was the distinctive sound of shattering glass, as bottles were thrown from cars. The tyres did more than yelp as the cars went up and back through the main street of the town. It was summer, and night had come slowly. By the early hours of the morning there was a pattern to the noise. One or two cars would roar through the town on the way to Mick's place, turn around the monument, tyres screaming, and then with their heavy V8s and loose exhausts roaring, it or they would go up the road to the far end of town, where they'd do a similar turn and repeat the process.

Where was the policeman? Mick telephoned. There was no answer. He'd be out on a job somewhere.

By about three in the morning, he'd had enough. The relentless pattern had established itself to the point where as he lay in bed, trying to sleep, he could almost count the minutes from one set of tyre squeals to the next as they left the far end of town from a standing start to come up to his end and do their squealing turn around the monument.

When he put a half a dozen cartridges in his khaki pants and slipped on a pair of sneakers, he went to the big red gum that stood right beside the track, just before it reached the monument. It was only a hundred yards or so from his house, and it was in the shadow of that tree he squatted as he slipped the two cartridges into his father's shotgun and thumbed back both hammers.

It was just about eight minutes, as he had come to work out, till the car was due to come back, and as it turned on the road around the monument, under full braking, its body rolling and lurching till it was nearly standing on two wheels, it would have to travel at its slowest as it passed the big gum tree. Mick knew exactly what its path would be, its driver's window just a metre or two from where he crouched in the black shadow, gun muzzles in the air.

Yes, it came. He felt relieved and almost welcoming as he saw its lights approaching, and then, when he heard the inane laughter, heard yet another thrown bottle smash on the road he and his neighbour would travel next day, heard the shouted foul language, he found his mouth was clamped tightly shut.

As the car went past him on the warm summer night, the driver's window down, exactly as it drew level with him where he squatted in the lee of the tree he fired both barrels simultaneously, the gun muzzles pointing carefully upwards, aimed away from the car and back slightly in the direction he had walked from.

The roar and the muzzle flash startled even him. He reckoned it must've frightened six months' growth out of the drunks in the car.

From that moment, everything seemed different. It's true, there was an increased scream from the big red car's engine, but that was only while it was leaving. This time it didn't come back. Then there was quiet, for the first time in hours.

Mick slept a righteous sleep that night, and it was understandable that he was sleepy and didn't hear the commotion next morning. It was his neighbour who was calling out and pounding on the door. Their two houses stood side by side in the open, no others nearby, and in the morning when he woke, as Mick raised himself on one elbow, the first thing he would see through his window was the road with the monument in the middle of it. That morning, as he saw it, he grinned to himself and thought affectionately of his dear old dad's hammergun, before wondering what the racket was about, surprised at his neighbour, not usually excitable, he thought.

He ambled to the door in his underpants, to see not his neighbour alone, but the policeman as well. It was the neighbour who was knocking because the policeman was busy, up on the already hot flat tin roof next door, keeping moving and looking intently down onto the iron, carefully picking small objects off it and putting them in a plastic bag, and looking black with anger.

"Got him up there searchin' f'r evidence," his neighbour thundered at Mick, following his gaze. "Reckons when he finds it he's gonna throw the book at 'em. He knows who they are, got 'em down at the station now. Can't find the gun, but, not yet, anyway.

"Struth, Mick," the usually placid neighbour went on, still bellowing, facing up the steps as the nonplussed Mick stood on in his underpants, saying nothing and trying to gather his woolly thoughts, "I'm layin' charges. I put up with it when they was lairin' up an' down the road, and I put up with it when they busted all them bottles 'n' that, but I'm buggered if I'll put up with it when they shoot shotguns at me house!"

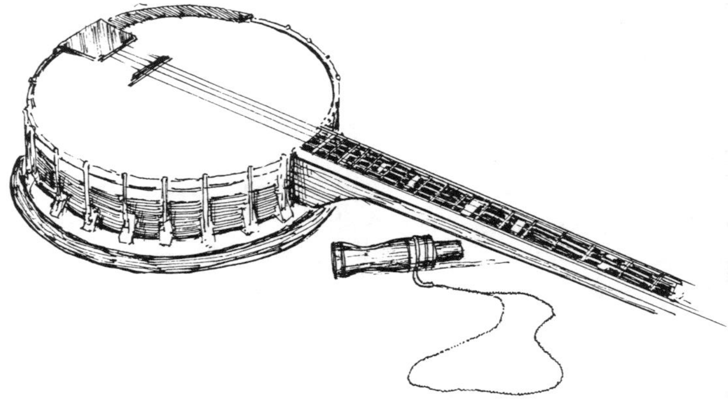

The Music Man

There's a lot of music in the bush. Most of those who find the need to go there don't need to be told about it. Maybe it's the best thing about a weekend away rabbit shooting, or whatever other kind of hunting it is that appeals. There aren't many of us who don't like to lie there in a sleeping bag in the dark, and listen to the sounds the nights make.

There'll be those who listen to the quail whistle in the warming spring months, as I do, and those who've heard the whoosh of the air displaced by the wings of the wedgetail when he bounces so unexpectedly out of the long grass in front. I believe I'll also have company when I say that for me, no sound in the world matches the rapid, beating whistle of ducks' wings at dawn.

The hush of the bush is music in a key of its own. The cities have plenty of noise in them, and I suspect that as much as for anything we go bush for the peace and quiet. But there are other kinds of music in shooting as well, a lot of plain, ordinary old talent. Some of the great shots have been competent musicians. Fred Kimble, who invented the choke bore in America last century, was a violinist. Vance Bourjaily, who wrote one of my favourite books, *The Unnatural Enemy*, was a jazz saxophonist.

A while ago I laid my hands on a four-string standard banjo, handmade not long before by an old man. I bought it, played it, appreciated it, and knew I had to find him. It wasn't named, but the craftsmanship was second to none. The wood in it was like a fine gun stock, and it glowed with the deep radiant lustre that only best quality wood can have. The test of many stringed instruments is how well they stay in tune. This one had the arm made of solid Madagascar ebony, the only chunk I've ever seen, cut lengthwise in half and then made into a laminate of six ply, hard and true, and it won't have warped when my grandchildren are considering their musical future. One look at it was enough to see that the man who made it loved his craft and was fully engaged by it. In the hands of an expert it would give infinite pleasure, and have about it the kind of timelessness that we all find in the guns of our dreams.

It wasn't all that hard to find him when I set about looking. He was recognized around the town by a few musicians as an artisan worthy of respect. I'd only prepared one question for him: how was it that in this age I could manage to buy a piece of his fine workmanship for a miserly hundred dollars?

He was seventy-three years old. All his life he had worked with wood and music. Years before, he had discovered he had a talent for making instruments, but he wasn't widely known. The ones he made were important to the people who owned and played them, but that was about the strength of it. The name that he inlaid into his creations wasn't a known one, because he didn't have the money to advertise himself and create a reputation. In a word, he wasn't acknowledged, and so he practically gave his work away. In appreciation of the fact that I'd sought him out to discuss the instrument of his I'd bought, he gave me an ebony bridge to fit it, and to match the arm he'd carefully crafted. A few months after I met him he was dead, and the secrets of his hands died with him. What a waste.

****

On the river, among the backwaters where the ducks fly, old Laurie was a legend, a music maker of another sort. All the locals used to love to get invited out to shoot with him and his son. An invitation like that meant a good bag, because Laurie was one of those rarities in Australia today, a duck caller.

They told me about him often. He'd sit in his hide and call in a flock of teal that hadn't given any appearance at all of bending his way. Then he'd stand up with his creaky old side by side and shoot a bird with each barrel.

He'd sit straight down and lower his head, and when they were about to lift over the trees at the far end of the swamp and be gone for good, he'd quack seductively and swing them round, bring them back, and do it all over again.

Struth, I thought, when I first heard this, no wonder the locals liked going shooting with him.

I always wanted to meet one of the old-time shooters who could truly talk like a duck, and so be taught the secrets that seem to have been increasingly lost the further we've come this century. After years of practice, I reckon I frighten away about as many birds as I lure in. So I went looking, and tracked down his son. I had to introduce myself, and we sat out in his yard, in autumn, it was, and watched the sun start to swing slowly down. We had a good yarn, when he told me about the way he'd accompanied him and shot alongside his father, and through his spare and laconic words I peered into the river country and glimpsed many a sunrise. I could hardly contain my impatience, though, and as soon as it seemed half polite, I asked him: maybe he could introduce me to his father?

The son looked solemn, then rose from the yellowed cane chair, and he stepped off the veranda and cut a couple of lines in the dust of the farm's back yard with the edge of the sole of his boot. No, I couldn't meet his old dad, because he was in hospital. He'd just had a stroke, and he wasn't up to it; by the look of it he never would be again.

Then we were both sad. As much to change the subject as anything, I told him how lucky he'd been to have a father who had taught him how to call ducks to the amazement of everybody who saw him at work. I suppose I was still hopeful someone was going to take me on as a pupil.

The son of the second music man looked uneasy, as if he was out of place in his own yard, and his gaze firmed away from me, went towards the red sun, as he drew more lines on the ground while another parcel of our folklore blew away with the dry leaves in the yard.

All those years by his side, numberless autumn mornings as those matchless tones had coaxed wary waterfowl to the hide, and he'd never bothered to learn. He'd taken him for granted and one day it became too late.

What a waste.

Squaring Up

Bob is on the mend. For a long time he lay a quadriplegic, but then the force of his mind and heart and the strength of his marriage and his family began to tell against the weakness that had overborne his previously active life.

Today, years later, he walks. He moves about his farm in a vehicle and his neighbours no longer have to put in his family's crops for them, the way they did, uncomplainingly, without fuss, for several seasons.

They all thought he couldn't do it, but he proved them wrong and perhaps more than once a detached observer would have concluded his courage was such that given time he had to win.

****

Bob had always ridden a motorbike around his big station property. He'd been in many a spontaneous race with his mate, Brian, and they'd almost grown up together, with a common hunting interest and blocks of land not far apart.

They'd shot together in the nights to clear the land of foxes, and they'd spent long afternoons on the rabbits that were always pests. They'd covered a lot of ground in each other's company, and shared reloading equipment.

One day, Bob went out to ride his boundaries. He left fairly early in the morning and he hadn't been gone half an hour when, at a pace that his dog could have run at, the motorbike had collected a piece of heavy fencewire and the front wheel had locked up instantaneously.

Afterwards, as he lay and stared at the ceiling, something he was fated to do for a long time, he said that he felt nothing when he hit the ground. The damage had already been done to his back by that time, because of the sudden wrenching of the handlebars. Even before he hit the hardened red earth, his body was limp as rags.

He set his mind to wait all day, knowing as many an injured bushman before him has known that if he was to survive, this was his first hurdle, because it wouldn't be till much later that he was missed, and someone would come searching. He had time to go through this many times in his mind, because he was utterly incapable of moving his body. He knew what this meant, of course, and from that first hour he had to make up his mind to hold on to his sanity, something he was to have to do afresh many more times in the years to come.

He managed it, though, and eventually there were headlights at the end of his longest day, showing him at last that someone had come for him.

In the time that followed, his friends found him initially distracted and only slow to come to grips with the contraction of his life. Restriction must obviously be worse for the strong. He was encouraged, and bit by bit a life developed for him, but it was one between four walls, and at first there was more numbness and little sign of the grim survival instinct they all knew he had. Everybody did what they could, but inevitably it seemed like not enough.

One day, Brian went around and there was a difference. Bob had started to talk about shooting. He brought up the .17 he'd only used a few times before his accident, and indicated that he was determined to grow well and go shooting crows again.

Brian pointed out that he'd hardly ever done any crow shooting, only in the one or two years when their numbers had been very thick and they'd taken their ripping and tearing toll on the lambs.

This didn't seem to mean much to Bob. He wanted to do it anyway. Brian thought no more of it and reckoned that a sign of interest in the old life was an advantage and should be fostered at any cost. Whenever he had the opportunity, he widened the talk from farming and crops to take in rifles and shooting.

He found over a series of visits that there wasn't a time when the subject of crow shooting didn't come up, and Brian ended up saying that he was a bit surprised at all this interest in a kind of shooting that had never much figured in the district or in their personal repertory. When he idly asked why, there was no satisfying answer.

Later they rated it as the beginning of Bob's long recovery, but at the time they were not to know what it signalled. Instead, they were frankly amazed at the intensity of his retort. He told them that he had to become well again to shoot crows, that it was his life's imperative and nothing short of it. It was central. It was what had to happen.

One day perhaps the moment was unguarded, and the reason did come out. He'd been talking with Brian, who again asked why this crow shooting interest had suddenly come to take on such dominance. Quietly, Bob said nobody could know, nobody could ever know, not unless they'd been where he had. He'd lain on an untravelled road for thirteen hours entirely motionless of frame, when his loudest shout didn't register as a whisper, with the only movement he could make an urgent blinking of the eyelids that also gradually became exhausted — and all the while, one by one, the bobbing, darting crows with the shiny, hard beaks were cawing, growing bolder, dancing blackly, ever closer to his face.

Bombed or Shot ?

It was well into the quail season, and a fine one it was turning out to be, when domestic pressures prevailed and there was no more escape. The house had to be painted before winter set in. It had the ring of an ultimatum.

There hadn't been too many problems up till then, and he'd been able to go out the necessary twice a week, and sometimes he cribbed a third trip. He and his shooting mate lived on quail through the season, and they took advantage of it too stock their freezers. They both owned contented if tired dogs, and the neighbours came to their barbecues and appreciated the hard work they'd put in to make them possible, quail being a delicacy for any non-shooter.

To have it brought up short by the need to do a job like that was an annoyance, but one that he could accept, being retired, because at least it wouldn't cramp his style altogether. At least, that's what he was thinking till he fell off the ladder.

In the surgery the doctor, a family friend, told him that of course he'd be sore, at his age he'd have to expect it, but there was probably nothing broken. He made it clear he did want to look at his lower spine, just in case, and so an appointment was duly made with a radiographer.

When the film came back and the receptionist called him to the surgery to collect it his own doctor was away, but in the doctor's usual thoughtful fashion he'd left a note saying he ought to take the x-rays along to the local hospital and have them looked at there. If there was any problem, they'd be sure to pick it up.

This was all very annoying, but he supposed it had to be done, so he did as he was told, the quail paddock inviting, the paintbrush beckoning, his dog wagging its tail absently and wondering what all the delays were about. He went straight from the doctor's surgery down to the hospital, in through the casualty door, handing the x-rays over to the sister in charge, and in his self-effacing way he asked if someone could take a quick glance at them, because his own doctor was away and wasn't able to do it.

She was very understanding. She took them from him immediately, said they'd been busy, but there was a lull in the activity and with any luck at all she'd easily find Doctor and see what he could do. When she set off, he began pacing up and down past the nurses' station, so he could look in through the glass, and before long he watched the sister scurry back into it and use the telephone. It was a big place, and there seemed to be a lot of movement. Evidently the doctor couldn't be found. He was impatient. His back was still a bit sore, but he told himself that was just from aggravating it by all that painting over his head — when he should've been quail shooting, he thought ruefully.

The door opened again on the other side of the glass and the man who appeared to be the doctor came in. The sister rose, took the big beige envelope to him, and handed him the film, scrutinizing it with him as he held it up.

Immediately she shot a glance back over her shoulder through the glass and suddenly the house-painting quail shooter knew he should be a worried man. There is no expression quitle like that of a worried hospital nurse. Her eyes were wide.

She came straight out. "Would you like a seat?" she asked without a pause.

His adam's apple rose and fell. "No, thanks," he said. "I'm in a bit of a rush, actually. I've got work I have to...."

"Look," she interrupted, "why don't you just sit down over here? I'll help you." Before he could protest, she took him by the arm and led him to a convenient chair, put him in it, then turned her back on him and was gone to the other side of the thick glass. Evidently, he thought, turning pale, whatever was on the film was too good to miss. A bead of perspiration trickled down his forehead, and as it reached his eyebrow the doctor turned and looked straight at him. It was a piercingly bad sign.

The sister came back out, briskly, in response to a brief exchange with the doctor.

“An explosion?” she said, eyebrows up. “Was it an explosion?”

He felt suddenly faint, but he tried to keep cool. If he gave in, perhaps they’d want to put him in a bed, and do doctor-things to him.

“No,” he said. “No explosion. Whatever made you think...?” Before he could finish, she had gone. He stood and looked carefully in through the glass and he found he was using both hands in wringing out whatever life might have remained in his old cloth cap. The two of them were deep in discussion, ignoring him. He saw vague visions of how sick he must be, how badly injured his mid-section, and his mind raced to find limits. Would his walking be harmed? Would his spine deteriorate? Would he be able to shoot on Friday, as he’d planned, or would the paralysis have already struck him down by then?

Suddenly she made him start and the vision he was having of his impending funeral disintegrated. She was in front of him, looking down, her face not sympathetic.

“Shot?” she was saying. “Were you shot?”

“No!” he said. “No, I wasn’t shot! How could I be shot? Who’d want...?” — but she was gone again, to put her head together with the doctor’s, so they could feast their eyes on the film once more.

Who would he leave his gun to? How long did he have? The doctor was shaking his head. The sister was looking grave. They’d want to keep him there. Who’d collect his car? Who’d be the one who made the telephone call to his wife?

The man himself came out, with measured steps.

“Look,” he said, “you have to be honest with us, or we can’t help you. Who did this to you? How did it happen?”

He held up the x-ray, and there they were, the unmistakable dead-white marks of metal, scattered right throughout his lower middle — strangely, all seeming to be the same size.... in fact, just the size of number nine quail shot. The doctor and the nurse were on the verge of discovering that a quail shooter swallows a lot of that in a good season.

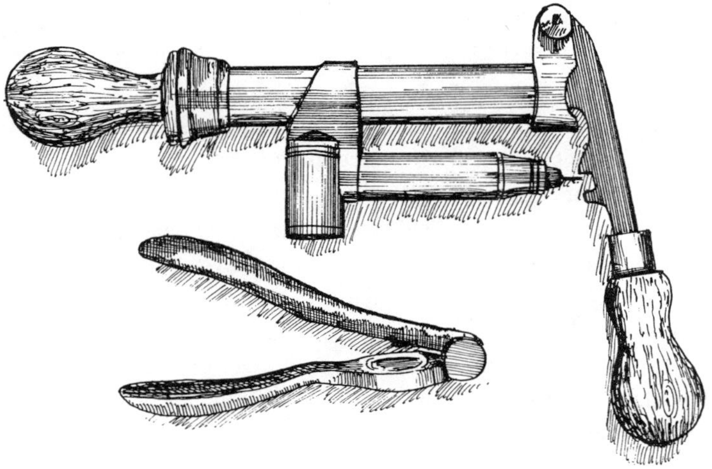

Nugget

He was an old man when I knew him and older when he died. Right up until then, he didn't just shoot ducks. He handled them with artistry, played on their habits the way a good musician plays a fine instrument, as though it's a privilege. I realized later that he knew we're entitled to no more than a loan of swamps, to use them respectfully while we're here.

He came from a family of pot hunters, where they blew them off the water and were all the happier if they could wait for two or three to line up first. He never did that. He told me so, and I believe it, because I saw him shoot them on the pass, dipping wigeon and wing-pumping shoveller. Even if he hadn't told me, I'd have known it, because he handled them so well.

When he'd pulled off a long shot, and after those who watched would be forced to stand stock-still, noticing the still of the dawn because the bird had such a long way to fall through the hush of morning red, he'd have picked it up and he'd shrug off the compliment for the shot. Instead, he'd look at the duck in his hand, and he'd nod and always say the same thing: "I s'pose his time'd come."

His mates knew and respected and worked with him but they were reluctant to shoot with him. Perhaps they felt that if they took a place too close alongside him they'd be doomed to go hungry. I doubt it, though, because he had too much courtesy. I think instead that the average shooter can only stand to see just so many of the highest, fastest birds fly over someone he's standing beside, and find that their time has come.

They said he'd mined in Africa, and maybe that was part of the reason for his name. This story was supported when a couple of old-timers remembered the time many years before when his brother had detoured to the little town to visit him, after being back in Australia and calling in at the biggest gun outlet in the state, there to buy a revolver to take back to Africa with him to wear at his mine. He'd insisted that it be nickelled, to resist the tropical corrosion. They'd seen this revolver, and to them it cemented Nugget's provenance.

There were others who argued that his real claim to a reputation was that he'd used the name to shoot under at the old live pigeon matches, banned in '56. Perhaps this explanation would account for his love of Legia Stars, those fiercely expensive old paper cased high-brass live bird loads that were filled with nickel-plated shot and surrounded by mystique. They were his one luxury in life, and when they went off the market it didn't seem to matter to him, even though he shot ducks every Saturday of the season and he never used anything else. He had a stockpile of them somewhere, and with them he turned his birds over end for end, dead in the air, until after a morning's shooting he'd cleared the opposition out of a little patch of swamp. They'd get sick of him and splash off somewhere else, seeing him doing it again and again, taking the only black duck out of a flock of teal with his first barrel, then turning out the lights on the biggest teal, while anybody nearby was lucky to toss in a futile barrel as the flock flared.

Perhaps hardest of all to bear was his casual acceptance of his neighbour's awe as he'd pick up his birds, maybe only twenty yards apart. "Thanks, mate. I reckon their time'd come."

He more or less shot in the company of a number of the locals, or at least he had a beer with them after they'd all retired from the swamp. There were the postmaster, the baker, a couple of farmers, the undertaker, and the district lawyer.

After a while, it just seemed that he'd stopped going out of a night. Somebody chipped him about this one afternoon in the pub, and he only gave a slow grin and said he reckoned that by the time night fell, he'd had enough of that day, anyway.

One other time someone asked him how he was going, and he drily said he wasn't going far, because he reckoned he knew more dead men than live ones.

Then when he disappeared for a while nobody paid much attention, or at least not until the duck opening, and it's at that point they started to wonder, because he hadn't missed it for more than sixty years. Before they'd all grown used to not getting an eye wiped beside their favourite stands of kumbungi, he turned up, and shot as always through the season with the easy style of the natural. But they saw his step was heavy and his face was grey, and he avoided the hard wading.

No one said much, but they probably all knew, just the same. He didn't bite back so fast in the banter when they gathered at the local hotel on Saturdays after the bag had been plucked. He'd have a beer, the same as he always had, and he'd amble back to his humpy, the simple bush shack that he'd lived in for longer than ghost gums had cracked at night.

It was the undertaker he finally spelled it all out to, at the end of the season.

After he told him, he was hobbling and shuffling, barely able to walk, and so he was when he admitted himself to the hospital for the first and last time.

Nugget had lived in the town for decades. He'd built his own shack, and been content to eke out a sparse living doing casual work in the district; nobody knew of any relatives. He had no life outside this ambit. In the accepting and practical way of the bush, his mates went to his hut to clean up, because they knew their old friend would never do it for himself.

As he for his part lay dying, they for theirs showed they recognized that life goes on, and they packed his personal belongings, the few there were, in tea chests: there were camp utensils, crockery items, lots of leather, and there were the tired waders that he never bothered to wear in the local, shallow swamps; there were rabbit traps, a game bag, and near-historical shooting paraphernalia with purposes they couldn't readily identify, all sorts of scattered odds and ends like the ancient and blackened cartridge roll crimper that probably didn't work.

In the second room of his hut, the one he used for storage, they found seventeen pinewood cases, the print faded, but all marked "Legia Star", and they must have smiled, a little softly. When they came to move them, to their surprise they found that they were empty, every one. Not a cartridge remained. Perhaps it was a coincidence. But they guessed that he'd taken himself to hospital as the only practical thing to do, the rational act of a man who realized that, yes, his time had come.

No Longer with Them

After the old man took himself to what he knew was the last bed he'd lie in, it was at the featureless end of the duck season, and the dank beginning of winter.

His mates gathered at the pub and they talked about how with Legia Stars the crump and whoosh of his old full choked Cashmore's thirty-two inch barrels used to be easily picked out across the swamps when it told of bushmanship and skill, satisfaction and a full belly.

As hunters and fishermen, their daily life betrayed their attitude to the questions of destiny and death. They missed him, all right, but they weren't morbid about it. Why should they be? — he wasn't. Even if they had been, it wouldn't have helped.

They spoke about him hesitantly at first, while they were slowly adapting to the idea that he wouldn't be turning up again to shoot from his favourite spots; as a little time passed, then they missed him less privately, and they spoke more freely about him, with their increasing perspective. After all, he was only doing what they all would do, in time.

They laughed about the day he missed three birds straight — though nobody could remember the name of who it was that witnessed it. They remembered the times they'd gone away to some shoot-by-invitation, maybe after the opening;

he always shunned a tent and slept in his swag. Or again, perhaps, they'd head off somewhere together again on the eve of the second opening, though it was later in the year and cold. He'd wake up, be out of his bedroll, his cartridge bag prepared the night before, and be gone in a minute and a half. He'd head off without breakfast and when he'd leave the camp in the dark he'd usually say pretty much the same thing to his mates, urgently sucking black billy tea, and burning their lips. "A man come here to shoot ducks. Orter get on with it." Everything else was said by his rickety Cashmore.

Because he was singleminded, he'd put up with the discomfort and he'd find the best spot, sockless feet in old canvas shoes, not bothering with waders in even the worst of weather. No cold water would prevent him from the dozen or so supreme moments the morning would hold as he hooked down whatever speeding waterfowl the skies threw at him.

If in their discussion they seemed a little awed by his prowess, then that was all in order. Their admiration might mask their sadness at the imminent passing of a friend.

All the while, he himself was in a hospital bed, playing out his final act, and when they visited him they saw how his body had been tossed in the tide, and how at last it shrank at the rupture of the gates that had dammed up the years.

He owned practically nothing. Even his gun was shot loose, worn out. His funeral, though, had long since been paid for in advance, and he wanted one thing to be clear. This he established on the first occasion when they all came together and visited him in the quiet country-hospital ward, on a Saturday afternoon. He said that he'd left enough with the publican to shout for the bar on the day of his burial. He had it in mind to extract a solemn promise from them to remember this, and not unnaturally it was the undertaker he turned to so he could make his wishes known, and to find some help in it, his last request. It seemed little to ask, and the undertaker agreed, not without a shade of embarrassment, in front of them all.

As his skin faded to merge with the colour of the bedsheets his eyes grew brighter.

They visited him from time to time when they could manage it, usually singly. When they knew the end couldn't be far away it didn't need the saying. They knew it well enough, and so by arrangement they all trooped in to his bedside together on another Saturday afternoon to pay what they feared would be their last call on the man they remembered as the finest high duck shot they ever knew.

He was pleased to see them and in a burst of unexpected and burning energy he told them all at once that he intended to have his coffin stopped on the way to the burial so that the mourners could go into the hotel and have the round of drinks that he'd already ordered and paid for.

At this point his intention suddenly became clear. The undertaker had agreed to his request before, but he had no idea of the specific way that the old man had in mind to ask for it to be carried out. This came, in fact, as something of a shock. For a start, it wouldn't be legal.

So the undertaker found that he was suddenly thrust in charge of the little group, and they stood there at the bedside quite abashed. He felt obliged to make the old man understand that it would be much more appropriate if they were all to go back from the cemetery and meet at the hotel after the service, and so he quietly put this to Nugget.

The old man amazed them with the ferocity of his response. He wouldn't hear of it, and he insisted that they had to stop the funeral on the way to the cemetery, and have their drink then, and not do it afterwards.

He was tired and weak, but he wouldn't be moved from his request. Eventually, while the others looked at the ceiling and at the floor, by then wishing they were somewhere else, the undertaker explained in detail, though he avoided it as long as he could, that there were legal problems with the idea of bringing a funeral to a halt and leaving — he called it 'the deceased' — standing in the road while the mourners all stopped and went into a hotel.

Nugget was very firm on what he wanted, and he wouldn't change his mind. Past all argument, he firmly continued to insist on his last wishes being met. He kept arguing that this was his dying request of them, and they had no right to deny it, something that the men gathered there found very hard to dispute. It was all made worse by the fact that they were embarrassed by the coldness of talking in front of their friend about his imminent death. When they left, they hadn't won.

Then the lawyer had a try. He went back a day or two later, because as a group they'd all trooped out in the same defeat, and he hoped that on his own he might be able to talk sense to the old man, whom he thought was confused. He explained again, on his own, quietly telling his mate how he'd had to return to make clear to him that their friend the undertaker couldn't break the law and stop the funeral even if he wanted to, because there were health regulations that he had to abide by.

The old man, wasted and becoming fainter in physical presence, had somehow become more powerful in the force of his personality. Perhaps he had drawn on the strength of his friends, calling on a lifetime of shared hunting memories and common experience in the swamps of the district. Perhaps it was just his natural strength of will. It cost him a lot, but he continued to state that it was his express and final wish to have the procession stopped on the way to the burial, and not on the way back, so that his friends could go as a group into the hotel and have a drink together at his expense. They were his hunting mates, after all, his friends through the decades.

Finally, the frustration was too much. He might have been a lawyer, but he was still a man of the countryside and a plain speaker. Exasperated, he said at last, "Nugget, what's the difference? You're going to be dead, mate. This is your burial. This is it. It'll all be over. We can have the drinks on the way back from the funeral. If we have them on the way home, what's it matter?"

The old man had it out in the open at last. He rose up an inch from the pillow, and he spoke his words in his usual measured way, though as he did it seemed to the lawyer that he'd stood up in the bed and was shouting.

"If you do it your way," he gasped, his breath barely holding, and his voice rising in pitch, "then I won't be there with you, will I?"

Other Blokes' Dogs

It was quite a figure he cut. After he'd splashed through the mud and water and then come in out of it, his hairy limbs were quivering and dripping. He'd put the dead teal down. There was a wild gleam in his pale eye as he cast rapid looks around the dawn sky to see if any more might have been flying over. His wet nose was quivering with excitement and he could even have been dribbling a bit.

That was my shooting mate. His dog cut a striking figure, as well, and we'll come to him shortly.

****

I've always believed in my dog. I'm also pretty wary of other people's. My dog is trained and obedient, and it's only in the strain of company, and under the bad influence of other less intelligent canines, that he may occasionally weaken and do something just a fraction less appropriate than it ought to be.

I know how well he works, how brilliant are his retrieves and stylish his points. Other people in their moments of uncharitable weakness may call him wilful or even disobedient. But all creative genius in humans has a certain eccentricity about it so it's hard to understand why folk don't recognize it in my dog.

Here's an example. I'd been quail shooting one day and I'd finished up and then cleaned the afternoon's bag, eighteen or twenty birds that I was carrying back from a dam's edge to the car in a bucket. The farmer drove up and we both stopped for a yarn. While I was talking to him I saw him looking past my shoulder, and he gabbled at me and pointed to my dog; when I turned round, I saw he was obediently — as always — in the sitting position, beside me and the bucket.

The farmer told me a bit indignantly that while we were talking, the dog had leaned over, removed one of the birds, and swallowed it whole, just quietly slipped it down the hatch without chewing, neat as you please, and then sat back up straight. He said the job was so well done it took him aback, and he even mimed the way it happened for me a couple of times. That was helpful.

For some reason he was offended at this interesting and derivative act. He didn't think the dog was entitled to the quail, and he said so, as well. Knowing dogs as I do, I was able to see a little further than the farmer, who was plainly too hung up on more pedestrian sheep and cattle dogs with their prosaic ways.

No, my dog was just independently exhibiting a little learned behaviour. He'd seen me eating them and enjoying it, and so he just decided to ease into trying it himself, and not overdoing it, he picked an appropriate time and slid one quail down the hatch, just like taking a pill — a quail pill, so to speak, perhaps the dog equivalent of taking a tranquiliser. Because he's seen me do that — I do it often. Particularly when dog training.

****

I wish other people's dogs were as imaginative and far-thinking as mine. Sadly, it's not always the case.

I went duck shooting with my mate, the one I started to describe earlier, before I got sidetracked. We shot good bags that day, too. If only my mate had held up his end, there's no telling how many we'd have ended up with. We shot all sorts, big black duck and plump teal, hardhead and wood duck.

We'd started at daylight, and when it was time to finish, I ended up with the hard job — as usual — of packing the dead birds into a sugar bag while my mate enjoyed himself and splashed around in the mud and the water, picking up the decoys and winding up the anchor strings before packing them away.

Around behind a clump of saltbush, when I thought I had them all gathered, I found the evidence of an evil deed.

On the ground, spread out in a fan shape, there were two duck wings, port and starboard. In between and a little to the south, there was a pair of duck legs. Underneath those there was a row of big, heavy duck tailfeathers. There wasn't anything else ex-duck at all.

My mate's dog was stretched out, head on paws, and wearing a happy expression. He'd crawled around behind the cover offered by the heavy growth, out of sight, and made a meal out of a duck that was half mine!

I couldn't do much else; I called the owner over, and I pointed to the shameful little pile of leavings, and I said, "Well, I've got the *ducks*, but what do we do about the duck *pieces*?"

You'd wonder how a man could be silly enough to have a bloke like that for a mate, wouldn't you? He looked at the tell-tale detritus, and he kept a straight face.

"Ah," he said, "we keep 'em for spare parts."

****

It's not hard to see where these misfit canines get their bad attitudes from, is it?

My dog would never do that. He's too well trained.

Anyway, I know he didn't do it that particular day. During the shooting, while all those confounded birds were making that racket falling down into the cold water in front of the hide, he'd done the sensible thing, found somewhere warm away from the worst of the noise, and gone to sleep.

No, it's other people's dogs that cause all the trouble.

Someone Pulled the Plug

There are days that it's impossible to forget. I was standing in a swamp a while ago, looking at the teal go through the dead gum trees. There were more in that single flock than I'd ever seen at once before, and I shot one out of the front of it, took the gun down, raised it and shot a second from a third of the way through, and then put it down again, and if I say I was content to watch the rest fly past, I might actually mean I was too stunned by the size of the mob to try reloading for a third.

It was later when I walked up onto the hill above it that I saw it was a natural sump. Modern farming practices had starved it of water, but this particular year someone had pulled the plug a bit further up the way. As a result, the water had run down, making a huge lagoon of just the right depth. The dog had to step carefully and search out the higher footing to avoid going under as we went along into it. In places he'd hit a channel and as he'd go in his ears would splay as he fell down through the water and had to swim.

He didn't mind. He could see what he was in for. In and out the best path through the broken-down gums, round the outgrowths of lignum we went, trying not to get lost. He didn't have to worry about spiking his waders. I do. If there's a snag anywhere, I'll find it, or it'll find me; it'll leap out at me just below the waterline, and the tear it makes will be three-cornered. This allows for one whole leg of my waders to fill up with water, and I adopt a lopsided gait even more curious than usual, with my feet as always finding little loops of tree roots to hook up on.

In those kinds of places there are always walls of one kind of resinous growth or another that tower up and create impassable impediments, ones that interrupt an approach to the tall tree picked out as a marker to walk to.

With luck there'll be a bit of a rise in the earth or an internal bank to walk on. I found one, that time, and though it meant there were more lignum bushes to go round I found the footing firmer. Dog at heel in case of snakes, I went to the heart of it.

There were water hens, and a flock of straw-necked ibis. Frogs called as evening came on, and the terns as they floated in gave their peeping cry that contrasted with the croaking normally associated with the swamp.

I put up two snipe, protected now, with their raucous and startled call, and watched them flare with that floating and effortless flight. They're insubstantial, somehow, and it seems fitting that collectively they're called a wisp. Good thing they're protected; I'd have missed them anyway.

The swamp was so lush it even smelt green. The life it supported was extraordinary. Flock after flock of teal matched the similar sized flocks of sandpipers with their aerobatics. It's a fine thing, the mob mentality of a flock of birds. They play follow the leader to much better effect than people ever can. The bird at the back is making its turn right along with the one at the front, so the whole flock moves together, pulling in the same direction. It's a pity the shooting organizations a decade or two ago couldn't have taken a lesson from a flock of teal, and all swung the same way at the same time.

Even I could shoot a feed with that much air traffic, sitting on a little knoll under a bare gum tree by a bush with a couple of hatfuls of dirt scooped out to make a hole to put my feet in, and a fair-sized bag to hold my sixes.

Life is simple with a flight line just out in front, a dog to one side, and a gun that's an old friend. To attain that kind of simplicity, though, it must be by the water. And for anyone to be sitting in front of the water, there needs to be a farmer up the way with a suitable supply of it.

I hope that for as long as I'm alive I can still find a place to have that kind of simplicity, and that somewhere, not too far away upstream from me, there's a farmer, willing to say he believes this year he might do without the crop that bit of country would grow.... and then to let the water have its way with the dry earth, as he pulls the plug.

Nowhere to Hide

Joe Louis said it of Billy Conn, when he was going for his rematch with him in 1942: “He can run, but he can’t hide”. I didn’t know that, the day I first heard it. He must’ve had a clear vision of his quarry in the ring, been singleminded. Later, it was to have significance for me.

****

We were going to shoot somewhere up near Buloke that year, we decided. We often did that at the opening, had a couple of smaller backwaters near the bigger one. All the old crowd’s gone, now. It was a long time ago. I don’t know how long, but I was still shooting a hammergun, if that gives some idea.

Anyway, it was just what we did in those days, and I suppose if we hadn’t moved away it’d still be just what we did. We made the plans, we decided where to meet, and we went about our business, with maybe a hint of a smile coming along a bit more readily, the sign of a lifting of our spirits in the course of the hard working week. The days seemed longer then than they do now, but it must be just the passage of time that causes that.

He had to come from the south of the state, across the big row of hills, a long run with the tight little road and its bad camber weaving round blind corners along the tops of them, bleak and windswept, muddy and treacherous, stuck up high and featureless in the air. When he drove into our camp that night, he came to the spot we'd agreed and he found us, our hammocks swinging from the trees, the billy on the fire, the congenial lies already getting under way. There was an unmistakable air about him of a man who was relieved.

It hadn't been raining where we were, down in the swamp country, but those late summer storms come on hard and fast, in a flurry of black and grey, and they're often gone as suddenly as they came. For those not in the middle of one it's hard to remember how ferocious they can be. When he arrived, even in the firelight, helped by the odd kerosene lamp we had hanging from a tree branch, we could see he was white-faced.

Nobody knew what to say. His temper was never all that good, and we didn't want to say the wrong thing and stir him up. He was still rangy and lithe. He'd been a welterweight in his time. The only sign of it was his nose; I suppose he must've stuck it too far forward for a very brief moment on one or two occasions, long enough to get it bent, but other than that you'd never have known it. He was middle aged, but all the time I knew him I had the impression he was in his prime, and always he gave the unquestionable sense that he was afraid of nothing. At least, not until then, anyway.

Well, under the good humour and the easy wash back and forth of the talk of our plans for the next morning, the stumps we were going to shoot from and the time we'd have to get up and who'd boil the billy, all the myriad things we'd been itching to say all week but wouldn't admit to without the excitement of the impending opening morning shoot, he didn't have much choice, and he loosened up a little. Despite himself he probably found it infectious, that excitement, and in time he had to let it out.

Not long before midnight, somebody, I don't remember who, coaxed it out of him.

When he'd been half way across the hills, the storm was suddenly on him, well under way all around him, and his nerves must've been tight as he felt through the steering wheel for what the wheels were doing on the suddenly-greasy road, and the rain quilting down as the darkness of the rising night moved in and mixed itself with the leaden storm grey.

He'd driven into it, no sooner remarking to himself — there was nobody else with him in the car — that he'd come about half way when suddenly it turned nasty, and out of the thick and swirling late summer rain there was no benign sheet lightning, but instead great licks of forked lightning started carving up the sky.

We've all seen that before, but this time was different. He was hit. There was a clang that he said nearly deafened him and a flash that must have been unforgettable, and for some reason it earthed before his eyes on the car, in the middle of the expanse of metal immediately in front of the windscreen. Seemed to me like a funny place to do it, but that's what happened, and I reckon it unsettled him in a way he wasn't used to. He took me over and together by torchlight we looked at the burn on the steel, and the blackened, smeared and crazed paint that together made up all the sign it left, this bolt from the black.

I asked him how he'd felt when it happened.

When it came, it was the only reference I ever heard him make, in all the time I knew him, to the experience he'd had in the ring. He just looked at me as though he wasn't sure who I was, and he flicked an eye back at the ugly slash standing out on the car's paintwork in the muted light and he said something I've never forgotten.

"Like the ring," he said. "All the room in the world to run, but nowhere to hide."

Yes, Louis on Conn. Funny, though, at the time I didn't know that, and I thought it was original.

A hilltop in a thunderstorm — nowhere to hide, in all that wide open space. I suppose to him and under the circumstances with the night blazing jaggedly around him it must've been a long and lonely passage to our camp; he was there, exposed in the storm and the wet, and he was trying to be somewhere else, where it was calm and dry, so the only solution was to put his head down and get on with it. Perhaps that has its parallels with life in general, given a minute's consideration.

I read somewhere that lightning strikes the earth about a hundred times a day. It might, too, but that wouldn't make it any more welcome when it does, though, would it?

****

Next morning, I stood as we all did in those days, out in the open, in the water, and gazed up into the sky.

There were half a dozen or so of us, maybe ten, I don't remember, and all in a ragged line a hundred yards or more apart, lined up north and south across the long swamp. I was the last in the line at the northern end. I shot a few birds in the early light, and when the first meagre puffs of wind blew out the dark I found myself outranged a bit and I had to be content instead to watch them fly — they were all teal that year, I remember, we hardly saw anything else — and as they often do on the big waters, they just took themselves up higher and higher. This left the best shots to fetch them down and the lesser ones to try.

Well, you know me; I'm one of the lesser ones. But I do like to watch the birds stretch their wings. When they're straight overhead they look like they'll get lost in the great dome of the sky. I always turn on an internal pep talk, reminding myself that the overhead ones are closer than they look, to make it seem a bit easier, not that it ends up helping, most of the time.

After I'd missed another half dozen or so birds, climbing too high with only the gentle breeze, I decided it was time to make my way in. I ought to be able to say I had the presence of mind to realize that they were too tall and too hard for me, though it's more likely I was just running out of cartridges. Anyway, I'd collected a feed, and that's the name of the game, but as I made up my mind to head off, it happened that then I saw the highest bird of the morning on the approach. It's funny how they stick in the mind, some birds, and for some reason become unforgettable.

The only black duck I'd seen, it came under enemy fire half a dozen times as it pelted toward me up the swamp. It lifted two yards higher with every barrel. Did that bird pour on the coal? I heard the double salute from all of our mob, two barrels each as it flew on north, toward me, last in the line; when it came to be my turn to try, I knew they'd all be watching.

In case anyone reckons I shot it, the truth is I missed it twice, both barrels, just the same as everybody else.

No, I didn't shoot it. The bloke behind me, not from our party, the one with the ancient single-barrel and the slouch hat, off to one side by a dead red gum, he was the one. He killed it dead in the air and it never even twitched, just somersaulted once, which is exactly the way it should be.

But the funny thing is it was the only good shot I saw him pull off all morning. Time and again I'd seen him shoot at easier birds and never even take a feather.

****

Plenty of room to move, that bird, and nowhere to hide.

And they wonder why I go hunting, the neighbours. They're prone to that kind of speculation, living in the city. I think they don't know much about some of the world's realities. Maybe they wonder what it is that I do, out in swamps, before dawn, alone with the mosquitoes and whatever conclusions I can draw about what goes on.

They don't realize that I can go duck shooting, and as one lone black duck goes skimming past, high in the sky on a timeless morning on a day long ago, I can see you, me, an ex-pug with a flattened nose, a white face and a scar of burnt paint on his car, and a wizened little man in an army jacket and a slouch hat beside a dead red gum, all playing out the whole comedy and tragedy of life.

There's all the room you could ever ask for to run in, mate, but....

The Army Major

Why do you shoot? Yes, and why do I?

When you go into the swamp, do you become more acutely aware of the sounds and the sights and the smells of the life that seems to be richer there than in the city? Are you more inclined to see it all through different eyes when you're surrounded by the green and blue mantle of the day away? I think I am.

I wonder whether I get closer to the core of things, somehow, with a dog and a duck call. I don't understand why either of these should take me any closer to anywhere, but that doesn't mean they don't take me there. I don't understand why my dog retrieves with such zeal, but that's no reason to stop using him.

****

One morning a few years ago, Marty was preparing for the duck shoot that came up every few weeks of the season. He had the respect of the other blokes, because he could read the birds, and usually find his way under a few when the time came. He wasn't infallible, but he shot his share, since he knew their habits. When the farmer who owned the swamp went to Marty with a job for him to do, he wasn't surprised. He'd done it before.

Marty knew the swamp. He knew the places where the birds flew along the old submerged fence lines, where they passed the dead gums, where they lifted to cross the trees, and where they were likely to set their wings and drop their landing gear to put down on the water and find safe haven. He'd shot over it for years.

No one took offence when he made suggestions about who should stand where, or which section of the swamp should be left alone for this shoot or that. He was a quiet sort of fellow and never inflicted himself on anybody.

On this particular day the man asked him if he'd mind looking after a visitor for him. He said that he was a decent type, no trouble to have around. He was an Englishman, actually, a major in the English army. One or two blokes had found him to be a bit pukka, but perhaps with just a few passing words to him they hadn't looked too deeply.

Marty said he would, of course. He'd had bigger responsibilities, he thought, and if the worst came to the worst then he could put him into place on the morning and then quietly take himself off to shoot somewhere else. There'd been a time or two when he'd had to do that, anyway, and, truth be told, that was often the way he'd rather go if he had a choice.

So they were all there on the morning of the shoot, before dawn, and the major was clipped, polite, but not standoffish. Marty went wading with him to the spot he'd selected, a stand of trees that usually took a bit of beating. From where they were to shoot, they could look across to the next clump of heavy cover, a place that Marty would shoot from himself on many mornings.

They spoke very quietly, matching their tones to the hushed setting the way we always do on a duck swamp before dawn breaks, and they didn't say a lot. But the major, a man called Crawford, did seem determined to make one point. For all his quiet and soldierly bearing, he had a love of the outdoors and of shooting. He uncased a Churchill XXV, a very fine game gun and worth a lot of anybody's money, and Marty heard him out as he said softly by the interior light of the car that he wished he had time to use it more often. He was careful to give his thanks to Marty for taking the time to look after him on that day, because, he said, it was important to him. It was the last day he could have to himself before he went to his next army posting, which could last any length of time. Not long after he said this, the false dawn passed, and the real one arrived. They had not much distance to walk till they were in position in the water, and it seemed that they were in for a good morning because in no time at all, two teal, always the early starters, zipped their way in, one a little behind the other.

Marty thought he saw them first, and, the major being his guest, he turned to tell him that they were on the way. As he opened his mouth to speak, something made him stop. The major had eased his feet around a fraction in the direction of the point where the two ducks would be most vulnerable as they flew past, and he seemed to shift his weight and lean that way. So Marty said nothing, on a hunch.

They'd both done the right thing. He turned to the incoming teal and smoothly shot the rear one first, well out, corrected his feet again, and effortlessly shot the second dead in front, so the two splashes came one on the other.

Marty saw him do this, and straight away took himself over to the other trees, there being no more need for words to be spoken, and he let him carry on with it, his last hunt. He left next day for Northern Ireland, and in a week he was shot dead.

****

I think of him sometimes, Major Crawford, in the early morning of his last shoot, as he stood in the swamp, alive to the sounds that only he could hear and to the sights that only he could see; and I wonder whether he managed to get any closer to the core of things.

I hope so. I really do.

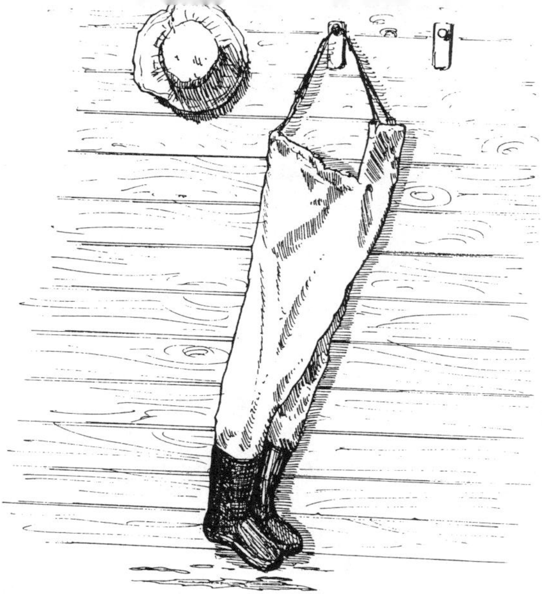

Alby Didn't Like Max

Alby didn't like Max. Max didn't like Alby either, mind, so there's not much point in thinking that there was anything lopsided about it. It was unashamedly mutual. There's no better explanation for it in life than to say that's just how it is, sometimes. Brothers-in-law, they were. It was only a fluke that they were both shooters.

Max believed Alby couldn't shoot to save his life. He thought he was just a bushie who spent his time paddling round looking for a duck to home rule, and if he couldn't find one he reckoned he'd get out of the boat reluctantly, because it involved work, and then he'd go and do the same thing to a half-grown rabbit somewhere.

At least, this is the kind of charge that Max used to make in the local hotel when he'd brought his sister down to visit, while Alby was feeding them all, and in the evenings listening to Max tell everybody how most things around the place should be done.

Max was very witty. As he drove into the homestead yard, he invariably had the window wound down, and he used to say aloud to everybody in the car, in a voice that carried out to his hosts: "Here we come, ready or not, and when we've eaten you out of house and home — we'll leave." One day his sister told Alby that the two men might have their differences, but Alby ought to remember that Max's friendship with him had stood the test of time. Alby drily remarked that the same could be said of galvanized iron outhouses.

All the same, Alby accepted Max's peculiarities the way he did most things. He even accepted the way his visits nearly always coincided with duck season.

It bothered him a bit because he had a feeling that when one of them aligned itself with not the season but the opening then he'd be very unwise to take Max to any of his best places; this feeling suggested that Max might well come back with half a dozen of his loudmouthed mates and jump the fence on Alby, to steal his spot in the future.

Max's mates were like that, unfortunately. Alby never said so, but they couldn't stop him thinking it, and he privately classified them all, including Max, as club shooters — a low name to call anybody, in Alby's opinion, which was why he never said it out loud.

Max shot all the target disciplines and he had the guns for the lot. He pursued club meetings and energetically burned powder in the search for better scores. When he shot game, sometimes he did it a lot less well. Alby just privately classified his performance as patchy at best, in the way most shooters will take a view of the ability of anyone they shoot alongside.

Alby, on the other hand, took his battered Browning semi-auto with the pitted half choke barrel and used it against everything that was legal, brought it home to eat, and up to the time of these events never gave a second thought to the fact that the only couple of times he'd shot clay targets his scores were south of disastrous.

He probably never would have, either, if Max hadn't spoken once too often in the hotel. I don't even know what it was he said. Just another of his amusing quips about how bad a shot his brother-in-law was, I suppose. Who knows what makes people crack? Catastrophes assume different proportions in men's minds.

That afternoon, Alby brought Max home from the pub, in time for them to ready themselves to shoot ducks in the morning. The season being under way, he knew he'd see some good birds, after they'd already had some small hunting pressure, and he had no obligation to take Max to a good spot where he might later do some damage. It wouldn't be hard to find a modest shoot without risking too much.

Already in his mind, the plan had formed by the time the two of them arrived home. He let his brother-in-law go in, and making some excuse he drove to the house of his mate and borrowed his cheap side by side, a spare gun that he had occasionally shot. He didn't even hear his friend's gibes about giving up his battered old semi-auto just so he could go back to the stone age, but simply slung it in the car and took it home as soon as he could carry it out the door. He needed a gun that had a break action.

On the way home he stopped the car on a quiet track away from all housing, and lifted the gun out. He inspected the bores by the car headlights and when he saw, as he expected, that they were clean, he took a cartridge out of the glovebox and put it in the tight barrel, and then discharged it harmlessly into the air.

All he had to do then at home was make sure he knew what brand of cartridges Max was shooting. He had a look in his kit, still in the back of his colourful big four-wheel drive, and discovered they were red factory loaded number fours. He had plenty of once-fired empties just like that.

Next morning, with the two of them kitted up, before dawn broke he took Max with him to a spot on a lake not far away which had a special aspect to it; it was a fly-out route for the birds, and when the shooting started and they gained height, they'd often circle the swamp once or twice and then make for this exit, where they'd provide very testing shooting. There were never any close birds there, but that was what Max needed, Alby told him, to demonstrate once and for all what a good shot he was.

It's fair to say that Max had never realized how much Alby had looked after him in the past, always ensuring he was put under birds he could handle. But those times had finished, the night before, in the hotel.

He pulled out the side by side, and away they went to the small stand of dead trees that Alby had been watching for weeks. Max was as brash as ever, and during the long wade, he gave Alby a hard time about his choice of gun and pointed out how much he himself was going to enjoy a good duck shoot using his new under and over with all the gold inlays.

When they reached the stand, the sun was rising. Alby had told him there was no point in being there too early. What he hadn't told him was that he wanted no easy birds, in case it brought his confidence up. He needn't have worried. It was a still morning, and the birds started flying high in the air straight away.

Alby let Max miss the first few hurtling teal, barrel stretchers, before admitting quietly that he seemed to have left his cartridges back at the car. This suited Max, of course, because he could give Alby more of a shellacking about yet another of his failings, but Alby just replied that he'd watch Max shoot and see if he could learn something.

The initiative sprang away from Max. He immediately offered cartridges to Alby, but the quiet butt of most of this cocky humour just declined, said he'd have the chance to go out again in a few days after his brother-in-law had left, and encouraged him to get into them while he had the chance.

Nothing throws most of us off like being carefully watched. Alby stood behind Max, so he could see where he was shooting. When he'd missed the first few, Alby observed that he was speeding up his swing to catch them and was only a little behind, so he started giving him helpful advice, and that had the desired effect and made him miss all the more.

The day grew brighter, the birds flew higher, the shooting echoed round the swamp, and it wasn't long before Max had missed them from all angles, and was even wishing he'd brought more ammunition. Alby permitted himself the quietly spoken observation that he wasn't sure that having more ammunition would do him much good. Once again this didn't help matters, and at that point Alby asked Max if he could spare one cartridge because he thought he might have a shot after all.

Max tried to hand over more than one, but Alby refused to take them, and told him to carry on, seeing they still had a bit of time. He took the cartridge and as Max turned for his next shot, he dropped it quietly down his waders, content to wait.

Max shot on. Alby, when he told me about it later, said he knew it was a gamble, but to take it he only had to be behind him out of sight and ready. So he was. What he didn't know was how neatly Max would oblige him.

It was just a plain difficult day. Alby said to me he was glad he hadn't been shooting, because they really were hard birds. Still he'd bargained that eventuallly Max would have to hit one. Ultimately, he did. What Alby was grateful for was that he left it half way through the hour or so's shooting time in the morning before he managed it. That was just the gods smiling on Alby.

The moment he pulled it off, and the bird folded at that thoroughly respectable height, his instinct was to turn behind to Alby and make sure that he'd seen it. Alby was watching, all right; the instant he saw the bird stagger he moved his gun half way to the shoulder, as though he was bringing it down after having fired.

Eyes on the bird and ignoring Max's expostulations, he took the side by side down and opened it, extracting from the dirtied left barrel the single red empty cartridge case he'd carried into the swamp in his top pocket and placed in his left barrel, unseen by Max.

As Max turned to him, and he was pulling it out, then looking past him, watching the bird splash into the water, he said, "I b'lieve that's the way it's done, Max."

He didn't have to do any more. They only stayed another half hour, but if they'd lingered all day, Max still wouldn't have hit another one, his confidence was so shaken.

On the way back, Alby asked Max if he'd like to drop into the pub, but Max declined, because he felt like going home.

Black Snow for Christmas

It was December 24th, not a hard date to remember. It wasn't hot, either, as it almost always is by then. At that time of year the heat can sear those not fully used to it in the more inland country, diminishing the attraction of a good rabbit shoot that might well involve a walk of a long way. The walk is half the fun for me. The other half is what the day will bring, because we never know.

The property manager told me they were there, a couple of varminters with centrefire rifles. He didn't make a lot of it, just gave me a rough idea of what was happening when I met him to say hello on the way through.

I appreciated that. Some owners get concerned about having two groups of shooters on a property at once. A lot of the time I can't see the sense in worrying about it, myself, just as long as I know they're there. If a fellow with a shotgun can't hear roughly where two high power rabbit rifles are at work in a few thousand acres of rolling hills then he shouldn't be let out alone.

What he'd told me was simple enough. He was suffering more than his share of trouble from crows. They were thick on the place, and he nearly started foaming at the mouth when he filled me in. At lambing over the last two years they'd reddened their hard beaks, and he was afraid it would be the same in the coming season, so every time I had the chance, he instructed me, I should shoot one.

I've been asked stranger things. I was the guest, and they weren't protected there. They can be terrible pests in some circumstances, singling out a ewe with twins, and diving on them one after the other, making her run back and forth, back and forth, until she drops. If she goes down beside one, they'll take the eyes out of the other, and if she falls in the middle, then they'll turn their attention to both.

So I thought his request was fair enough, and I put it to the back of my mind when I set off, kicking logs and drifting towards the edges of cover in clearings, looking for the telltale brown eyes, and the flash of russet where the light passed through an edge of fur.

It was half a day of that. We were looking for different kinds of country, those rifle shooters and I. It was obvious they'd be high on a hill somewhere, making sure they had a view overlooking some warrens, while for my part I'd be moving in the watercourses and on the flats. We didn't exactly get under each others' feet. There was plenty of space for us all, and it was late afternoon before I even heard the cracking of high intensity rifle rounds.

They were at the top of a long gully, and I was heading their way. I didn't have too many choices if I wanted to keep going. I had to cross that gully, and from a vantage point I could see they covered it all, so instead I picked a line and came up behind them to ensure that I could make a safe approach. I gave them a shout as soon as I thought they'd hear me from under their earmuffs, and they waved me up to them and both pulled their bolts.

A simple shotgunner like me wouldn't pretend to understand bipods and spotting scopes and reticles and mirage, but there'd be no misreporting if I said they had a couple of pretty ferocious .22s that were bringing the far side of the gully a lot closer than it might have been without them. One of them was a Swift, I remember, and it was loaded to the gunwales, its owner said happily.

They knew exactly how far a bullet had to travel to the spot they were shooting at over the way, and told me. I forget just how far it was. They knew the gully and had measured it accurately some time before, so they could be sure how much to allow for bullet drop at the distances right down the valley in front of them.

It seems they knew the property backwards and went there often. Usually when they left they were carrying a pile of headless rabbits to take away and clean. But on this day, they'd come along to the wide ravine and found it holding an untidy pile of half a dozen dead sheep that had been dumped there a while before, just long enough to earn the very sharp interest of every crow in the district, those same crows the property manager had it in for. And the manager was a mate of theirs.

They'd taken the first few off the flyblown mounds of wool, and they were getting their eye in by the time I rolled up. I think they soon grew to appreciate the audience, and it spurred them to competition. One thing's for sure: it wasn't a safe place to idle away the hours if you happened to be a crow. If he'd been there to see it, the manager would've been a contented man.

At about this time, not long after I'd arrived, a huge wedge-tailed eagle had made it his business to coast down idly and take pride of place on top of the highest woolly mound that was an expired sheep.

It would have seemed to me that no bantamweight crow would've been likely to see the need to argue with the heavyweight of feathered predation, and the rifle shooters must've thought the same, because they said that this new development must surely be the end of their crow shooting, and just when business was looking up.

It wasn't so. There was a dead tree, standing up over the whole scene, and when the first crow landed to present a target sitting on one of its bare limbs, they'd have hoped the shot passing over its head would frighten the eagle and drive him off.

There being no shortage of crows, they soon found he ignored the roar of the high velocity round as it passed a couple of metres above him to strike noisily home.

They were fragile bullets, they told me, and that was why they disintegrated crows. It'd be hard to call it much less than that. I soon wondered why the usually wary black birds kept on coming in and perching at all, but they did. Crows can't resist a mound of rotting wool with a sheep carcass in it somewhere.

Not being a rifle man, after a few examples I concluded that when you've seen one crow dissolve in a black cloud you've seen them all, so I gave the spotting scope a nudge and took it off the tree that the crows were coming to, putting it instead onto that eagle to have a look at him while all this was going on.

It might seem strange, but they always look to me like they're wearing pyjamas. There's more than a touch of absurdity in this, because they're such imperious birds, the way they strut around with a fixed stare, as though they think they're generals. They look like they think they know it all, and their pyjamas flap in the breeze and make fatuous their solemn expression.

I can see him now, General Eagle in dirty brown pyjamas, looking up vacantly as though bemused, his mind somewhere else, impervious to the reverberating sound around him, but not to the mists of coal-black feathers; every time another crow was vapourized they came down in clouds, sometimes catching his attention and making him move his head, to look up and around yet again, with those characteristic quick little jerks.

It must have put him off his stroke, all that way deep into the inland of Australia; it wasn't what he was expecting — snow at Christmas time, we don't usually have it, and black snow, at that.

The Politician

In a small provincial town there stood a parliamentary electoral office. It serviced a wide area of the red country, and there was a time when it was as well-utilized as many others of the town's premises, the barber's or those of the noxious weed board.

The position of the local sitting member was once thought to be secure, the job lasting for a long time if not for life and drawing a degree of respect from the locals which indicated that despite the obligatory good-natured leg-pulling at barbecues and other town events, the encumbent was nevertheless well accepted.

There was a point when this ended. There was a subtle change, barely noticed at the time. It happened when a younger man took the seat after the premature retirement of the previous one had brought about the need for a by-election. A lot of people continued to take it for granted at first, but in a while there was general agreement that the new man was different.

It started off as just a feeling, but it was fostered and it grew. Like those before him, he still went to the high school sports, but he was putting in an appearance. He still opened competitions at the local show, but when he put on the apron in the cooking section he was doing it for the camera, not because he belonged in the community.

This was clear enough to most long before the debate began over the new gun laws. He'd always maintained that he was a local, and he always said he defended his people, but they saw him not as becoming more sleek, not as becoming more oily, but as though he had less of himself invested in the district.

He didn't support their rights. He said he would, and many of them made it clear to him what they wanted, but while he gave lip service to them, his more extended absences from among them told in the end, and they knew they had no representation to speak of.

Old Angus considered this for a long time. The locals seemed to think it was now to be expected in the behaviour of a modern politician, but Angus was unable to accept that, and because he was outraged by what the government had done to the lawful gun owner, he developed a burning interest in trying to categorize what it was that had gone wrong. When he was asked what was ailing him, he said wrily that he was suffering from acute politico-melancholia.

A great observer, he never did talk much about the slide in political morality. He'd had his view of it for a long time before the gun prohibitionists started thrusting their talking heads onto Angus's television set. Then one day he saw his own member of parliament in a television studio somewhere. It was an environment so alien to the people he was supposed to be representing that it might as well have been a foreign country. He sat in a plush chair, pontificating gravely and taking a public position against gun ownership, and it was then that everything Angus had suspected was made clear in his mind. He had not enjoyed the advantages of a university education, but the breadth of his reading might have surprised a jumped-up opportunist, and it was the words of Henry Ford that came to him: "I would like to communicate to others the calmness that the long view of life gives us." Angus was a patient man.

That said, this behaviour was still the last straw. Enough became enough. He washed his hands of the man, spoke badly of him rather than not at all, and wrote him off as having no use to the community.

The politician's value sank. There was no watershed, no particular day when it was all over, but instead just a decline over a long time of the little goodwill of his remaining.

One day, Angus had to go to the city. A rare event, it coincided with his birthday, and he thought it gave him an opportunity equally unusual. Before he went, he telephoned a good mate of his who worked in Parliament House, and they had a brief chat. Yes, his friend said, he'd be happy to oblige.

Then Angus rang his niece, the one with the access to the laser printer in the newsagent's office. He asked her if she'd copy a message for him. She said she would. He asked if she'd print it out on clean, crisp paper, and find him a good quality envelope. She said she'd do that, too. Naturally, it was to be a matter between the two of them.

He retired into his study, and he tapped out a line of type on the old manual that he used on occasion for his important correspondence. This he took to her, and she duly copied it. To her surprise, it was the name of the politician that Angus asked her to put on the envelope.

With this secure in his inside pocket he went to the city, and next day, mid-morning, he made his way to Parliament House. He met his mate, whose job took him daily into the parliament, and made sure that he had access to the politicians' pigeon holes. When he was certain of it, he asked of his friend nothing more than to put the addressed envelope with its simple message in the letterbox it had to go to. He was confident that it would happen straight away, and it was appropriate because parliament was sitting. Angus had thought this was as good a time as ever, because it would've been a pity to waste a trip to the city.

And now there's only the matter of the note.

Angus didn't know very much about the politician. He did know one thing, though, and that was the certainty of skeletons in his political closet. Someone of his ilk must surely in that respect be predictable. Angus didn't need to know him; what was more important was that he knew his kind of man.

Angus didn't have to do anything himself. He realized he was not strictly telling the truth, but it was a white lie, and it was sweet when he wrote it. The anonymous note, his revenge, his birthday present to himself, simply said: "I know who you are and I saw what you did." The politician's past would surely take over from there.

Hunting at Night

I deserve to be called unorthodox and I've always been willing to admit it. I do a lot of hunting with my german shorthaired pointer at night.

His image is on the back cover of this book, and his name is Barkis, which is a literary joke that nobody ever gets. It takes a little reading of Charles Dickens to know that in *David Copperfield*, David receives a lift in a cart with a silent old man, and they go along for a while with nothing said, until right at the end he speaks, and says he has a message for a lady known to David — "Barkis is willin'".

I chose him out of all the litter because he had dignity, not jumping around like all the rest. He stood back and thought me over for a while, before deciding whether or not he'd tolerate a permanent connection.

He was five months old. He might have had dignity, but all the way home from the kennels he sat in my wife's lap and sucked her finger.

****

Is this dog willing? He never heard the proverb that he who measures twice only has to cut once. He might not have all the answers, but as a fellow I know said at the dinner speech of a less than popular colleague leaving for greener pastures, we might not always agree with his opinions, but at least we know what they are.

Yes, he's willing. In the calm of the predawn hours, before the wind that wafts over the decoys blows the grey light towards his kennel, he'll sense my stirring in the house. Or perhaps he'll smell the gun when I move it. He's willing enough to let the neighbors know that we'll soon be on the road, and he does it in style.

They deeply appreciate it, of course, his warbling at four in the morning being a reminder that if they weren't so ridiculously lazy they could be out catching pneumonia, and taking double rises on teal the way I'd like to. They respond with gifts; I get perplexed when the boots I find in the yard don't match, but some of the heavier objects have made useful doorstops.

****

I love to watch him work hard, back and forth at the steady, grinding pace of the distant caster, nose to the ground, tail at a steady beat. I often wonder how far those four feet travel in the course of a day's shooting across big, bare stubble paddocks, unrelieved by trees. Not even the spiky stubble wearing at them will slow them down.

I remember one hunt in particular that was a real test of any dog, six days straight, and Barkis no longer in the bloom of youth. There was I, covering ground as best I could, leaning sideways towards him in each tack of his two hundred yard casts. Big fields mean wide runs, and a dog with a couple of kilometres of plains in front of him may just keep on going instead of staying close. Along behind comes his master, tottering clumsily along through the clods and around the thistles on half as many legs as it really takes to cover ground.

On the sixth day, after we'd all been shooting our bags over him, it would be understandable if he got tired. So there we were, struggling, trying to stay close in one of those wide loops that took him well out. Suddenly he hit the riveting scent of a close, tight-sitting bird. He looked across to see us making for him, and focused back on the job. We kept coming, but it was a long way, so he did the obvious thing. He sat down on the job.

You've heard of a setter; perhaps I've got a new line of dog here, a sitter. Mind you, it was a good, staunch point, gravely carried out, unflinching, in fact, and when we caught up we found two quail right under his brown, wet nose, which completed a gentle arch all the way to his rump, planted firmly in the stubble.

I'd run the camera out of film, but at least I had a witness. When we kicked the birds up, we took one each and shot them both.

****

When ducks set their wings and decide that the middle of my decoys is the place they want to be, I like that, and I can live with it without grumbling or looking for a change of scenery. When rabbits are bursting out of tussocks and disappearing behind rocks for the fraction of a second it takes me to miss them with a load of sixes only to reappear hale and well on the flats before going end for end when I finally hit them with the second barrel — well, I can put up with that, too, and a casserole to follow.

But it's when I'm shooting quail that I'm happiest to be alive. There needs to be a bird in cover, unseen, and a pale gold winter sun, with a dog staunch on point telling me where I ought to be. Yes, I know it's not my dog on point, because he's too busy running along under his floppy brown ears half way into Gileses' next door. But it's somebody else's dog, a dog, and that's all that matters. Barkis is willing. Got bad habits, but he's willing.

****

One of life's mysteries is how a quail can zigzag his way out of trouble without appearing to. A cylinder shot pattern at thirty paces is a forty-inch diameter proposition, and yet when the bird rises and I shoulder the gun, it's only a flick of his wings that shifts him to the right, and so my shot passes harmlessly on his left side. Next I summon up the mental picture of what was taking place and become aware that his floating jink was about the width of his wingspan, only a foot or so, and he should have fallen easily within the span of my shot pattern, unless I shot hopelessly to the left of him. But he flies on unscathed, and as he passes forty yards I fling in the second barrel, at the same time as he gives another little jink, but this time to the left, so my quarter choke, which at forty yards also has a diameter of forty inches, passes harmlessly on his right side; did I shoot just as hopelessly to the right of him? Or did that little wing dip take him further than a wingspan away from his perceived line of flight?

For all my pondering on the problem, what I usually end up with is no quail, two empty cartridge cases, and a dirty look from the dog. Perhaps the flight of the quail is like the clay bird's, full of optical illusion. But one day last season the illusion spread far enough away to reach my dog.

We'd shot all afternoon at hard, testing birds that had risen at a fair distance. Barkis, I've already admitted, has been prone to a few bad habits that a dog of his age is entitled to keep. He got on a running bird, leaving its scent as it ran through the green pick in the stubble. He concentrated, keeping the wind full in his face, casting twenty yards at a time, but it ran, and wouldn't be pinned.

As he completed one tack, going to his left, another bird sprang up unexpectedly in front of me, flushed by my feet, and not the dog. So I shot it. As I did, he turned to begin his next tack, heard the shot, and at the same time out of the corner of his eye saw what he thought was a quail. He did the logical thing and made a grab for it. I said he had bad habits.

Unfortunately the blur of different colour on the green and brown carpet interspersed with stubble spikes turned out to be a clod of dirt, lying uncharacteristically in view. So the brown hound had a mouthful of dirt for his trouble, and looked pretty silly trying to spit it out. I had to stop walking to get the laughing over with. But dogs forgive and forget, and they can live with being told that real pointers don't snap at clods, or at quail either, for that matter.

I laughed at him another time. It was winter, and we were in yet more stubble, with a greasy wet green growth through it. All his young life we'd had poor years, and he's been a dog unexposed to the big coveys that occur in the good seasons — a singles dog, in effect.

We stepped into a wide paddock and I let him cast out into the wind, which he did with his two hundred yard tacks. He didn't know it, and neither did I, but there were more quail in that paddock than either of us had ever seen in one place before. As he ran, he was unaware that he was herding them up to a slight rise, the kind our quail often like to fly from.

On his third or fourth cast, he was running past the place they'd all chosen to mob up in, toward a second fold in the ground. At that moment, a big gust of cold winter air blew over them, and he had a bigger whiff of quail than his two brown nostrils had ever known.

His legs locked up instantly in a point, but I'd never taken the time to explain to him that dogs have a high centre of gravity, and he tipped over as he flew off the top of the little rise and skidded along the wet grass. He was upside down, but still in a point. I shot the first bird to rise near me, and broke up with laughter watching him try to rearrange himself and put the sky back where it belonged. After the worst of the fit had passed, I remembered my little double had another trigger, and so I shot another bird as the long rise went on.

I apologized to him for laughing, perhaps not convincingly, but our friendship's been weighed in the balance and found substantial enough to contain my outburst. In other words, I'm the one who feeds him at night.

One day a bit of mystery intruded itself into our shooting. A while back just the dog and I were working some hard country where the birds were all jet propelled and too touchy to take liberties with. They were rising ahead of him, and I was ploughing on with malice aforethought, all steamed up because I'd missed a lot of opportunities by being a shade slow. So I was all eyes, ears and suspicion, watching both the brown beast and where I was going at the same time.

As he completed a cast to one side of me there was the purr of wings in front, thirty yards to one side of where he stood, and before I was aware of it I'd mounted the gun, tracked the bird, swung through and touched the rear trigger, having judged it to be too far out for the first barrel. The bird, cruising along less than a couple of metres above the stubble, turned over once in the air and fell down on its back, wings spread.

That's all in order, it might seem, but there was something wrong. It took me a moment to puzzle it out as the dog ran to the bird and retrieved it, stone dead. It finally came to me, strange as it may sound; I hadn't fired. I broke the double to check, and there were the twin brass cartridge heads, with two smooth primers in them. I took them out. Yes, they were unfired. There was nobody else in the paddock, and I confess I looked around to be sure. When I cleaned the bird, there wasn't a mark on it.

As Red Skelton used to say, I just do 'em, I don't explain 'em. It gave me a crisis of conscience when I came to do a cartridges-to-kills tally at the end of the day. I have my diary in front of me: "Eighteen birds, twenty-six cartridges — one death by misadventure." It makes for a strange entry, but it was just another day we shared.

****

Then there was the time a friend and I shot in sudax, the waist high member of the sorghum family. We beat around in it like some lost tribe in Africa.

We had a few short of our bags between us when we called it a day, pounding our way to the edge, sitting down to do the plucking and cleaning. The dog went and dozed by the wheel of the car. Fifteen minutes later I looked up and he was gone. I stood, whistled, walked a bit, looked for the nearest water trough, assuming he was dunking himself in it. I found it, but no dog. It started me worrying.

Returning to the car, I drove around the whole crop, out onto the flats, and stood on the roof so I could look around at all points of the compass; no movement. But my friend, older and wiser than I am, went where I should have gone, out into the thickest part of the cover we'd been working, and found him there, on point.

I was glad that I wouldn't have to spend the night sleeping out in the car, waiting for him to turn up. I think I was more glad that I had a dog that would hold a point for half an hour.

Then I stopped and considered it. I concluded that it's like this. The dog is as much a victim as I am, and like me he needs to be pitied. I hunt because I have to. The fact is it was a pair of birds he had pointed in that heavy growth, so thick that he had them both locked in tight and the scent was strong. He didn't hold them there because he knew how to be a good quail dog, or by having exceptional determination to keep them there for his master to shoot, or even just to have his own way in the matter.

He kept on doing it for the same reason he kept eating and breathing. He just couldn't figure out a way to stop.

****

Both of us could be said to be victims to the same vices, the dog and I. When either of us is eating, polite people look the other way. We're both inclined to daydream, given half a chance, and the night after a good shoot, we both tend to twitch and yelp in our sleep.

At least I can count. For years I hoped the flop-eared hound would pick up the idea. Shouldn't think it'd be too hard — two barrels on the gun, two shots, (sometimes) two birds to find....

The sad fact is that his arithmetic has been a distinct failure. While it's nice to think he has faith in his owner after a shot's been fired, and he'll gallop out in a hopeful frame of mind, he was out of class the day they taught addition. He never seemed to pick up the difference between one shot and two. This might seem to be a nicety. Nobody expects a dog to carry a calculator.

When by some quirk of fate I put two birds together, though, out he'd go and very efficiently pick up one, to return to hand in copybook style. If it meant running over the first to bring back the second, then experience taught me to expect a momentary look approaching perplexity. Then the light would go on in his eyes — problem solved: he'd drop the one in his mouth where the first lay, leave it behind, and come in at full tilt with the second. Never look back.

One memorable day we were working ducks over a little pool and a half dozen decoys. In the whisper and crackle of wings I suddenly saw teal in front. I took the front bird with one barrel, and the shot string caught the one behind simultaneously. The flock lifted, and I swung on another, and to my surprise took him cleanly as well. Three ducks down on the ground past the pool; two of them were four or five paces apart, and the third ten yards further on, all in a line. Away went the finder-fetcher, straight to the furthest bird, for a stylish retrieve. He came as far back to me as the next of the three — and yes, wonder of wonders, he stopped, and picked up the second without dropping the first. He had two birds in his mouth — he'd learnt to count! I congratulated him. I congratulated myself. I took the two birds.

Would he go back for the third, that he'd just stepped so daintily over? He was convinced. It had never existed.

****

I'm allowed to grizzle about his weaknesses. I'm his mate, and besides, I saved his life. I shot with him last season, on the edge of a mangrove swamp, where the teal flew high and I was mustering my best swing to do justice to the occasion. One came past along the border of the mangroves, and I swept the gun out so far in front that the sight picture stays with me as I write. The teal crumpled in the air, dead, and came down heavily in the mangroves.

The dog was gone in a moment, into the heavy cover, and I watched him enter at a spot adjacent to where the bird fell. In five minutes there was no sign of him, so I sighed and went looking.

I'll never forget the vacant eyes, but more important I'll never forget the floppy ears. The eyes were puzzled because the legs and other bits and pieces wouldn't move, being bogged as he was to the point of complete immobility in the glutinous black ooze. The ears were so spectacular because they were floating on it. That's how deep he was in it. He'd have died there unless I'd pulled him out, which I did with the greatest of difficulty, and with the memorable squelching of the clinging ooze. It took me half an hour of washing in fresh water before I considered him fit for the car and he had a kind of well travelled and even beaten look about him for a few days as he no doubt pondered on what happens to fools that rush in where angels fear to tread, or where, if they must, they at least take water wings.

****

We do a lot of hunting at night.

A few days ago I took him to the vet, and only one of us came back. I think in a way I'd like to say instead that I took him out to where he made his fearless, huge, chest-on leaps into the cold water after the ducks he so much loved to fetch, and that there I had calmly done it for him, the last kind act of one good friend for another. He had done so much for me, after all.

I'd like to report that after we together watched a sunset there by the channel where the water passes a wide, sturdy tree, I'd buried him under it with some indefinable part of me, to rest quietly through the dawns to come, a little way below the whisper of the black ducks' wings, within hearing of the bush paddock where the quail sometimes give their haunting whistle in the evenings.

I didn't do that. I thought perhaps I could have done it, this last act of one good friend for another, but I may be like a lot of us in finding that I didn't have what it takes at the end. The vet couldn't have been more helpful, or more humane, and she knew how long to stay out of the room.

It's afternoon now, and I look across the yard to where his kennel stands; it seems surprising how misty the windows must be in this house, because I find I can't see it properly at all.

The pup is on order. But in the meantime, and for a good while yet to come, I think, we hunt together in the nights, the willing Barkis and I, the way we always used to. And I like the nights, I like them a lot better than the days. The days have a chill about them.

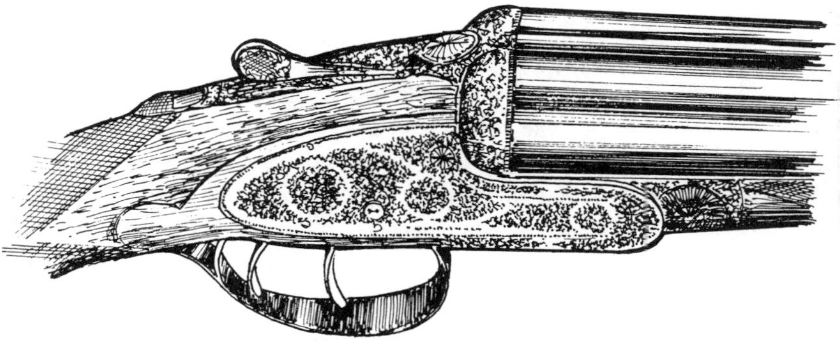

Seven Letter Punches

I never liked him. I never met him, either, but in this case I don't think that even matters.

He was a dairy farmer; times were no doubt hard. It was in the Depression years, and to some extent that's an excuse, but was it enough of one?

The average weekly wage for those lucky enough to have work would've been no more than three or four pounds at best, and by then the price of a new Purdey was close to a hundred and fifty, so however it's viewed there was a lot of expenditure involved.

When he ordered it there must have been the usual wait. Just the way any of us would, while it was in the making and then in transit he must have stamped around and daydreamed and probably worried over it as well. The waiting time's always been close to a couple of years for one, and added to that it would have had to come by ship, of course, a minimum six weeks on the water, and he would've been concerned about the salt and the damp, fire in the hold, heavy objects being dropped on it, loss on the wharves, and maybe even attack by buccaneers for all I know.

He wasn't a bad live-bird shot, from what I heard. I don't know how big his property was. It might be some mitigation for what he did, and thus be a help to my frame of mind, if I were to discover that he was poor.

Fred Crofter. There aren't many of the family about any more, and the couple I've met wouldn't know the butt end of a shotgun from the muzzle, anyway. But he certainly did.

When he ordered it I suspect that in his head there must've been a struggle as he grappled with the question of whether or not to spend the money, an interior monologue like many a competitive shooter has experienced before succumbing to the beckoning finger of the promise of better scores. He could've bought a best gun from some other company for maybe two thirds the price and practically no waiting time. There was no shortage of agents for guns by makers who were well thought of not only in this country, but in his district, and for good reason, too; he'd have considered the Boswells, often Purdey lookalikes that gave away to them nothing much in quality that I've ever been able to find, and the heavier Churchills, too, there were a lot of those made as pigeon guns for Australia — the Walter Betts Crown grade or the top of the line Holloways, all of them being high quality sidelocks, but maybe getting a bit too cheap for him there towards the end of the list.

He wasn't happy with any of those. He evidently wanted only the best, which doesn't suggest poverty, and he ordered the Purdey, self-opening, thirty-two inch tubes, full and full, with best Purdey fine scroll engraving, and those who've seen an example know how good that is.

The live bird matches were on every weekend within striking distance of where he lived. I believe he travelled a fair bit, too, and he took his competitive skill elsewhere as well, to shoot all round the area, towards the north of Victoria. I understand he made money in the matches, six birds at twenty-seven yards' rise, they mostly used to shoot. He'd have needed that full choke.

All right, then, I accept times might have been tough, but they couldn't have been that bad, because he still bought the gun new. When he took delivery of it I'm sure he had pride of ownership that any of us could have experienced. No argument.

All the same, does that justify what he did?

When he collected it, he stopped in at the general store. They say it was within the first day or so because nobody saw the gun any other way but in the state it was in after he'd done it, and probably half the men in the district, crawling as it was with live pigeon and duck shooters, would have been more than interested to see it as soon as it arrived. He'd have been sweating on it and he must've had plenty to say about it, maybe at the clubs, or at the stock sales, or even when they picked up his milk in the cool of the mornings.

I concede that there was no gun registration in those days, but there was less theft, too, and more sense of community, so I think protecting it was only part of his motive and it becomes puzzling to pursue that line of thought.

Anyway, the fact is he stopped at the general store. It was never a big town, so the store might not have been all that well stocked. I doubt that it would've been able to help him unless he'd made a special order in advance, not for something as little called for as what he was there to buy, so perhaps he'd already thought about it, decided what he was going to do; if he had, that only makes it worse, it seems to me.

He'd ordered them in advance, all right, steel letter punches, one-eighth inch: one f, one r, one e, one d — by now the picture must be coming clearer.

He must have taken the new gun carefully out of its oak and leather case, within the first day or two, and put it in the vice in his tool shed; funnily enough there were no signs of jaw marks, so he evidently took care of that by some kind of packing. But he took his seven letter punches and he went straight across the fine scroll, over the centre of the locks, not on one side but on both, and the discreet 'J. Purdey & Sons' was overshadowed by the ragged line above it of those seven stamps, all lower case: 'fred crofter.'

Nobody'd pinch it then, by hell.

No. Why would they they want to?

****

As I never met him, maybe I shouldn't judge him, but I can't help thinking that he must ultimately be considered a confused man.

In one way he was probably the same as the rest of us, in having a genuine appreciation of a good gun, even if he had trouble understanding it, and what in its advanced workmanship it stood for. It's possible he thought that what he had in his hand was a once in a lifetime acquisition, paid for by his sweat, and that it was his to do with as he wanted. But I think not.

I imagine the rise and fall of his hammer in the shed, over the finely etched locks, the thumping on the punches an attempt to search out a soul in the gun and brand it, to mark it as his own. I think he was a man who tried to wed his own mortality to a work of art, and somehow to gain for himself what none of us can have. He couldn't be expected to see a contemporary Purdey as having any sanctity of its own, it might be argued, and I tend to agree with that, because in those days the best handmade guns were both working implements and not uncommon, but he certainly saw something more in it or otherwise he wouldn't have acted as he did in his own clumsy way, trying to preserve it. Don't forget that he must have seen some beauty in it other than its monetary value because he did protect it against the jaws of the vice.

The fact is, of course, whatever it was he sought to preserve of himself, it didn't happen, because he's gone and the gun's not. It doesn't work that way, it never can, and the fact is that he ought to have known it, but he didn't. Strangely enough, that's what I think it is I hold against him, because he ruined a good gun and I bet he still didn't learn it.

I was looking at that gun the other day, and I grudgingly thought that just perhaps I could've found it in me to be a bit easier on him if he'd only had the good grace to shell out enough money at the general store to buy a capital F and a capital C, instead of being so mean and only using the small letters all the way through both names.

But I'll tell you what: I doubt it.

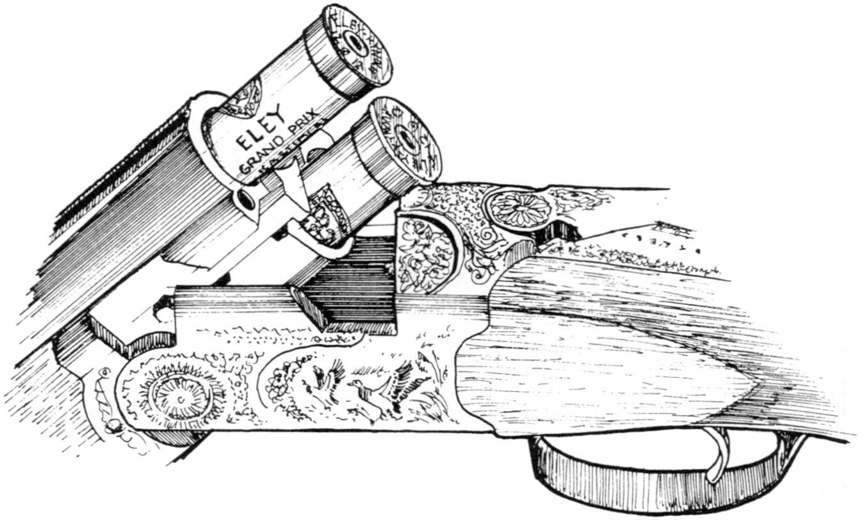

A Grand Prix Man

One day I had to go into his garage for something. We started talking, so I wasn't paying all that much attention to what was lying around in the usual shed-clutter. When I thought about it later, I could've sworn there weren't cases and cases of shotgun ammunition standing round, though. Surely I'd have noticed.

That's why it puzzled me when we met at a sporting clay shoot a while later, and we started talking about quail and dogs and then cartridges, it being nearly the season. I gave my preferences, we all have them, and the talk rambled over where the prospects looked good and what reports were coming in from which spies where. And neither of us was giving away a thing to the other, of course.

Then the discussion came back to cartridges. All his quail shooting was closely tied up with the old Grand Prix, I learned, and I didn't think a lot of it at the time. He told me just how much he enjoyed them, and I thought of the cardboard, the old roll crimp, the distinctive colour. They used to be everywhere in the fifties and I knew them well, but that was all a long time ago. The name had been a watchword and many were peeved at its passing. People developed strong attachments to cartridge brand names then.

At the time, he simply said he hoped he had enough of them to see him out, and that he thought he did have.

Later on, I talked to a few others, and one of them mentioned how much shooting this man actually did — a lot, it seemed. They reckoned he lived on quail through the season, and had his freezer stocked after it. That made me start wondering. They stopped making those old cardboard loads in the early sixties. They went to a star crimp for a while, still in cardboard, and then briefly on to plastic, but everybody knew the character was gone and they were no longer the same. To be shooting the original Grand Prix all season long for life... and he was a fairly young man. I hoped he hadn't had some bad news from the doctor.

I thought back to his shed, and there was still no tag in my memory of it that could seem to be attached to a big stockpile of relatively rare old cartridges.

It's not the kind of thing to lose sleep over, and I'd have thought no more of it till one day for some reason or other I had to go into his work, and I met him in his office. He was cordial, and again we chatted, and it was hard not to notice the two fired, yes, cardboard, roll-crimped Grand Prix cases standing in the middle of the desk.

I certainly didn't tumble to it without some help, when I first saw them. I might've been in a hurry. Probably I'd never have mentioned it even then, except that they managed by their own means to rope me in. There was something about them that I found stirred the memory of my own childhood. It was Grand Prix cartridges that I remembered most myself. It happened just as I leaned across his desk; I felt drawn to them, and even till that point I hadn't realized the source of their charm. Suddenly they seemed to come strongly to my attention then and I mentioned the two of them there, sitting on the smooth wood.

He smiled. He relied on the old Grand Prix to get him through the season.... He thought he'd have enough.... I asked him outright how his supply was going. Not bad, he said, not bad. Two at the beginning of the season, and depending on the year, and how damp the weather, another two towards the end, and that was usually enough to do the trick. At that rate of expenditure there should be enough to get him through.

Four cartridges? Enough for the whole season? Not many quail in that. It seemed that his use for them couldn't have been the conventional one.

Yes, he told me, four was enough. Plenty. With that and a tiny smile, he picked up the two empty cardboard cases, holding them together immediately under his nose, and with his eyes closed he inhaled deeply from the old fibre-wadded cardboard tubes, lost for a moment, gone from the office, perhaps visiting his childhood the way I'd suddenly flashed back to mine, sniffing the unmistakable aroma high. As he put them back into their place on his desk, his mind came back to the present and once again he engaged with me in the world of work. It was then I understood how four cartridges could be used to last a shooting man the whole way through a season.

Ray

Part One - Silver Service

It's easy to take a shine to some people, and occasionally impossible to avoid it.

He lived on a little farm, not too far from the sea, and that's how it all came about. In lots of places along the coastline round where we'd gone on holiday, there were rock caves and little islands, and these constitute habitat. In habitat, wild things live.

When I met Ray, I'm afraid he wasn't happy that this is the way it goes. I happened to drive past his farm that time, and there it was, an unforgettable picture with him in the centre of it, stalking up and down in his pea paddock, a mass of impotent anger, waving his arms at a huge blue flock of pigeons that swirled and settled, swirled and settled.

His wet, grey hair untamed, Ray was wearing rubber boots, though it was high summer, and these were complemented by a pair of shorts safely described as less than dashing. Other than that, all he was wearing was a liberal and glistening coat of sweat and a wild look in his eye.

He was out in what we discovered was his back paddock, set away from any houses; I thought that however well he was doing with these pigeons by running up and down shouting, with a pocketful of traploads we could possibly do a bit better and help him out. We'd climbed out of the car, my mate and I, and had a word with him. I doubt that we would've, but the clincher was a sign he had on the fence, proclaiming to anyone who chose to drive past that he'd laid bait for pigeons. When we saw that, it suggested that he was in serious trouble from the airborne marauders.

So, we'd stopped to have a yarn. He didn't waste any time. He said nothing would please him more than somebody lending a hand to clear some breathing space. He had a crop to protect, and it was getting on to late afternoon, feeding time for pigeons. He looked up in desperation as they whirled overhead in readiness and he told us that in a few more days of that heat the crop would be harvested and gone, but just at the moment it was in danger of being carried away pod by pod beforehand. I reckoned if he kept up this activity in the heat he'd be the one carried away, but I didn't say so.

He looked towards the sea, where the rocks and the cliffs gave shelter to the birds, as we all knew. It seemed to be a cruel part of nature's plan that Ray's father a half century before had bought property in what would turn out to be such a vulnerable place, leaving his son to bear it now while the old man, quite senile, sat on the veranda back at the house and nodded and dribbled with laughter while Ray ran up and down outside in the sun, risking heart failure.

With Ray's permission gladly given, we took the guns out of the car and stood in front of a row of trees, to try to catch the shade, and we folded up a couple of passing birds. I don't think I ever saw a man as tickled as Ray when he saw that happen. He jumped from one rubber-booted leg to the other, and hooted with happiness. Feral pigeons are pests. We were only doing our civic duty, and didn't see fit to get all that excited about it, but it was plain that it hit a button in Ray so that every time he saw a pair of pigeon wings fold up terminally in mid-air he couldn't keep his mirth in.

They were persistent, those birds, because they'd obviously been feeding there a while, and in just a few minutes we had a fair pile of them. The whole time, Ray scuttled around and watched in open-mouthed happiness. Nothing made him more joyous than the sight of a feral pigeon dissolving in a puff of feathers, unless it was two doing the same thing.

In our holiday in the district, we'd been driving back from shooting a round of skeet at a little trap club we'd found when we'd come across him, and so we had with us open-bored guns that were just murder on them, and after half a case of assorted ammunition had gone skywards with malice aforethought our feral foe perceived there wasn't a lot of future in being a pigeon on the spot at the time, and the big flock broke up and went home, seawards.

Every last one of them that tumbled in the air brought a whoop from Ray, just an innocent expression of almost childlish glee. It got louder as we went, so that neither of us dared to miss and disappoint him. By the end of the day if we had something to say to him he'd only answer in monosyllables, and I realized with a chuckle I couldn't restrain that it was because he'd gone hoarse and a grunt was the best he could offer.

The sun was low when they'd stopped flying. We were all hot and tired. Ray was a mass of sweat-streaked dust, and with an energy belying his years he bounded out in his rubber boots and against the declining sun he made an unforgettable picture as he scooped up pigeons, all unbanded, of course, we'd been careful to look closely at a few before we got going, and started throwing them into a woolpack he'd brought over for the job. The wildlife authorities had tried to clean them out of the rocks, we came to learn, but they'd found it too hard to control their numbers, and every limp bird was a gift Ray hadn't expected. Suddenly, with the last of them still left to gather, he jumped in his vehicle and roared away in the direction of his sheds.

It wasn't clear to us why he'd bolted, but we broke down the guns and finished tidying up, packing the birds in the bag he left with us, and followed him over to find the place where he wanted these possibly poison-fed birds to be left.

There he was, less wide-eyed than before, solemn, still running with sweat by then on the way to mud, brown as a tree, and gravely waiting for us to pull into the yard. He was like a grimy traffic policeman as he pointed us to a stop outside a Moreton Bay fig tree outside his sprawling, cluttered and filthy work shed, located a domestically suitable distance from the house. To enter too roughly seemed like it would've brought it all down around our ears, so we went in gingerly, as he stomped ahead and made the way.

With a gravity he hadn't previously seemed capable of, he motioned us deeper into his hideaway. There, as the sun set on the dusty summer landscape, still croaky, he solemnly uttered one word — 'Gentlemen!' — and with a flourish in a style any head waiter would be proud of, he swept in front of us with an ornate silver tray, and handed the two of us large crystal bowls, in which there reposed generous servings of white crab meat nestled on beds of fresh green lettuce. The forks, too, were solid silver.

It was then I noticed the filthy old refrigerator in the corner. All the rest, the serving-ware, was a marvel too complex to brood on. I asked him nothing, just accepted it, though I mentally connected the white crab flesh with the big boat sitting in a shed we'd passed. We ate as though it was the most natural thing in the world, to stand chairless and eat a gourmet dish in the bowels of a musty hovel while coated in a mixture of sweat, grime and feathers. He waited in complete silence till we'd both finished every morsel of it, and took the tray from us.

In his oddly formal way, he then invited us back again, and seeing we were to be in the district another week, obviously we accepted. The two of us spoke at the same time, stopped and began again, when we consented to come. With that kind of start, it seemed fair to say, we'd both worked out it'd have to be too good to miss.

Ray

Part Two - A View from the Front Line

Ray had decided to live in those rubber boots after he dropped a farm implement on himself and damaged his foot so it was badly misshapen; less flexible footwear was never again to suit him. Many would find it hard to think of a misfortune like that, just another of the numerous hazards of farming that we in the insulated city don't have to pay attention to.

He'd had to sell off his property bit by bit, to stay afloat, and over the years its boundary fences shrank in retreat as market gardens and hobby farms encroached on the district. It must have been like a defeat for Ray.

Softly spoken, vehement and intelligent, he seemed to be just the living example of the battler. His skills, like those of so many farmers, were diverse, and he could turn his hand to anything. He was politically informed, and astute, too, as folk on the land often are. He was an incongruous man, as anyone would've seen if they'd stumbled on him lying half buried in some truck repair job, wearing the inevitable rubber boots and shorts, and struck up a conversation with him.

At best this is only part explanation of why he didn't tell my mate and me about the pig sty, though.

We went back four days after we met him, as we said we would, and the crop he'd been trying to protect from that huge flock of pigeons was looking a touch ragged. Couldn't be helped, he said; he'd tried. He came out briefly to be polite, and then he was gone, that second time we were there, and we separated along an old fence line to shoot what we could of these persistent feral raiders that had spent the whole time regrouping.

We were a long shouting distance apart, and there were enough birds to shoot at to keep us busy, so I didn't pay all that much attention to what my mate was doing. I'd heard his gun discharging, and just when it was that I stopped hearing it I'm not sure.

I turned around when I was no longer conscious of it, and I saw him a hundred paces or so from where I'd left him, beside an old, thatched pig sty built in the days of Ray's father. He didn't have many pigs, just a few, and many of the sties were unoccupied. This one stood aside from the others, and it was obvious my mate had gone over to it looking for cover so that the incoming birds wouldn't discern his outline.

As I watched, he started to perform a cute little dance. I can't say it was something that I was accustomed to watching him get up to in a paddock.

I did a double take. At first I couldn't see what it was all about, but then I saw him run a dozen quick and jerky steps to the stock trough nearby, and to my surprise, though the wind was quite cool, unlike the way it had been a few days before, he started to tear off his clothes. His arms were going like a windmill, and there was something frantic in his gestures, but they weren't ones being made to me. He was fully self-absorbed. There were birds flying over his head and I opened my mouth to warn him almost by reflex, as though they were the ducks we often shot together. Then I realized that I couldn't even see his gun, so it had to be lying on the ground somewhere, and I knew then he must've been in trouble.

I made my way over as quickly as I could. He'd moved close to the abandoned sty, all right, and he was black, his whole body a seething mass of fleas. I've never seen anything like it. He couldn't fling himself in the stock trough because there wasn't enough water in it, so he had to content himself with hopping crazily from leg to leg while he wrenched off all his clothes and lashed his limbs and trunk with a hastily wetted shirt. It seems that it's a known phenomenon that fleas inhabit old-fashioned thatch sties after the pigs have stopped using them. It was high summer, when fleas are very active.

He was off work for a week, and the whole time he shivered and broke out in hot sweats alternately. In his misery, he counted, and he had one thousand four hundred and fourteen flea bites. Twelve months later the hot sweats would still come on him without warning, drench him and leave him shaking, maybe with a fever, particularly at night — and just possibly at the very memory of the day.

Ray strolled out later and cackled quietly when we told him what'd happened. "Ahhh, the fleas, that'd be right. I meant to mention that...."

But that's not what I really remember him for, either. The episode with the fleas should've warned me.

The next week, though we'd left the district at the end of our holiday, I took the trouble to make the drive back alone. I'd liked the shooting. The pigeons were still flying. They were bound to have been, as long as there was anything of that crop left standing so close to the bird infestation.

Ray, cackling, happy to see me, took me to a wide open paddock not far behind the house, and showed me how it was possible to see the flight line of the feral pigeons coming from their rocky cliff faces on the sea shore half a mile away. They'd come in and turn into the paddock not far from where he left me, and make ready to land in what was left of his crop.

This time armed with a closer-bored gun, I picked off a couple of high passing birds while Ray watched, and again I saw that transported gleam in his eye when they puffed feathers and fell out of the air. I thought he was going to stay again, as he had when we shot in the paddock south of the treeline a fortnight before, but I looked and he'd gone without delay.

Leaving me to it, I thought, in the interests of efficiency, and I reloaded, making a mental note to switch from trap loads to some sixes if the next birds didn't come in lower.

I must've had twenty or more birds on the ground with that many more having flown on, saluted, when Ray suddenly bobbed up in front of me, having come up along a fold in the ground from the house.

"How are you?" he called. "You all right?"

"Never better," I yelled back, reloading, and didn't wait for a reply as I shot another high incomer. I looked down to where he'd been, but he'd gone as suddenly as he came.

It occurred to me that he wasn't showing the same interest as he had at first, but I had my hands full, and I was enjoying myself too much to worry.

About the same time elapsed, and then I heard him call again. This time he'd come up a different way, and he was behind an old tank when I turned and looked for him over my shoulder.

"How are you? You all right?"

Action re-run. "Yes, Ray, I'm fine." Then he was gone.

The birds weren't as suicidal, that was obvious, but I was still getting good shooting, if harder than before. It kept me too occupied to wonder what he was up to when he turned up again with the same question.

"How are you? All right out there?" This time he called from beside a tree, further back than he had been last time, and at first I couldn't place him. I had to scan the horizon, past the outbuildings, past the only other dwelling in my field of vision, a big house just outside the borders of the property and getting on for three hundred yards away.

At the time I couldn't help but wonder at the number of feral birds that were there. A few years before, there'd been an uproar in the district when somebody'd finally given in under the strain and laid serious, heavy-duty poison, leaving raptors and dogs and Lord only knows what else dead in the swathe it cut through the food chain. They'd never caught him. I thought how clean an option shooting is when compared to that, and I was settling into the task with relish when there he was again.

"Hey," he called, "are...?"

"Yes, Ray," I interrupted; "I'm fine. Come on over."

But he wouldn't, just slipped away again, leaving me to do what I was good at, I thought, a bit smugly, amused by then. It didn't occur to me what he was up to.

When it drew to a close, I tidied up the slain on my own that day, and when I'd finished I wandered back to the sheds to find him and pay my dues.

He was in the yard and saw me coming. He seemed to brighten up, somehow. He called to me.

"How are you? All right?"

"Ray," I said, "I'm fine. In the pink. Happy as a hog in a wallow. Sparking on all six. What'd you expect?"

He gave such a jump when I said that that I suddenly knew I was onto something. He seemed guilty.

"Why wouldn't you come out today, Ray?" I asked him, and he stumbled when he tried to reply, and he started to stammer a bit.

"Hey, come on," I said, "do *you* ever shoot your own pigeons when you're getting in strife?"

"Yes, yes," he answered, far too quickly for me to be impressed. "Often. Often!"

"Where, Ray? — where we were the first time we came?"

"Ohh, yes," he said, "often out there. Often."

"Where we were last time, then, Ray? Do you shoot there?"

"Ohh, yes," he said, "often out there, too," but I could see he was uneasy and was hoping he'd thrown me off the scent.

"What about today, Ray? Where I was today? Do you shoot a few there as well?"

He threw a nervous look due north. I had him.

No answer.

"What about out there, Ray? Do you go out there?"

I had him stuttering.

"Well, I.... er.... don't go shooting.... er.... there.... er.... all that much...."

Again the nervous look to the north. There was nothing there but a straggling last bird, pink in the setting sun, and that lone house.

"Why don't you shoot there, Ray? Why not?"

He shifted his gum boots in the dust and he fiddled with the single button remaining on his shorts, as again I saw his eyes dart to the north.

"Is it that house, Ray?" I asked, and I saw it hit home. "Is it your neighbour?"

"You're all right, aren't you?" he came back at me, for the dozenth time that day, as if he didn't know. He could see I was fine. He had a crop under such attack that it had just about been lifted out of the ground while he watched. Here he had a tame shooter who fell on him full of goodwill, and attended to the problem for him out of civic pride and a certain peevish dislike of pigeons gone wild. I know how they can breed. About every two months if they really get going.

"Come out there with me next weekend, Ray," I said, "and we'll roll a few together."

"Well, now, next weekend," he said, "what day in particular would that be...?" as he started to hedge.

I went in for the kill.

"That neighbour of yours over there, Ray," I said, nodding northwards, and I saw him flinch, "what is he?"

"What is he?"

"Yeah. What is he? What exactly is he?"

"Well, ahh.... Well, he's back now."

"He's what?"

"He's back now. He was away. On holidays."

"That's well and good, Ray," I said, "but that's not what I asked. I asked what he is."

"Well, he's.... ahh.... he's.... a birdlover."

The light came on.

"A birdlover, Ray?"

"Oh, yes," he said, a little relieved it was out. "He's definitely a birdlover. Quite definitely. He's certainly a birdlover."

"Well, then, Ray," I said, "he might like feral pigeons, would he, then?"

"Ohh, yes, yes," he said, emphatically, "he certainly likes pigeons. But you're quite all right, aren't you?"

"Ray," I said, "of all the things we've established this fine day, the first of them, the foremost, numero uno, is that I've never been better in my life. I'm hale and I'm hearty. I'm on top of the world. Now, tell me, what is there about that house over there" — and he winced again — "that makes you think I shouldn't be?"

"Well," he said, trapped, looking wildly round him, "well.... I've occasionally — er, *very* occasionally — ahh.... found that.... er.... while shooting pigeons in that particular paddock.... which as you can see is in full view of his house.... er.... that he.... er.... does have a bit of a tendency to shoot at me a little with his .303...."

The Man Who Shot Alone

He hadn't thought of him for years, but one day he went to a sporting clays shoot, and there he was. They'd shot together in the past and just fallen out of touch. There are those we have more in common with; they're the ones we don't seem to grow apart from so readily.

Anyway, there he was, after all that time. He was standing up as large as life when Doug went to pay his nomination fee. Doug was half way down the gravel path that went to the canteen, kitted up ready to shoot, when he suddenly appeared, off to one side, looking pensive. It was a surprise, though a pleasant one.

At first, Doug thought they saw each other simultaneously, but when he reflected on it afterwards it occurred to him it could have been that he was spotted first. However it happened, they soon found themselves at a table in the canteen catching up on history. They covered guns in a few minutes, talked recent dogs, and before they knew it a half an hour had gone. They decided they'd better nominate if they wanted to shoot, because it was getting late.

He looked a bit embarrassed when they stood up — Doug noticed it straight away.

"Hell," he said, "I'm goin' mad. I left my wallet on the bench at home with my handicap card. A man's lucky to remember the gun."

No problems. Doug was pleased to be able to help out. It was almost a way of saying to a mate that he was glad to have caught up with him after all that time.

So that he wouldn't feel at odds, Doug told him that for the day he wouldn't bother entering the competition himself, and he'd shoot clays-only as well. He went and paid the money for both of them, and arranged for them both to go into the same squad while his new-found old friend went and collected his gun and cartridges from his car.

They didn't have too bad a shoot, considering, and it went fairly smoothly for Doug. He hit most of what was thrown for him, and when they finished their first round he was wishing he hadn't been shooting clays-only because he thought he might've won something.

His old mate didn't shoot too badly, either, though Doug was pleased to see that he had the edge. By the end of the day Doug had the idea that his friend wasn't really as good at the sporting clays business as Doug was. He just slowly picked up the notion, for some reason. Maybe it was because he didn't have all that much idea of the cartridges he needed. When the target to be taken was a close one, Doug had some special skeet loads that worked a treat, and he offered some to his mate, who looked a bit sheepish but took them and did pretty well on the stations where he needed them. Doug had a few heavy loads he kept for the second barrel on the long shots; he shared those as well.

At the end of the afternoon they stood around having the usual yarn, and before Doug knew it they were making arrangements to do a trip away to a quail paddock the following weekend. At some stage, Doug happened to say that he still loved to shoot quail. His mate had sparked up at that and said he had a good quail paddock working, but the only trouble with it was that it was a fair distance away, but as long as Doug didn't mind travelling a bit for his birds, well, he'd been looking forward to having a go at it, kind of saving it up a bit... And so Doug agreed, and they finished making their plans before they went their ways from the target ground.

As his mate was driving away, and Doug was opening the door of his car, a fellow who knew them both a bit, but not a lot, walked past him and grinned at him, and shook his head. His name was Ernie. Doug always reckoned he was a bit of a know-all. At least, that's what he told himself.

"He shoots on his own. Don't you know that?" Ernie said this over his shoulder, and he laughed. Then he kept walking. Doug decided that whatever this meant, he wasn't going to pay any attention.

****

The following weekend he rolled up bright and early to the appointed address. In a tangle of guns and slips and shooting jackets and vacuum flasks, his old mate greeted him warmly and they discussed the road they were going to have to take, what time they'd be back, and which dogs they were going to leave behind and why. If they chattered and repeated themselves and fussed around a bit before they went out for a day behind a good pointer, they wouldn't be the first to get excited at the prospects they saw in a cloudless day without the worries of work.

Doug was just about to raise the question of which vehicle they ought to take when his old friend brought it up himself. It seems that he had a utility truck that he'd brought home from work. It was his to do what he wanted with on the weekend, and there was no sense in using a private car for the job if the boss was kind enough to smile on them this way.... He grinned his easy smile and before ten minutes had passed they were rolling out the front gate, hoping they hadn't forgotten anything.

They'd discussed the destination in detail. His mate seemed to be very keen to make sure that Doug knew exactly where they were going to, and Doug was impressed with this, taking it as a sign of confidence in him. We're all prone to suffer from the idea that somebody's going to steal our best shooting spots. Evidently his mate was showing him a lot of trust.

They had to go all the way to the state border. It was a long trip, and they needed to step along on the highway and make a mile if they were to get some serious shooting done that day. They'd only been driving three minutes and his mate turned to Doug, looked him full in the eye, and yawned loudly. Two minutes later he did it again. Another minute passed, and he yawned a third time.

Unexpectedly he'd flicked the wheel, directing the vehicle off the road and onto the apron. "Geez, I'm tired," he said, and yawned again. "I think you'd better drive."

In a moment he bounded out of the driver's seat, flicked his long legs a couple of times and appeared at the passenger door. Doug took the hint. He slid across behind the wheel, positioned the seat, adjusted the rear vision mirror and then was ready to take over. He hoped his mate wasn't coming down with an autumn virus of some sort, but he seemed to make himself comfortable there in the passenger seat and in the space of about four beats of a quail's wing his mouth was wide open and he was snoring happily.

In settling himself into the long drive, Doug ran his eye over the unfamiliar instrument panel, looking at the dials, and he saw the clock, noted the time, checked the heat gauge, which was fine, picked up the chest of a big, brown dog in the mirror — he looked fine, too, riding well back there in the nest they'd made for him — and then his eye fell on the fuel gauge. It was right on empty.

His mate had gone out like a light. He didn't want to stop, because he might wake him, and he obviously needed forty winks, he'd gone out to it so fast. There seemed nothing for it; he'd have to stop and risk waking him. No choice. Otherwise they'd never get there. He pulled in at the first service station he saw, and succeeded in keeping the dog quiet, despite the doberman lurking in the shadow just inside the door of the garage. He was pleased with himself for that. He was a considerate man, Doug.

Over two hours later, they pulled into the last turn, a dirt road they'd both discussed back in town, and the sleeping beauty woke and stretched.

"That feels better," he said happily, and then, looking around: "Where are we? — ahh, nearly there. Good."

Doug was glad he felt better. He thought they were going to have a successful hunt, and he didn't want anything to ruin it.

They did have one. Permission arranged by telephone in advance, they had no need to waste time, and once at the paddock they were behind the dog in a few minutes. The birds started to rise, and they shot in good harmony. Doug didn't take long to be glad they'd decided to make the effort of the trip.

By the time they sat down to an early lunch, they had nearly half their bags and looked like wrapping the day up successfully. There hadn't been a cloud on the horizon, and Doug found himself wondering why his companion didn't do more of his shooting in company. Because it was true. He wasn't ever invited around to the houses of the fellows he shot with, by the sound of it, not even to their reloading sessions in the inevitable backyard sheds, and none of the regulars talked about passing a Saturday afternoon with him. He remembered what Ernie had said. He shoots on his own. But yet he knew what to do. His dog was trained. He could hold up his end when it came to shooting a fast bird, too. And his gear was beautiful. It was a best gun he was shooting, worth a pretty penny. It had the characteristics of a riddle.

Soon it was the end of their short lunch break, and they stood up to go back to work. Doug couldn't help himself. He grinned at the pleasure of it, watching scudding clouds and feeling the cool autumn breeze, and when he suddenly became aware that his mate was frowning, he had to ask what the problem was.

"Ah, there's a nice little lot of birds here, Doug," he said. "I wasn't expecting so much shooting. I've just run out of nines. Thought I had more, but they must be in the other car at home."

Doug was happy to help out, and said he had plenty. It was a fine day, and it was a pleasure to be able to stand by a friend he hadn't known was his. He picked a couple of boxes out of the back of the ute and handed them over, and away they went.

When they finished the day, the birds all cleaned and packed, the dog long since asleep, they were happy men, and if he was tired on the way home his mate didn't show it. He drove the work utility all the way without a hitch. They arrived home in good time, not all that long after dark, which would've pleased their wives, as well, and if Doug had been asked how to have a more pleasant outing, he wouldn't have been able to say. He picked up his own car and gave a warm goodbye to his mate; they each kept a bag of prime, fat quail, and he doubted if it could've worked out any better.

He was at another sporting clays shoot the following week. Pulling up at the top of the hill, he was pleased because through the windscreen he saw his mate, standing down on the flat below him, looking a bit tentative, near the nominations desk outside the canteen.

As he stepped from the car, it was Ernie he heard, though, again, his raucous voice booming all over the ground.

"Howyergoin', Dougie? Hear you did some quail shootin'. Whaddyer reckon? Does he still shoot alone?"

This was more than annoying to Doug. He stood up out of the car and he was just about to tell Ernie a few things, but as he did, down the hill he saw his old friend give a little start and a hesitant wave as he obviously saw someone he knew, going to nominate for the day's competition. He saw the long figure sidling up to him and his head bobbing and weaving as he got closer.

Ernie followed his gaze down the hill.

"Does he still shoot on his own, then, Dougie, or did you fall for it?"

"Fall for what? What do you mean?" Doug asked, not so snappy now, watching the scene down the hill, thinking he'd seen it somewhere before, as the new man his old mate had nailed was taking out his wallet, looking distinctly cornered.

"Did you fall for it?" Ernie boomed again, grinning. "He's the meanest man in town. Did you fall for the old "Hell-I'm-tired-you-better-drive on the empty tank routine?"

A Duck in a Tree

I nearly always like people who come from farms. They have a pleasing air of reality about them, and it's as though they're not in any doubt about what they came from, and what they're going back to when it's all over, for that matter.

He had that quality of acceptance and he came from a farm. He had lots of encouragement to shoot. They all helped him, the neighbours, his brothers, his uncles, his father perhaps more than all. The reason they all shot was possibly a little more complex than the glib thought that struck me when he was talking: they all grew up hunting because they all grew up eating.

There was certainly that in it, too. There were quite a few mouths to feed, and the river was wide and it was close. A walk there with a gun would yield a few rabbits, the odd duck. Sometimes when the water spread out, it would even produce a few snipe.

His father was unlike many farmers who brought their families up to hunt only for the pot, though, because he shot quail. A bird this size was thought by many to be not worth the hunting. Little do they know.... This fact suggested to me that this father in particular had a good grasp of the subtlety of what is taught by flats and tussocks, valleys and standing water, to young people who walk them carefully with a gun in hand.

Anyway, he had no shortage of teachers and no dearth of opportunities, this boy, and he had the time and the will, so in his lifetime he shot a lot and he came to do it better than most.

Naturally, in the beginning it wasn't so. At first, as it is with all of us, there was a little slot in his head that was readying itself to take the key of the hunt, which had to go in and be given a half turn, so that one day he'd find himself with a code of ethics and a set of values to shape and test what he was to go on and experience afterwards in the field with others like himself.

This happens to many of us, but it isn't always a load of fun. Any lesson life has to teach us might be a painful one, and it is life and death that the hunter deals with, after all.

It was a .410 his father gave him, and with it came the solemn instruction over a long period to the effect that it was a man's right to hunt, but it came with responsibilities. It was a little gun, but it had been made to kill, and it was for serious purposes. All this he had learnt as part of the family's currency. When he was duly deemed fit to take it out alone without shooting his foot off, he soon fell into the way of patrolling the river and walking the flats after game. In early mornings on weekends and after school at dusk he covered all the property, and peering in the tussocks from time to time he'd roll a rabbit or even two, and when his mother saw a rabbit or hare after his bigger brother had helped him skin it behind the tool shed she'd yelp with a delight he remembers to this day, and his father would wink at him when the stew was being ladled out; perhaps it was just his imagination that the piece on his plate would be bigger than even his father's.

One afternoon he was walking as quietly as he knew how through the fallen timber by the side of the river when he just happened to look up. He wasn't in the habit of it, because he'd never found much in the sky to shoot, but this time he did, and to his surprise he saw he was being watched by a black duck sitting on a heavy branch beside a hole in the trunk of a tree.

It seemed high to him, but it was well within the range of the little gun, and when he flicked it to his shoulder and fired, the duck never knew what hit it.

He took it home and met his father in the yard. Swinging it jauntily, he expected that evening to be the focus of a lot of well deserved attention, as he had always been with the rabbits he'd brought home before. Unlike them, ducks were real game; his father and his uncles went out duck shooting on a few special occasions each year, and he wasn't so slow that he hadn't sensed the way they used the duck as a yardstick to define how good somebody was as a shot. Here he was, with a duck of his own, and he'd never even been allowed to shoot with the men yet! Surely he would, now.

He remembers his father saw him coming as he entered the yard, and stopped what he was doing, and he emptied his hands slowly, deliberately dusting them off on the backs of his thighs. He approached his boy as though there was a load on his mind, and asked how he came by the bird. His voice was grave.

He didn't raise it, and he didn't upbraid or scold. He just pointed out that it was springtime, and he asked the boy exactly where the duck had been when he shot it. When the boy explained, he dropped down on his haunches, and he talked to him in the voice he usually reserved to tell him about funerals, acts of bravery in the war, and family secrets. It's notable the way the boy remembered that tone of voice long after he became a man whose own children had grown up and left home.

What his father told him was that it was out of season, that seasons were declared for good reason, that the black duck was sitting beside her nest, that there were chicks or at least eggs in that hole the boy had described as being next to her, that just as undoubtedly they would now die, and that even more inexorably there was nothing anybody anywhere could ever do about it — except never, never do it again.

He related all this to me, this boy no longer, as though it was yesterday. Running his eye up the wall of the room we were in and gazing at the ceiling, he said that even now he could look up and see that hole in the tree any time he liked. I believed him.

He said a couple more things. He told me that his father explained the shame of wasting meat, and decreed they'd eat the duck, but only because it was there and it was fresh, not because it was right; it was just more wrong to throw it away, seeing it was already dead.

The other point he made to me was subtler than that. He said that in his long shooting life, he'd had the opportunity to take a lot of ducks. In those days of a long time ago, in some quarters there wasn't all that much notice paid to the formal dates of the hunting season; nevertheless, he said, that solitary hen black duck that appeared unexpectedly by a hole in a tree above the head of a boy with a .410 had saved the lives of a lot of chicks in time to come.

I asked him how she tasted.

"Sour," he said.

And I thought to myself that it needed a good father to wait for the right spring day to find the hunting slot in the head of a boy, and see the key, in this case a black duck, and then give it half a turn.

Doing it Right

I saw a black labrador working the other day. It was a bitch, sleek and lean in a way many are not. I suppose that was because she's owned by somebody who cares about her enough to discipline her eating.

Oh, but she could retrieve. She went straight out, but she never did it before she should. She came directly back, with the bird undamaged, every time, and the things that happened in between would send a duck purist misty-eyed with emotion.

Many dogs can retrieve, but the heavy-duty waterfowlers who live on black duck just love the labrador, and there's good reason for that. Over the years they've made themselves an unparalleled reputation. There's just a style they have, an application and grace that those who haven't seen are left the poorer for.

It may not look like it takes a certain view of the world to be a dog that rides in a punt or sits in a hide, and then in a flurry of mud and the water shaken from a sodden coat gives up a bird to her master. It may not look like it takes patience to sit by a pair of legs in waders, belly down on black ooze, head down on command, even the lively tail under orders to be still.

No, it may not look like it, but it does. It takes love, trust, loyalty, even flair. When I stood up in the hide to take a teal on the curl, if I was silly enough to miss

I wouldn't soon forget what I'd see when I next looked down into those big, brown eyes. A man can only stand so much reproach.

I don't know what made my companion ask me why I so much love dogs. It'd suit me best if he somehow saw it in the way I watched her work, or in the way I must've smiled when she brought a big, robust bird to his hand, and gave it up to him as a matter of honour and pride, and not duty or habit.

Some time there, along in the morning and between birds, he did ask me, and we sat in silence as men do in duck hides, and bit by bit the question worked itself along in my mind, towards a place where a coherent answer lay. I sensed it was true, but as it so often is, till challenged on it I'd never properly thought about it. He was right. I don't just like dogs. They mean more to me than that.

Why hide it? It must've been obvious anyway. But I couldn't come up with much of an answer at the time because I didn't know the reason. I'd left my own at home, so I could let him work his, and I'd done it as a mark of respect. Perhaps he understood that; it would please me if he had. So I did try to tell him, and if I can remember properly, it didn't come out all that convincingly. I think I stumbled around amongst a few issues like faithfulness, steadiness and training, and maybe I hinted at style and practicality and simplicity. All the same, I knew I hadn't hit on it just then, in the field, the deeper reason.

That came later, in the restless dark when I was supposed to be asleep, just before I went out again a week or two later, to shoot over another good dog, the real reason thrown up by the subconscious, almost in a dream state, just the fates making good and sure that I didn't go on thinking it's too simple. It never is.

****

It was twenty-five years ago. Thirty. I was doing something different, then, and as it happened it was playing jazz in various dives and places where people go for entertainment. This particular one was on the coast of New South Wales, in a holiday town, and it was New Year's Eve, not my favourite day of the year. There are too many people out of control, and it makes me prickly when I see it.

The town was — and probably still is, though I haven't been there awhile — a long, strung-out affair, with two clubs that sold a similar brand of merrymaking. It was perhaps a bit over two kilometres along a straight stretch of highway between the farthest points of the town, and both these were clubs, open till the early hours, and till I don't know when on a New Year's morning.

The crowd was just getting wound up when a man came in with a seeing-eye dog that sat patiently by him at the bar. Where there's a stage with some elevation, the band can see it all. He drank steadily for three hours, and when he was properly drunk, the barman at last set out to put an end to it by refusing to serve him any more, and quietly telling him to go home.

At about this time I asked someone who knew him what was behind it all, why he was blind, where he came from.

It seemed he'd been a well respected builder, and one day he was driving his work vehicle when for some reason he lost control of it, and it rolled. He was carrying building materials in the back, and a bag of lime, of all things, was what came through the window at him. Possibly that was what knocked him out. At any rate, when he came to, it had broken over his face, and his eyes were gone.

The locals, in the spirit of small communities everywhere, had rallied around him, and they bought him a seeing-eye dog. It was a black labrador bitch.

On this night, he didn't so much walk up and down in front of the bar; he paced and soon he started stalking. He called for more, but the barman stuck to his decision. In time, he began to rage, but it didn't work and he still got nothing.

Finally, he delivered his ultimatum to the embarrassed staff. If they wouldn't serve him, then he'd take his business elsewhere.

The only other elsewhere was at the end of the two kilometres of dark highway, and he and his dog were used to walking so he wasn't intimidated by it. It was an hour or two into the new year, and revellers raced up and down the roads. There was no lighting. A warm, dense rain had started from a thickly clouded sky, and the man turned to his dog and told her that he wanted her to take him to the other club.

By this time, the place had gone progressively quieter. Movement slowed, 'St Louis Blues' came to a grudging stop, and in a moment he flared, this joyless and angry man. He was wearing black, symbol of his own melancholy, and his clothing matched his dog, who was his best friend, though sadly I knew he'd never seen her.

It's even conceivable she had a sense of her own blackness, as well. She'd heard the rain, and for perhaps the first time in my life it occurred to me as it would do often enough afterwards that intelligence is a far cry from knowledge. It was very, very dark outside.

There's an echo of his raucousness in my mind, his roaring at her, hoarse, gauche, a figure of pity, and my inner ear still hears his strident insistence to be taken to the other club, to be in the rain, to be in the dark, to run the gauntlet of the long, wet road and with her by his side, the two of them to be splashes of black on black.

She wouldn't do it, that proud little labrador. She took him into every wall in the building, but not to the exit. He ranted at her, and she patiently threaded her way around the floor to take him to yet another corner where there was no door.

It was then that he hit her. Around the whole of the open area there was a hiss of breath taken in, people disconcerted; some shifted from one foot to the other, and some looked away. Hitting her didn't work, and she led him to another corner, still mutely disobeying him, despite the blows that turned into a savage beating.

She set her face and bore it. Eventually, someone took her away from him.

****

So there it is. It may not add a lot to the sum of human happiness, but it's an honest description of the time when I saw a fork in a road, and a dog went down one path while a human took the other.

In the finely etched profile alongside waders grey-black in near-frozen mud, I admired in a labrador bitch a quality I saw once before, powerful enough to make me love dogs. I could say that it was just another case of the dumb animal remembering what the developed human had forgotten. But I believe I can do most justice to it if I stop after describing it as purity of purpose, that's all.

Two Pensioners

Economically it may not make all that much sense for a pensioner to shoot quail for the pot, not with the cost of ammunition, fuel, and the wear and tear on the car. Perhaps even less so when the german shorthair he used was close to being a pensioner, too, all of eleven and with a limp that troubled her more than occasionally. But he did, or, rather, they did, and never a bird was wasted. Sometimes they'd take their Victorian limit of twenty and it was hard to tell which of the two of them was the more content.

It was another of those perfect life-matches, the kind where nature's done the work and spectators are welcome to come along afterwards as long as they don't ruin things by talking. Because that's what it was between these two pensioners, man and dog, she of what he called the choke-bore nose. They suited each other only too well.

George had been looking out carefully, he told me wrily, for April the 18th, his 84th birthday, because they'd promised him a full bottle of lemonade. It happened that the quail season was open; just as well the 18th didn't fall on a Saturday, or he'd have been the only one not at his party. He told me he did end up receiving the gift all right, but he enjoyed the one he had on the Saturday even more.

He said that nobody's too old to learn, and he was one of the very few people

I've ever come across who was able to say this unashamedly and mean it. His birthday came round on the Sunday, but the day before, just as you'd expect, he had the other pensioner out with him in a paddock somewhere doing what they both did best.

Stinkweed, it was, and very heavy. On this occasion, when she pointed, he did what he'd always done, just barely consciously checked the wind, and went in confidently, gun at port, finger lying by the triggerguard and thumb on the safety, with his eyes well up, expecting the bird to spring high and be caught by his peripheral vision.

Nothing.

He stepped back and forward in front of the dog's nose, and the movement would usually be expected to flush the tightest sitter, but instead of that, or the dog moving up to follow a dislodged bird that had started to run, she stayed resolutely still and refused to change her mind.

In the exchange that took place while they were trying to educate each other about the matter, he mentioned to her more than once that the marriage lines of her parents were in significant doubt, but she held to her point of view. She waited till he'd done all the man-things, like trying to nudge her off the point, making to walk away and calling her, dropping down beside her to peer into the tangle of weed she was pointing, and finally in desperation heading downwind in a curve to see if the bird had moved out of her scenting range and foxed her.

She just stayed on. When she'd had enough of his silliness and she was sure he was watching, she burrowed her head deep, then deeper into the tangled weed, and came up with a quail chick the size of an acorn, which she presented to him ever so gently, her tongue arched, holding it up and out at him completely unruffled and healthy, and the look on her face he could only describe to me as being supercilious.

In the hope of avoiding further humiliation from her, he didn't let her see when he released the chick as closely as he could to where it came from. And not wanting to intrude any further on this disconcertingly late-season feathered family, as he stood up slowly from his creaky knees he prepared himself to creep away from the scene and hunt somewhere else. A man looks silly going out of a paddock on tip-toe, he told me later. Even as he rose he was making up his excuses so he wouldn't have to hurt her feelings. He thought he might kid her back to the vehicle for an early lunch, and pull the wool over her eyes that way.

When he stood, casting around the horizon trying to spot her moving form, he discovered she'd already taken herself from the paddock, no cradle-snatcher, thinking perfectly well for herself that it was not an appropriate place to be working in, and he hadn't seen her at once because she was sitting quietly at the fence waiting for his command to be allowed through it, when he finally got round to catching up with her.

He asked me ruefully which of these pensioners was educating which, enjoying every delicious moment of the tale, but it was a rhetorical question, and all I could say to him was that when I'm his age, I hope I have half her sense of humour, half his good grace — and that there are still dogs so fine.

Henry — a Correspondence

There's an old cleaning rod of highest quality that lies across the back of my workbench, which is where it will always stay. It's ebony, for a shotgun, one-piece, and so without the more usual brass ferrule for a joint, midway.

It came to me from Henry's estate, passed on to me by his widow. I sold a couple of guns for her, and she wanted me to have a memento for myself, so I took that, and gratefully. Henry had already given me something else, and I didn't want to seem selfish.

It had all begun when he wrote to me on the recommendation of a mutual friend in a warmly restrained and unmistakably English style about some small reloading problem that he thought I might be able to help him with. His first letters held drawings of parts of his reloading press, meticulous, orderly representations of an unusually focused mind. We exchanged letters; before long they contained other representations, philosophical ones, and I admit that in my own there were invitations, to draw him on. Soon I found myself incorporated into the company of someone who was to stand out in my life, and yet we never met.

I knew and trusted Henry from the first, and it didn't seem necessary to meet him. I found out about his wife's dogs, his holiday house, the touch of arthritis in his hands. He went to pains to photograph his guns and send me pictures, and we discussed the provenance of his little Franc Sodia ejector game gun, bought new from Ferlach when he went there after the war to track down Nazi war criminals, which he did for five years.

Its quality was a sign of his own refinement. Only the old men, the most skilled, were left in that quarter at the time to manufacture guns, the young having had their training ruined by their going off to fight, and the few pieces they did produce over that period were very fine. He had it handmade to order for his father, and sent it home, only to inherit it himself in due course. The cleaning rod had belonged to his father, so was much older.

The subjects we covered at first dealt with this country's pathetic politics, but then went back as far as Napoleon, of whom he wrote with a surprising depth of knowledge, and in his understanding of Wellington I soon caught more than a whiff of martial insight. He took me on a whirlwind tour of history, and I found myself happy to go. He taught me what I suspected, that politics have never been especially different from the way they are here, now.

In time I found that he had fought in the Special Air Service in World War Two, and had been captured by the Nazis. He wrote only sketchily about his war, temperately, with a neutrality and an understatement that masked his experience. He wrote of being 'questioned', but he neglected to stipulate the unspeakable things that were done to him, and these I had to find out later.

He tended to relate a lot of his war experience to the hunt, but in retrospect that was possibly just his way of ensuring that I understood without being patronized. It's rare for the truly erudite to talk of instinct. Perhaps it offends their sense of procedure. But Henry did, and he told, for instance, of the way that Diana leads the modern shotgun shooter to the flight path, and that observation marries with instinct to put him under the bird. He wrote of this not to make me an instant expert on mythology; he wanted instead to order his own reflections on the time he led a raid on a suspected enemy radio installation in Italy, when on a hunch of foreboding that he never could explain, he pulled up his small force and, instead of going in, ordered that they keep watch on it, an isolated farmhouse, for all of a day before proceeding, and then to their surprise when evening fell they saw six times their own number of enemy file out of it, and away from the ambush they had nearly walked into. Diana indeed.

So at that time, I didn't know exactly what they'd done to him, the Nazis, but I found out later. To use the words I was given, they'd passed their time 'altering his dentition', bit by bit, while he was held captive in a cell.

There was no bitterness in him, though. His intriguing mail revealed to me an insightful observer of late middle age. Hunters, I had cause to reflect as we wrote, seldom resent death. They understand it only too well, and like others who live close to the rhythms of the earth, they generally find harmony in the picture, and then the gifted among them are capable of conveying it to others. In Henry's case, his dignity never made his gentle teaching ponderous.

****

I drove interstate when he'd judged it was time, and had given permission for them to tell me so by telephone. It was just four months into the year. He'd refused to let me go to him any earlier, and, as it turned out, he managed the whole process just as he wanted it, almost to the minute, certainly to the hour.

When I arrived at the house, I found I was seeing it differently from any of the other times. We'd spent six weeks together just that Christmas, gone back over it all, taken it apart, put it together again, and I'd hugged him long when I left, the first time for many years.

That was why I hadn't been so concerned about not going back until he was ready to send for me. I could have gone anyway, but I respected his wishes and waited till he gave me the nod. It was his venture, after all.

So from the time I had what I knew was the final call I wasted no time and pulled in at five that afternoon, and he thanked the women from the hospice, grinned his cheeky smile, sent them away, and asked that I take him to his chair in the sitting room, and when I did, I turned to the piano beside him, because I didn't know where else to turn, and I played to him his old songs, the jazz standards, in two flats, three flats, four, not many quicksteps because it wasn't the moment for cut time — or so I thought. Instead, I went into ragtime and stayed as long as I could, till my concentration flagged, then Irving Berlin, Gus Kahn, all I could think of that he liked, a last gift from the twenties, with many a diminished chord, and when I looked down it was not yet seven, and I found I was unmoving, focusing for some reason on his hair, nearly white, seeing how it was still thick and waved, and only slowly I realized he'd taken his final leave of me, sitting there beside me, my father.

I had chosen his epitaph, a line from Shakespeare: "Take him for all in all, he was a man, and I shall not see his like again."

****

When this and its consequences were over and I'd returned home, I tried to fall back into my routine, and in catching up with the pile of mail I had to apologize to Henry. I was distracted, I said, and perhaps wasn't myself. Sadness, I found, is a lapping tide of grey. I explained the break in my letter writing, and told him that in time, no doubt, perhaps a few more weeks, I'd focus again and the world would seem the way it used to.

I did relate to him the way my father always spoke of crossing the Styx, with broad humour and a self-deprecating snort. The hospice women in turn had told me their stories of him, and from what they said I decided with gratefulness that they'd ushered him carefully and respectfully to its banks.

I remembered his lessons; he taught me to train a dog. "Not much to it," he'd say. "All you've got to do is be smarter than the dog." He'd grin when he said this, and then the impeccable behaviour of the dog in question would give it the lie for the rest of its life.

My first air gun came back starkly to my mind, an old break-action smoothbore with u-and-post sights, and the endless safety drill, carried out till he was completely sure of my predictability; I was only nine years old, yet when he declared me a safe gun handler he never interfered with my access to it and he never questioned me, nor did he have cause to wish that he had. And I stood taller for it.

Clearest of all were the early competitions we had, he and I in the booming sound shell that was the second floor of the old stable, handmade brick and exposed rafters that turned out to be made of fiddleback blackwood. He set a thin wire from the high crossbeam, the same one the punching bag hung from at the other end, then tied a tin on it, and swung it so I could shoot it moving. "That'll teach you timing," he said, and shot against me each afternoon when he came home from work, before the last light failed. When I could regularly beat him he lost interest because he knew the job was done.

It came back with poignance, that and more.

I went over what I saw one day at his work. No refrigerator available, he and other workers would all put their sandwiches in the same cupboard. He'd buy a bottle of milk and leave it in there as well. In winter, it would keep for two or three days.

One lunchtime they all found their food had been nibbled by a mouse. A long battle to catch it began. He bought a succession of traps, and used every cheese on the market. Then he tried other mouse-delicacies, including his secret weapon, toasted pumpkin seeds. They all failed, and the contest drew on. Nothing was safe in the cupboard.

That morning he came in, and made to pour into his tea mug from an open milk bottle taken from the cupboard. He looked twice and there was a small nose twitching in it just above the milk line. He poured some off and found the mouse;

it had crawled into the bottle, and had survived all night by standing on its toes with its nose out.

He hesitated a few seconds, then poured the milk out and caught the mouse by the tail. He washed it thoroughly under the tap and let it go in the cupboard.

"What else could I do? It stood on its toes all night so it wouldn't drown."

Six weeks later, he caught it in a trap, and honour was satisfied. I pointed out he could've had six weeks of sandwiches not nibbled, but he only said to me I still had to learn the principles of fair chase. I nodded wisely. I was only ten...

When he left, it subtended too much in my life for a while, and I let it buffet me. When it comes to the loss of a parent, no matter how prepared we are, we're not ready, and there's no painless way.

I'd written to Henry in the midst of this, and that's when he sent me the letter, this exercise in wise understatement, that I have in front of me to quote from:

"....Thank you for your letter. I can feel for you over your father's death, but may I say that I am glad that you are able to write as you did.

"I am afraid that the maudlin dictates of present day fashion have tended to hide from many people the simple truth that death is as much a part of life as is birth. I think that your father has been able to show you that one's inner self (call it soul, esse, or what you will) continues to be, though in ways we cannot fully understand, and to take a part in the continuation of all things as needed. I am also very glad that the people in the hospice service were so kind.

"There is a story which I have only told once before, recently.

"When I was a small boy, my father gave me the responsibility for cleaning and looking after my grandfather's service and dress swords (both in metal scabbards, and with the bugle of The Rifles worked into the hilts). I had never known Grandfather, who had died in 1908, though I had a photograph of him as an old man with a grey beard and a panama hat. He had been a very keen and successful rifle shot during his Army days, which I think had a good deal to do with my choice of career.

"When I was in the hands of the Sicherheitspolizei I began to doubt my ability to stand up to their questioning. At the time I supposed I had had a dream — a Captain in Rifles undress uniform, with pillbox hat and side-whiskers, came into my cell one night. He told me to treat my interrogators as ignorant inferiors but to point that out to them with the dignity and courtesy which my commission demanded. He said that there was no need to fear the consequences and that he and others of my family who had served the Crown would be with me, whatever happened. He seemed absolutely confident — and I think some of his confidence must have brushed off. Nothing seemed quite so confused and beastly after that.

"After the war, when I was on leave, I came across an old Regimental group photograph, one of those rigidly posed Victorian ones with names written underneath. I had not seen it before. He was there, a Captain, in the row behind the senior officers seated in chairs. He had sidewhiskers and a shaven chin, the man who had come to see me in my cell — so now I do not know if it was a dream. But that does not matter. However he went about it, he came to help."

Soon after the events described above, while they were shooting all the SAS men, his name was transferred off the death list and his papers falsified by a young Tyrolean woman, an operative in the camp, and in a short time Henry made his escape.

A little while after he sent me this letter, Henry himself died, but I was honoured by being one of only the two people to whom he had ever relayed these events. Now I have both his account of them and his cleaning rod.

It's not a sad reflection for me, this one, but more a celebration of a bond forged in the finer aspect of our common pursuit. He was an extraordinary man. No — they both were.... All three were, if you count the grandfather, and there seems little reason not to. I have no feelings of loss for Henry, but instead an abiding kinship. I wrote to the man who had the good taste to buy Henry's fine little double shotgun, and I fear I might have lectured him a bit, telling him who owned it and what his achievements were. It was important to me. I received a crisp letter from him in reply, which I found gracious because it conveyed a strong sense of the new owner's respect both for the gun and the man who possessed it last. It also reminded me that history is being made all the time. And that's the way it is, not such a hard thing to accept.

Having settled for the cleaning rod from Henry's estate, I then found that his less substantial gift was the more abiding.

I don't expect to see Henry before I cross the Styx myself; I'll probably never be brave enough for him to need to call on me. One thing I'm sure of, though. There's a duck hunter in the other hemisphere caught in a bad tide somewhere now, as it comes onto dusk, and his blood turns cold, the water to his thighs, as far away he believes he hears his wife scream; or there's a soldier in a country whose name I don't know trembling in shock as he squints through the blistering sun and wishes he could just run barefoot on broken glass to get away from what he now may face.

It's true that I have the fine old cleaning rod, made of ebony, but in their extremity, hunter, soldier, as they make a figure out, drifting through the mist, or in shimmer through the mirage, they may find that they have Henry.

Shenandoah

When I was fourteen, I said one day to nobody in particular that I intended to become a musician. My father heard me and he asked what I'd like to start on. I said I was thinking about the harmonica. He looked at me, a bit absently, I thought, and he said something I've never forgotten.

"The mouth organ? Can't everybody play the mouth organ?"

To this day, I don't know whether he was serious, and I can't ask him now.

****

There were many of them during the Depression, in what turned out to be a big clan of sorts, not so much big in the sense that there were a lot of them, but big because it covered such a large part of Australia.

The railway system was their network to nowhere, and in the time after the disappearance of his friend, Alvin, my father went his way alone. On the occasions I questioned him, he said to me nothing in particular of the way he felt about it, but I sensed the confusion he must have felt, even all those years afterwards. It was obviously lonely, an existence of disorienting motion through the world, hand to mouth.

He'd arrived in Sydney in spring, and in the way of the other hemisphere, he'd turned north in the hope of cooler weather. Many months later he'd discovered the error in this, and by then was heading south. He went slowly through New South Wales, always looking for work, and drawing closer to Victoria, he found it was turning greener as he went. It didn't seem to be so for everyone he met.

One day he'd hitched a ride on the tray of a truck. Two or three men were already on it, and they talked to pass the time. Eventually, they began to fall asleep, and in the night, in the manner of men everywhere, there was one who stayed awake because he wanted to open up and speak his thoughts.

His view of life was philosophical. Before long, he told of what it was like for him, his speech freed by the fact that there were only the two of them, and he was unburdening himself to someone he could hardly see in the starlight, and didn't expect ever to meet again. I don't know where he was going, or where he'd come from; none of that was passed to me.

What he did say with surprising candour was that once he had given up hope, that at the time life had become too much for him. He'd been travelling the roads, also alone, in a place not far from Gunnedah, and he'd been camped up there four weeks previously by a big billabong with a distinctive Y-shaped tree holding an eagle's nest at the north end of it.

He'd come upon a robust rope, and he'd suddenly made the dispassionate judgement that this was the day when his troubles would be over. In just a few minutes he could end them all. He'd taken the rope and walked towards to the water, because he had his eye on the big tree with sturdy branches that looked out across it. It's strange how we humans are always drawn to water, no matter what our undertaking. There's something near mystical about its appeal, certainly atavistic.

As he approached the big body of still water, he heard it. A man was sitting on a mound set back from it a few yards, playing 'Shenandoah' on a harmonica. It just floated across, he said, and captivated him. He stopped and in a few moments he'd sat down to listen, as though he didn't have much choice.

When he stood up, a long while later, he threw the rope into the billabong, because he'd decided he no longer had a use for it.

This all came out as he talked about the way things had been for him. He found it hard to explain why, but the experience, he said, just gave him what he needed to go on. And, yes, for some reason my father didn't disclose himself to his new partner in conversation, but indeed he'd been the one who a month before on a mound of earth by a billabong with a distinctive tree outside Gunnedah had sat and watched the sunset each evening, making his way there from his nearby camp, playing out the day and helping in the evening, making music to an audience unseen but approving, and dealing no doubt with his own sadness in the best way he could manage.

****

I was well into my twenties when I had an invitation I couldn't resist to shoot ducks for a few days in New South Wales, not too far from Gunnedah. I thought I had nothing much of the sentimental in me, and I was hardly of the age for it, but it was too good to resist. There'd be plenty who wouldn't see a duck hunt as a noticeably ritualistic event, but the pull of water has always been there for me, too.

Perhaps that explains how during my time in the camp I had reason to excuse myself one sundown and go off alone towards a little swamp set well back from the water we were shooting over in the mornings, and which I'd discovered when I'd had a fit of the afternoon wanders; in my top pocket that evening there was an oblong shape about the size of a small harmonica. I felt like I had some kind of a cycle to complete, as though perhaps I'd learn something I didn't know when those same haunting notes of 'Shenandoah' were again made to hum like dragonflies over a stretch of water somewhere near Gunnedah, but it was an intensely personal errand and I'm glad there was nobody to hear me when I took it out and sat down with it in the reddening sunset at the water's edge.

Nobody, at least, that I know of.

Shooting Them Still

He was eighty-eight when his tired heart finally stopped; he had been eighty-four when he went shooting for the last time.

It came out right for me, because I was the one who had taken him.

****

We went out among the rabbits. He didn't need asking twice.

I was surprised, actually, because I didn't think he was up to it. Sometimes his aches and pains appeared to eat at him, and although he didn't say much about them, he did tend to sit and stare at the wall and some of the time he seemed to be brooding. I suppose in the back of my mind I expected he'd refuse. When I made the offer, he accepted without overt excitement and equally without apparent misgivings.

It came together quickly. In a minute or two, he had the old game-scene engraved Thomas Wild in its tired leg-o'-mutton case sitting on the kitchen table — to his wife's annoyance — and then the cleaning rod out as well, to take the oil out of the bores.... A pair of walking boots and a knife, and the next thing I knew, she'd filled the flask with tea and we were in the car, me putting my money where my mouth had been.

He was a fine man and he'd been good to me when I was young. I didn't often visit, but only because I had little reason to go back to that part of the country. I did suspect that he seldom managed to shoot, though I know he fished whenever he could; when I told him there were good numbers of rabbits reported to me as being in the old stamping ground, I guess it just seemed obvious that I should offer to take him.

On the way there I thought silently about the way his eyes had troubled him lately. He didn't speak of that, either, but his wife had told me. I wondered if he'd be able to see rabbits in the long summer grass. I knew they'd have had plenty of stirring up, so they'd be wild and there'd be no easy ones.

The conversation wasn't joyful. He told me of how he'd not long ago given away his last handmade duck decoys, and they'd been left unappreciated to rot on a house dam. No malice had been intended. It was only because the recipient was of another age, and saw them as being expendable, like the plastic kind we buy in shops. The story hung over our talk like a misshapen shadow.

Then I started thinking about his knee. I suppose by his time of life he was lucky to have just one bad one. I didn't want to see him having a fall in the stones. It was hard country; I'd taken a couple of nasty stumbles myself in that terrain, and I didn't have to carry his weight of years. Walking in it was hard work, one of the prices we tender for good rabbit shooting, and I'd paid it cheerfully enough myself, but it only dawned on me a bit late that perhaps it wasn't fair to ask it of somebody else.

He was aware of none of my thoughts. He sat in the car with a calm expectation that I had it all in hand, and I'd soon be setting him down where the rabbits ran. I thought that from his point of view it was all straightforward; it goes to show how much I know. This I was soon to learn.

When we arrived, the grass after a good growing season was longer than I'd expected, though I knew the place well. There were a lot of rabbits there, but they were well trained in what to do when fellows turned up to shoot. The station owner only ever allowed shotguns, and the survivors had developed an accurate vision of what was killing range, and whenever they heard the tramp of feet they headed off past its outer limits without undue delay.

His old twelve gauge Wild weighed eight pounds, and the choke in it, both barrels, was ferocious. That was something else I was a bit worried about, whether he'd be adequately geared up for the conditions. He'd sold all his other guns, and it was the only one he'd kept, perhaps more because of its sentimental value than its practicality. It was his live-pigeon gun, made to specifications and bought new, ordered through William McKenzie, the Thomas Wild agent at Talbot, north of Ballarat, in the thirties. It had seen a lot of work at blue pigeons twisting their way out of traphouses under the taut gaze of a ring of betting men. It was as much a part of him as the arms that held it.

By the time we started walking I was more than just uneasy, because when we were on the spot there seemed to be a lot that I hadn't thought of before we left. I decided I had to make the best of it.

I tried to give him the easiest walking. I made sure to shout when a rabbit would break cover and head his way through the tussocks and the tall wild oats, often just a shadow that made the long grass wave. I worried about how solid he was on his feet, and I started trying to work the dog around in front of me, so that some of what it put up would be likely to run at him.

Perhaps I'd have done altogether better to remind myself that the young are better served by listening to the old than they are by patronizing them.

In a while, I realized that he wasn't paying any attention to me at all. I could've sent the dog out in front of me wearing pink knickers, and started a brass band playing when a rabbit was running at him, and it wouldn't have made the slightest difference. He was doing it his way.

I did work this out eventually, I'll say that for myself. So about then I fell back a bit and started to watch, which was no more than I should've done in the first place.

What gave it away was only something I observed by chance. I just happened to be at the right angle, and I saw him lean into a shot, maybe half an hour after we'd started walking. Of course, there'd been plenty of shooting up till then, and I'd seen that, all right, but this one time, there was a big flat rock, the grey volcanic of the area, and it was thirty yards past him, out of focus to me when I was watching him. It happened just to be there, obliquely over his shoulder from where I stood, and as he bent into this one particular shot, I had a sudden, almost startling picture of it, and I saw him, too, as I should've all along.

It was flat and grey and squared at the corners. There are many strange shapes to be found in rocks, and this one looked for all the world like a trap house.

As I saw this shape, and a rabbit on a straight run out on the flats at thirty degrees past it, I saw him lean a little from the waist, slowly, deliberately; I noticed a smidgin of a bend in his left knee, and his feet were much closer together than would be expected in a field shooter standing amongst rough stones in bad walking country. I saw nothing elaborate in his swing, but just a little flick of the muzzle, up and left, at a rabbit he'd purposely let go, well out, past the —

yes, well out past the traphouse, and away from the tussocks, in the clear. When it was eighty yards from me, and maybe fifty from him, he centred it so that it never knew what hit it.

I'm a slow but a thorough learner, and I've never liked to intrude on a man's privacy. I called the dog in and hung back, and when he looked around to place me he found that I was having some difficulty gutting one or two of the rabbits I was carrying. I let him move away, and as I watched on with the benefit of some distance, soon I was sure.

No snap shooter, this, and, yes, there it was again; he carried the gun open, broken over his arm, and when another one broke cover and bolted, it was the trap stance he took, and he had all the time in the world, it seemed, before he made the shot, again at the same range, with the same deliberation and the same deadly result.

As a live-pigeon shot, he'd been not a great one, by all accounts, but a good one, good enough to make money at it. He'd had more than proficiency with a gun, and at that time it was plain to me that it never left him, not even then, at what was in effect the end.

So I stopped trying to organize his shooting for him, under the warming late summer sun on the flats. He wasn't interested in the close targets. At his time of life, he felt he could afford to let go any that didn't please him, so he did. He was comfortable with just the gentle angles of the ones that ran well out. Anybody who wants to shoot summer rabbits in thick tussocks underfoot is going to have to wave the gun about like a mad conductor's baton; yet when they're let go, then it's easy to lose sight of most of them. The ones that do break cover, though, are as near as rabbits can ever be to the straightaways that pigeons are as they come out of traps, when they behave themselves and don't put on any antics.

So that was his wish. He let a lot of rabbits go, that day, but of the ones he chose to swing on, I never saw him miss.

First his feet, then the closing of the gun. As he gave a little nod in the direction he was going to shoot, it was as if he was calling for his bird, and fifty years had fallen from his back. If there'd been someone there to take my money, I'd have put it on him.

There was nobody there for that, of course — only me. When he'd had enough, I took him back to the car, and let him sit and drink his tea while I walked a way apart and skinned what rabbits we wanted to keep. He needed to sit; when he had, for a while, he came over to me, gentleman to the last, his legs a little uncertain, and offered to help.

I told him he'd helped plenty already, and sent him back to the vacuum flask for another one. Before he went, though, I told him that I'd watched him, and seen his secret. I had to divert my gaze when I was half way through saying it, telling him I'd been looking closely at a fine live-pigeon trap shooter at work, because when he heard the words his eyes misted over and I saw him swallow hard as the past rose up before him again — but the prospect of a second cup of tea got him out of trouble, and with that in hand and as he leaned against the car he watched the sun set while I finished the work.

****

He's gone now, and his wife told me it was his last time afield with a gun.

I'll always be glad I took him, and when I think of him and of the day, it brings on a little twinge of embarrassment, about the time when I made a mistake by trying to do something for someone who was busy looking after it for himself.

Because that's the way it was. His feet didn't stumble on that warm afternoon, and his knee didn't hurt; his eyes were clear and he didn't have trouble swinging the gun; neither were his chokes too tight, not where he was.

The rocks around were hushed in the light summer breeze, not because rocks can't talk, but because they didn't want to put him off his shot, not with the match still unwon, the money still in the hand of the referee, the outcome in the lap of the gods and the light beginning to fail....

He wasn't there at all, though I thought he was, thought he'd be prone to the many pitfalls, among the buckshot gravel and in the tussocks.

No, he was away doing business with the live birds, the old pigeon shooter, over some trap house in Clunes or Kerang or Kaniva, away where the ankles don't twist and the rocks don't slide. For a while there I tried to bring him back to where I was, but it was the wrong place and he had the good sense not to come. He put away what to him was a lesser reality for a stronger one, somewhere in his past. He listened to his own drummer, and he shot pigeons out of traps that afternoon, the way he always had.

And for all I know, friend, he could be shooting them still.